Critical Phenomenology

In memory
of
Jean Hogan

Critical Phenomenology

An Introduction

Elisa Magrì

and

Paddy McQueen

polity

First published in 2023 by Polity Press

Polity Press
65 Bridge Street
Cambridge CB2 1UR, UK

Polity Press
111 River Street
Hoboken, NJ 07030, USA

ISBN-13: 978-1-5095-4111-9 (hardback)
ISBN-13: 978-1-5095-4112-6 (paperback)

A catalogue record for this book is available from the British Library.

Typeset in 10 on 12.5pt Sabon LT Pro
by Cheshire Typesetting Ltd, Cuddington, Cheshire
Printed and bound in Great Britain by CPI Group (UK) Ltd, Croydon

For further information on Polity, visit our website:
politybooks.com

Contents

Detailed Contents

Acknowledgements

We owe the inspiration of this book to Anthony Chemero, who – back in 2018 – suggested to us a project on critical phenomenology for Polity. The extraordinary support we received from Pascal Porcheron, Ellen MacDonald-Kramer, and Stephanie Homer enabled us to turn this project into reality. We are extremely grateful to Pascal for his detailed remarks and guidance, and to two anonymous reviewers for their helpful and constructive feedback, which were essential for improving the manuscript. Susan Beer and Evie Deavall have offered us invaluable professional assistance during copy editing, to which we are highly indebted. Finally, we are thankful to Gregory Fried and Niall Keane for their thoughtful comments and questions on selected drafts of this manuscript.

This book would have never seen the light of the day without the help we both received from our respective institutions and especially our loved ones. In particular, Elisa wishes to thank the Humboldt Foundation for their support over the summers of 2019–2022 as well as the Morrissey College of Arts and Sciences at Boston College for a pre-tenure sabbatical term generously sponsored by the Philosophy Department of Boston College in autumn 2021. Her deepest gratitude goes to her family, especially her mother, Mina Cafueri, for her unwavering trust and understanding, especially during the writing of this book. Paddy wishes to thank Laura Duggan, who provided invaluable support during some challenging times.

We would like to dedicate our work to the memory of Jean Hogan, a young philosopher of great talent and passion, who thought deeply about the topics discussed in this volume. Jean received her MA in Philosophy from University College Dublin, where we both worked between 2015 and 2018 as post-doctoral research fellows. With this book, we hope to honour Jean's rare sensibility and her fine understanding of the multifaceted qualities of lived experience.

Introduction

But our humanity is our burden, our life; we need not battle for it; we need only to do what is infinitely more difficult; that is, accept it. The failure of the protest novel lies in its rejection of life, the human being, the denial of his beauty, dread, power, in its insistence that it is his categorization alone which is real and which cannot be transcended.

James Baldwin, *Notes of a Native Son*

Phenomenology is a philosophical discipline inaugurated by Edmund Husserl at the beginning of the twentieth century, and since then it has developed into an increasingly diverse tradition with a pluralistic methodological approach.

From a Husserlian viewpoint, phenomenological inquiry is typically concerned with the investigation of lived experience. This entails an analysis of *what* a subject experiences based on *how* such a content is experienced. For example, in seeing, I perceive things, living beings, people; in imagining, I represent to myself an imaginary object or situation; in judging, I understand how objects (or subjects) are related to one another in specific circumstances; in acting, I experience myself as willing to perform actions. In all such cases, my experiences are *about* something, which appears to me in a specific manner (that is, as a content that is perceived, remembered, imagined, understood, wanted etc.). Phenomenological analysis is the description of how such appearances (or phenomena, from the Ancient Greek *phainómena*) are given to consciousness. Yet phenomenology is a peculiar form of description in that it is concerned not simply with the different manners of givenness of appearances but also with their truth and objectivity. To this end, phenomenology carries out analyses of the conditions that make subjective experience meaningful, coherent, and valid.

From a phenomenological viewpoint, appearances are not discrete series of sense-data, for they are given to the self in a temporal stream, which is informed by sensorimotor awareness, feelings, affects, and habits, thereby constituting one's experience of the world. As such, experience is best understood as the specific orientation *of* a subject *towards* some object in the world (be it a thing or another subject; whether real or non-real) in a distinct manner of apprehension and comprehension (as in feeling, perception, imagination, thinking).

While all experiences have some share in intentionality, which designates this directedness towards an object that characterizes each stream of consciousness, classical phenomenologists have historically offered different methods to explain how meaning is constituted in experience, and how such meaning presents itself to self and others. For example, Husserl's phenomenology stresses that the meaning of experience presupposes a sense-bestowing consciousness, that is, the self *for whom* experience is about. Instead, existentialist thinkers like Martin Heidegger and Jean-Paul Sartre draw attention, in different ways, to the practical and situated character of experience, and how the values and beliefs that circulate in the surrounding world inform the background of perception, action, and belief. Despite the diversity of methods, common to classical and existential phenomenologists is the idea that experience cannot be accessed from nowhere, and that a first-person viewpoint is intrinsic to how we make sense of the world around us, including ourselves.

Such an inquiry into the conditions of possibility of experience is not a detached philosophical enterprise that is indifferent to the dynamics of interpersonal life (what phenomenologists call 'intersubjectivity') or to the socio-political world. On the contrary, phenomenology interrogates our position in relation to other selves and the historical world, investigating social understanding (including empathy and being-with others), communal life, and political action. Intrinsic to the aspirations and methods of phenomenology is a pluralistic approach, characterized not simply by fundamental differences among phenomenologists and their respective approaches, but also by a continuous striving for a more accurate, rigorous, and fine-grained comprehension of human experience. In this respect, phenomenology is informed by an acute awareness and comprehension of historical time. As Davis points out: 'from its beginning in Husserl's thought, phenomenology has consistently been defined as a response to crisis – a critical inquiry into the very nature of our being' (Davis 2020, p. 3). Indeed, from Husserl to Heidegger, and from Sartre to Levinas, phenomenology has been concerned with a critical evaluation of its own historical and intellectual landscapes.

This book is a thematic introduction to the subjects that are most directly related to the role of phenomenology in the analysis of socio-political phenomena, including the conflicts that emerge in a world riven with social inequality, political exclusion, and discrimination. This particular orientation of phenomenological research makes phenomenology 'critical' in a specific sense, as it pays close attention to how categories of social identity, such as gender and race, are involved in self- and other-experience. As we will show, classical and existential phenomenology have widely and extensively investigated the enabling conditions of human experience and its situated socio-historical character. Drawing on this body of research, contemporary critical approaches to phenomenology have further brought to light the entanglement between embodied experience, social identity, and power relations. Critical phenomenology thus seeks to better identify the context-dependent character of first-person experience, refiguring taken-for-granted assumptions about what counts as 'ordinary' and 'marginal' in everyday life.

To this end, critical phenomenology proceeds by interrogating the relation between body, social identity (involving race, class, gender, sexuality, ethnicity, nation, ability, and age), and interpersonal experience, focusing in particular on the role played by gender and race in constituting 'visible identities' (Alcoff 2006). These are the identities through which the subject presents itself to others as the bearer of a historical tradition and lineage, as a member of a socio-cultural milieu, but also as the embodied viewpoint of a social position situated in a web of different power relations. In this regard, the contribution of corporeality (or embodiment) to the constitution of meaning is one of the key elements that critical phenomenologists develop in close continuity with classical phenomenology.

The body represents the incarnate horizon that makes experience possible, but it is also the site through which social identities are made visible. By further developing and radicalizing insights of classical phenomenology on corporeality, gender, and race, critical phenomenology shows that bodily presentation and the socio-historical meaning it carries are inseparable from social understanding and political experience. Connected to this is an appreciation of the role of social identity, which is not to be reduced to a passive medium upon which external power relations are inscribed. Instead, social identity is thematized as source of self- and other-understanding that can cross socio-cultural boundaries and create wider and deeper opportunities for thinking and action.

From this point of view, it may be argued that critical phenomenology reflects an intersectional understanding of how the subject is positioned in the world. Intersectionality, as defined by Patricia Hill Collins, refers to 'the critical insight that race, class, gender, sexuality, ethnicity, nation, ability, and age operate not as unitary, mutually exclusive entities, but as reciprocally constructing phenomena that in turn shape complex social inequalities' (Collins 2015, p. 2). Collins' view is that social categories like gender and race overlap in the creation of social inequality in that they reproduce patterns of beliefs and discrimination that are socially created. At the same time, however, from a phenomenological perspective, those categories highlight distinct domains of experience, intelligibility, and social normativity. Contemporary critical phenomenology adopts an intersectional angle to describe the relation between corporeality, social experience, and social identity, relying on classical phenomenological concepts and arguments to distinguish between the different social structures that operate at the levels of self- and other experience. To this end, as we show throughout the book, critical phenomenology draws on feminist philosophy, philosophy of race, phenomenological psychopathology, queer and disability studies, expanding and enriching the interdisciplinary character of phenomenological research.

Due to the close and, we may say, genealogical continuity between classical and critical phenomenology, this introductory handbook introduces the field of critical phenomenology to readers who are not familiar with the classical phenomenological tradition.[1] Our goal is to map out the trajectories that lead from classical and existential phenomenological inquiries to contemporary critical phenomenological approaches. In so doing, we highlight how critical phenomenology both draws from, and seeks to further develop, the philosophical frameworks established by classical and existential phenomenologists. As we show, critical phenomenology is a rapidly developing area, which is contributing to the expansion and diversification of the reaches of phenomenology. Given how voluminous and diverse the phenomenological literature on such topics is, this book does not – and could not – provide an exhaustive survey or even a unifying systematization of the whole field, which is highly pluralistic and in continuous growth. Instead, we aim to facilitate the understanding of the relationship between classical and critical phenomenology, thereby outlining indications for future research.

In this respect, it is helpful to provide some background regarding the origins of the label 'critical phenomenology' in the Anglophone literature. To begin with, the denominations of 'classical phenomenology' and 'critical phenomenology' date back to Donn Welton and Hugh J. Silverman's collection, *Critical and Dialectical Phenomenology* (1987), which gathers the papers of the 1984 and 1985 meeting of the *Society for Phenomenology and Existential Philosophy*. In Welton and Silverman's collection, critical phenomenology is not a univocal or distinct type of phenomenological research but rather a pluralistic methodological approach that builds on the connections between classical phenomenology, philosophy of language, hermeneutics, critical theory,[2] and cognitive psychology. Thus, the term 'critical phenomenology' was originally employed in the Anglo-American literature to refer to an interdisciplinary dialogue between philosophical traditions quite different from one another. Among the traditions involved are dialectical philosophy (modelled upon Hegelian philosophy in the nineteenth century, which derives the meaning of truth from the analysis and resolution of oppositions) and structuralism (the school of thought, often associated with Ferdinand de Saussure's structural linguistics in the twentieth century, which explores the structures that constitute cultural objects). On this view, phenomenology is critical insofar as it lends itself to a dialogue with different disciplines and philosophical traditions concerning the theoretical and cultural norms that constellate society, language, and cognition. Moreover, critical phenomenology involves the analysis of the methodological frameworks of social and empirical sciences.

In a more specific sense, however, it can be argued that phenomenology is always intrinsically critical. In this context, Michael Marder refers to 'critical phenomenology' as a form of critique that is inherent in classical phenomenology. Such a critique 'exceeds the limits of strictly epistemological problems and affects the areas of ontology, ethics, and politics no less than its Kantian or Hegelian counterparts. Curiously enough, it does so thanks to the inextinguishable self-critical impulse that, like a spark, jumped from Husserl's work to that of his followers' (Marder 2014, p. 5). Marder draws attention to the systematic character of Husserl's critical project, which is not restricted to epistemological problems (that is, involving the relation between knowledge and reality), but encompasses a wide range of philosophical issues, including metaphysical and ontological questions (that is, concerning the nature and meaning of being) and morality (which is relevant for ethics and politics). For Marder, Husserl's phenomenological project provides the inspiration for a philosophical tradition that interrogates the fundamental concepts of epistemology, ontology, ethics, and politics.

Thus, early characterizations of 'critical phenomenology' in the Anglophone literature emphasize the pluralistic character of phenomenological research from a methodological viewpoint. In this regard, it can be said that the concept of critique is reminiscent of Kant's view of critique, which derives from the Ancient Greek word *krinein*, meaning 'to distinguish, to divide, or discern'. Kant identified the critical task of his *Critique of Pure Reason* with the analysis of the powers and boundaries of reason (Kant 1998, pp. 132–3). In so doing, Kant aimed to shed light on the nature of reason across all areas of human experience in order to identify the universal conditions of possibility of experience, knowledge, and morality. Such conditions are called transcendental in that they are not derived *from* experience, but are constitutive of our experiential viewpoint and universally shared by all rational subjects. Thus, for Kant, transcendental conditions are a priori rather than a posteriori. One of the main aspects of Kant's critical approach was to resist and challenge the passive acceptance of unexamined assumptions and doctrines about knowledge and reality. To this end, Kant famously distinguished the domain of *phenomena* (objects of possible experiences, involving the use of sensibility and understanding) from *noumena* (objects that sensibility cannot reach, therefore they are possible only as problematic concepts, that is as intellectual objects or things in themselves).

Kant's original concern with methodological boundaries is not to be underestimated, as it was primarily an appeal to rigorous analysis. Like Kant, Husserl cared about philosophical rigour in the effort to describe and analyse the constitution of the self-world relation. At the same time, however, classical phenomenology is critical in a deeper sense than Kant's, and this is paraphrased by Husserl's aspiration to go 'back to the things themselves' (Husserl 2001a, p. 168). Starting with Husserl, classical phenomenology entails a fundamental revision and transformation of Kant's critical project. This concerns the critique of the different types of presuppositions or assumptions that limit an adequate thematization of the domain, form, and structures of lived experience, including its alterations and contingent aspects. Accordingly, early approaches to critical phenomenology stress that classical phenomenology is by nature critical in that it questions epistemic, ontological, and historical presuppositions that guide the study of consciousness, being, meaning, and truth. The flourishing of phenomenological research in these areas certainly testifies to the reaches and potential of the phenomenological tradition as a lively, methodological form of critique.

Over the past decades, however, as phenomenology has been more widely and extensively engaged by social philosophy, feminist philosophy, philosophy of race, and medical humanities, 'critical phenomenology' has come to identify a field of research that is more directly concerned with the relation between self, social experience, and social norms, including the critique of the social presuppositions at stake in such a relation. The methodological approaches underlying this type of research are quite different from one another. While some approaches are more consistently aligned with the traditions of classical and existential phenomenology, others are more directly inspired by the model of genealogical critique put forward by Michel Foucault in the twentieth century and, more recently, by Judith Butler.

A genealogical critique interrogates how systems of beliefs and concepts are generated in specific normative contexts that impact the thematization of the very notion of 'the subject'. As Foucault writes: 'One has to dispense with the constituent subject, to get rid of the subject itself, that's to say, to arrive at an analysis which can account for the constitution of the subject within a historical framework' (Foucault 1980, p. 117). Overall, Foucault denies that one can describe the structures of experience from a first-person point of view without attending to the ways in which individuals are positioned in historical contexts that are largely dominated by power relations. The challenge, therefore, is that genealogical critique seems to resist the methodological distinctions that are central to classical phenomenology, especially the distinction between self and world.

While contemporary critical phenomenology is, to a large extent, inspired by Foucault's and Butler's concern with the socially constructed character of power relations, it does not thereby obliterate the role of the subject in the analysis of experience. On the contrary, critical phenomenology puts forward constructive analyses that bring self, world, and power into continuous, reciprocal relation. One of the most relevant aspects of this new critical turn (to which we return in more detail in Chapter 1) is a relative turning away from the methodology of critical theory in favour of an approach that prioritizes the analysis of embodied experience, drawing especially on the works of classics like Maurice Merleau-Ponty, Simone de Beauvoir, and Frantz Fanon. In this respect, the critical turn in phenomenological research is deeply informed by the insights and methods developed by classical and existential phenomenology, while also aspiring to produce a new form of sensitivity to contemporary reality and social issues. To borrow from James Baldwin's reflections on the novel in our epigraph, critical phenomenology's primary aim is to identify, describe, and potentially liberate ways and forms of being human in the social world, without thereby categorizing them into rigid structures.

In this respect, Gail Weiss, Ann V. Murphy, and Gayle Salamon, the editors of the first collection of essays explicitly dedicated to critical phenomenology, argue that critical phenomenology is 'an ameliorative phenomenology that seeks not only to describe but also to repair the world, encouraging generosity, respect, and compassion for the diversity of our lived experiences' (Weiss et al. 2020, p. xiv). On this view, critical phenomenology represents a philosophical practice that seeks to make phenomenological concepts and arguments relevant for the comprehension and critique of social identity, shedding light on the constitution of plural identities as well as on the experiences of living at the crossroad of multiple cultural and social worlds. The ultimate ethical goal of philosophical inquiry, which Frantz Fanon defined as a 'new humanism', is taken up by contemporary critical phenomenology not just as an ongoing reflection on phenomenological practice, but also and more fundamentally as a response to the imperative of describing appearances rigorously in order 'to see them anew' (Salamon 2018, p. 12).

At the same time, it is noteworthy that the concepts and arguments that feature prominently in contemporary critical approaches to phenomenology are consistent with contemporary phenomenological research on illness, disability, and political experience (which is not usually defined or does not call itself 'critical'). Accordingly, the term 'critical phenomenology' can be used to denote an aggregation of interests in phenomenology towards the analysis of embodied experience in relation to social and political phenomena.[3] Such a critical engagement with classical phenomenology allows a re-appraisal of the critical themes and arguments that belong to the phenomenological tradition, providing a continuous engagement with the possibilities of phenomenological discourse. As a result of this, just as classical phenomenology does not represent a homogenous set of theories, so too critical phenomenology is nowadays a rich, diverse field of research that is constantly developing in dialogue, and sometimes in tension, with classical phenomenology. Therefore, the question 'What is critical phenomenology?' requires, first of all, a clarification of the critical scope of classical phenomenology and the reasons why phenomenology is relevant for the investigation of social reality. This is a theme that we address in Chapter 1, where we also present the methodology we use in this handbook.

The book is divided into six chapters. Chapter 1 introduces the meaning and scope of 'critical phenomenology', starting with an overview of the methodological challenges posited by Husserl's phenomenology. We thereby draw attention to the emergence of critical phenomenology in contemporary philosophical discourse, examining the key differences between classical and critical approaches. In particular, we illustrate the key critical insights of classical phenomenology (specifically the critique of naturalism and the suspension of the natural attitude, the critique of historical tradition, and the critique of alienation), and how they have been inherited by critical phenomenology. On this view, critical phenomenology is distinguished from classical phenomenology by a sustained focus on the relation between self and social identity (as in Linda M. Alcoff's account of 'visible identity'), by the intersectional character of lived experience (as in Shannon Sullivan's view of 'transactional bodies'), as well as by the critique of the natural attitude (as developed by Sara Ahmed and Gail Weiss). In so doing, critical phenomenology pays attention to how narratives can be employed to shed light on the intersectional character of social identity, without reducing the intelligibility of lived experience to narrativity.

Chapter 2 illustrates the phenomenology of corporeal experience, focusing on three main forms of embodied experience that emerge in classical phenomenology (especially in Husserl, Sartre, and Merleau-Ponty), namely bodily awareness, the distinction between the body-subject and the body-object, and the habitual body. We show how these dimensions of corporeal experience are developed by critical phenomenology to inquire into the relation between embodiment and social experience. In particular, we focus on phenomena of bodily stigmatization (as in Luna Dolezal's account of body shame), bodily alienation (as in Gail Weiss' and Dorothée Legrand's analysis of distorted body images), and normalizing practices involved in illness and disability (as argued by Havi Carel and Robert McRuer). The chapter thus introduces both classical and contemporary critical views of embodiment, including the ambiguous role of habit and the intersection between phenomenology of illness, critical phenomenology, and disability studies. The concepts and arguments here developed also serve as a foundation for the analysis of self- and other-experience that is presented in Chapter 3.

Chapter 3 articulates the affective, embodied, and ethical dimension of intersubjective experience, focusing on the concepts of empathy, being-with others, and intercorporeality. Starting with an overview of the concept of empathy in Husserl, Stein, and Scheler, the chapter examines the relevance of the self–other distinction in the context of empathy as well as the relation between empathy and personhood. On this basis, critical phenomenology emerges in relation to the concept of learning to perceive and recognize other subjects not only within, but also against, dominant social backgrounds. In the second part of the chapter, we deepen this relation between intersubjective experience and the social context by considering Heidegger's and Sartre's concern with (in)authenticity. We show how Heidegger and Sartre bring to light critical aspects of interpersonal experience, but also how their analysis fails to take into consideration more fine-grained cases of ambiguous belonging to multiple social and cultural worlds. We contrast such an approach with María Lugones' account of world-travelling, which offers a richer angle to look at empathy and being-with others from the standpoint of those who inhabit multiple social identities. In the final part of the chapter, we focus on the relation between intersubjective experience and ethical sensibility by drawing on Merleau-Ponty's concept of the 'flesh' as well as Levinas' view of sensibility. We illustrate how such concepts have been employed by critical phenomenologists, especially Kelly Oliver and Alia Al-Saji, to articulate a critical account of ethical vision.

Chapter 4 introduces the phenomenology of gender, showing the relation between critical phenomenology, feminist philosophy, and contemporary gender theory. The chapter begins by illustrating classical phenomenological accounts of sexual difference and gender, and how Simone de Beauvoir's insights into woman's experience lie at the crossroads between classical and critical phenomenology. We then explore the ways in which Beauvoir's feminist phenomenology has been developed by feminist thinkers to reflect on the ambiguity of gender and its relation to unquestioned social norms. Specifically, we refer to Iris Marion Young's analysis of female bodily experience as well as to Sandra Bartky's work on domination, which explores how gendered experience can become a source of, and function to maintain, women's alienation. The chapter connects the phenomenology of gender to the analysis of gender and power developed by Michel Foucault and Judith Butler. It concludes by reflecting on the expressive and non-alienating power of gender by considering the phenomenology of trans experience as well as of sexuality, with a focus on the work of Sara Ahmed.

Chapter 5 is an introduction to the phenomenology of race as well as to the concept of racial identity. The chapter begins with an analysis of Frantz Fanon's work on racialization and the 'fact of Blackness'. Fanon's influential work explores the effects of colonialism and racism on Black subjects, and how this is functional to creating a system of political oppression.[4] Fanon's account in *Black Skin, White Masks* is also explored in terms of its dialectical approach to the relation between subjectivity and race. In the second part of the chapter, we describe the phenomenon of racialization by looking at contemporary works in philosophy of race inspired by Fanon's work, including Charles Johnson, George Yancy, and Alia Al-Saji. We also present the connection between racialization and the phenomenology of whiteness, drawing on Ahmed's work. The chapter concludes with a discussion of the irreducibility of racial identity to the phenomenon of racialization, focusing especially on Anzaldúa's concept of *mestiza* consciousness and Ortega's view of the multiplicitous self.

Chapter 6 brings together many of the themes covered in the preceding chapters through an exploration of the domain of the political, including the phenomenology of social experience and political action. Starting with an overview of classical-phenomenological accounts of communal life, we consider the ontological foundations of the concept of political space in Hannah Arendt. We then show that Arendt's philosophy paves the way for contemporary critical approaches concerned with the relation between embodied experience, political spaces, and social injustice. In this regard, drawing especially on the work of Lisa Guenther, we explore phenomena of social alienation (such as social death and social invisibility). In the second part of the chapter, we consider phenomenological engagements with Miranda Fricker's account of epistemic injustice. This helps to illustrate how systems of political silencing and exclusion operate by producing disempowerment; that is, a diminishment of political agency that targets the epistemic and interpretative abilities of individuals and groups. Finally, we examine how critical phenomenology sustains an account of solidarity and coalition among women that centres on a positive appraisal of vulnerability. We conclude by considering how vulnerability and precariousness can be part of a project of coalitional politics by drawing on Butler's reflections on the power of public assembly.

1

What is *Critical* Phenomenology?

Between an 'objective' history of philosophy (which would rob the great philosophers of what they have given others to think about) and a meditation disguised as a dialogue (in which we would ask the questions and give the answers) there must be a middle-ground in which the philosopher we are speaking about and the philosopher who is speaking are present together, although it is not possible even in principle to decide at any given moment just what belongs to each.

Maurice Merleau-Ponty, 'The Philosopher and his Shadow'

The promise of interdisciplinary scholarship is that the failure to return texts to their histories will do something. [. . .] We must remember that to 'not return' still requires the act of following, we have to go with something if we are to depart from that thing.

Sara Ahmed, *Queer Phenomenology*

In his 1945 Preface to the *Phenomenology of Perception*, in raising the question that was destined to plague generations of philosophers, namely 'What is phenomenology?', Merleau-Ponty argues that it would be impossible to reduce phenomenology to a simple label. The difficulty at stake concerns not just the characteristic diversity and richness of the phenomenological tradition, but also the methodological issues posited by the founder of the phenomenological tradition, Edmund Husserl. It was Husserl, on Merleau-Ponty's view, who conceived of phenomenology as 'the study of essences', namely, of the invariant structures of experience. Yet it was also Husserl who established a method of inquiry that goes beyond the mere description of essences in order to tackle the embodied and situated character of subjectivity (Merleau-Ponty 2012, p. xx). To understand what Merleau-Ponty means by this, it is essential to note that Husserl's phenomenology is a systematic study of both our natural (or pre-philosophical) experience of the world as well as an attempt to achieve a phenomenological stance concerned with objectivity and truth. Such a stance allows the philosopher to think about the fundamental correlations that exist between self and world as well as about the essences of objects.

Building systematically on Brentano's breakthrough, Husserl was originally concerned with the project of a descriptive psychology that would identify the main forms and structures of that 'being directed to' an object that is distinctive of consciousness. This is what Brentano called 'intentionality'. Thus, discourse about intentionality, intentional life, or intentional acts should not be confused with 'intention' (the purpose we have in mind when we carry out actions). Intentionality is instead the most fundamental fact explored by phenomenology. Husserl gave to such inquiry the distinctive character of a rigorous science that deals with objects from the viewpoint of our experiential access to them, investigating only what belongs to the subject's experience, without imposing or adding any external assumptions to the phenomenon under investigation. In this way, he sought to secure phenomenology on a scientific footing. This amounts to establishing a method of analysis that is not influenced by metaphysical or scientific presuppositions, such as the Kantian distinction between phenomena and things in themselves, or the naturalistic belief that experiences make sense only as correlates of the brain's activity.

With the publication of the first book of *Ideas for a Pure Phenomenology and Phenomenological Philosophy* (also known as *Ideas I*), Husserl characterized phenomenology as a transcendental investigation of essences. On this view, phenomenology seeks to describe the essential and invariant structures underlying the experience of everyday life, spanning perceptions, feelings, and judgements, but also hallucinations and imagining. In all such cases, we are typically directed to an object (whether real or imaginary) that we grasp according to a certain 'manner of givenness', be it in intuiting, perceiving, imagining, remembering, or thinking about something. Guiding questions include: What makes imagining different from perceiving? How does remembering represent the content experienced in the past? In what ways are intentional acts founded (or based) upon perception? Answering such questions leads to an investigation of the essential structures of intentionality, including the a priori rules and conditions that are intrinsic to our apprehension of objects.

In line with Husserl's famous motto of going back 'to the things themselves' (Husserl 2001b, p. 168), subjective experiences are not to be thought of as lacking in objective reality just because they are subject-dependent. On the contrary, phenomena are conceived by Husserl as having a characteristic intentional structure based on how the object of experience presents itself to the self. This can be illustrated using the following example. Suppose that we look at the tree outside the window. On Husserl's view, it is possible to distinguish between three essential components underlying the meaning constituted in a given experience: the act of perception, the content of perception (the sense or meaning of the object), and the object (the actual tree in the garden). The sense of the object and the act by means of which the object is intended (in this case through perceiving) are called in the first book of *Ideas* 'noema' (pl. 'noemata') and 'noesis' respectively (hence 'noematic-noetic' analysis).[1]

The object perceived, the actual tree that exists independently of our experience of it, can be quite different from the tree that is grasped in the manner of perception (this because we may, for example, be hallucinating or having vivid dreams). In this respect, the intentional content of an act is not caused by the actual existence of its object.[2] At the same time, intentionality reveals an intrinsic relational character, which is the relation between the tree, as the bearer of our perceptual experience, and the manner of perceiving it. As experience occurs in a temporal stream that is spatially situated, such a relation is also dynamic: for example, the tree presents itself in different profiles or manners of appearances that refer to the perspective and bodily orientation of the perceiver. While the tree remains the same and exists without being perceived, the perception of the tree outside my window is a perception that is constantly changing: the tree appears now white under the snow, but it also presents itself in different profiles and shades as I move and look at it from various angles. Thus, the tree is perceived against the background of a manifold of different noemata or presentations, which are motivated by the different bodily activities that take place in perceiving. Ultimately, the tree existing outside the window is thematized as a being *for* a consciousness (hence, it is neither caused *by* consciousness nor included *in* consciousness).

To uncover the temporal, logical, and sense-bestowing nexuses involved in each stream of experience, it is necessary, on Husserl's view, to adopt a phenomenological method through which the philosopher temporarily brackets or suspends metaphysical or scientific presuppositions about the matter at hand in order to attend to what is immanent or intrinsic to a given experiential phenomenon. In this sense, the task of phenomenology is to describe the content of experience as this is given to consciousness. Such a task also requires the suspension of the 'natural attitude' in which we always live in everyday life. The natural attitude is a form of orientation in the surrounding world (*Umwelt*), which is constantly changing with respect to the self, as the world we inhabit is not just a world of objects but also a world of values and goods (Husserl 2004, p. 50). As Husserl writes in *Ideas I*, we live in a world of things 'on hand', namely things that are practically relevant, and we do not encounter human beings and animals as 'things', but rather as friends, foes, and relatives (Husserl 2004, pp. 49–50). Thus, suspending the natural attitude does not mean turning away from the world and our interaction with it. At stake is, rather, the attempt to identify and illustrate the intentional structures that make the relation between self and the world intelligible and relevant.

The analysis of the essential structures and variations that occur in the relation between consciousness and its intentional objects informs a large part of Husserl's concern with issues of meaning, essence, and truth. In this context, to speak of essences (or *eidē*, from the Ancient Greek 'forms', hence 'eidetic analysis') means to grasp the identity of an intentional object across the manifold of its presentations within a given domain, whether this is the domain of concepts (such as, the empirical concept of 'tree') or the ontological domains of nature and subjectivity (which involve physical and psychophysical beings). Transcendental phenomenology ultimately reveals that we are not only psychological or empirical subjects *in* the world, but also, and at the same time, transcendental subjects *for* the world. Indeed, the fundamental meaning-structures of intentionality disclosed by phenomenological analysis are universally shared by different psychophysical subjects without thereby overriding their empirical, historical, and socio-cultural situation.

By the time Merleau-Ponty was writing the *Phenomenology of Perception,* he had accessed some of Husserl's posthumous manuscripts stored at the Husserl Archives in Belgium, including the second book of *Ideas Pertaining to a Pure Phenomenology and to a Phenomenological Philosophy* (typically abbreviated as *Ideas II*) as well as relevant sections of the *Crisis of European Sciences and Transcendental Phenomenology.* Merleau-Ponty was also familiar with Husserl's *Sixth Cartesian Meditation,* edited by Husserl's former assistant, Eugen Fink, in close collaboration with Husserl himself. In these writings (unpublished at that time), Husserl explored more closely phenomena connected to the psychophysical constitution of self and other, including an analysis of the shared cultural world as well as reflections on the teleology or intrinsic purpose of European history.[3] This type of research brings to light the relation between temporality, embodiment, and intersubjective experience, including the possibility of empathy and the phenomenological foundation of culture. As such, Husserlian phenomenology appears concerned not just with the analysis of essences but also with the possibility of history, culture, and the whole sphere of pre-reflective experience (namely, prior to reflection and judgement), including affect and sensibility. Husserl's approach to such areas is based on a *genetic* method of inquiry in that it is concerned with the temporal and affective genesis of meaning-constituting acts. In this regard, Husserl was also interested in the possibility of a 'constructive phenomenology' (Fink's terminology) that would further reflect on the possibilities and limits of phenomenology as a practice of philosophical investigation.

To a large extent, Husserl's writings are characterized by an explicit ethical task, that of the cultivation of responsibility through the exercise of philosophy. For example, in some of his late works, Husserl argues that philosophical self-reflection (which is not limited to the analysis of self but also includes an account of intersubjectivity) builds into a stance of self-responsibility that philosophers take upon themselves for the sake of the moral improvement of humankind. Ultimately, Husserl's phenomenology is driven by an aspiration to self-transformation and practical renewal[4] that compels the critique of unquestioned styles of thought.

On this basis, Merleau-Ponty argued that the development of Husserl's phenomenology was not opposed to, but rather compatible with, the movement that aimed to 'place essences back within existence', as Merleau-Ponty writes (Merleau-Ponty 2012, p. xx). By this, Merleau-Ponty arguably hints at Martin Heidegger's phenomenological ontology as well as Jean-Paul Sartre's existentialism, which are directly concerned with the analysis of the situated character of human existence. In this context, to place essences *back* within existence means, on Merleau-Ponty's view, to practise phenomenology as an endless task of critical reflection. Such a task is necessarily endless, because it is not limited to the thematization of the modes of givenness of objects but also includes an understanding of the situated, historical existence of actual human beings. In this way, for Merleau-Ponty, the phenomenologists who carry out the reduction put themselves at a distance from the natural attitude of everyday life, and yet they can never step outside the situation in which they are involved. To this end, Merleau-Ponty questions Husserl's method, arguing that the reduction cannot never be complete, since our reflections are always part of a temporal flow *towards* the world (Merleau-Ponty 2012, p. xxvii). Differently put, bracketing our presuppositions does not put them out of play in the analysis of the experiential phenomenon.

Despite this critique, Merleau-Ponty does not completely depart from Husserl's method. In fact, Merleau-Ponty acknowledges that phenomenological concepts like the natural attitude and its suspension are, to borrow from Fink's terminology,[5] concepts that are used more operatively in Husserl's phenomenology than they are thematically clarified. Unlike thematic concepts that are explicitly conceptualized and distinguished from one another, operative concepts allow philosophers to *think through* sets of philosophical issues and problems. In this respect, operative concepts come to the fore through the way in which philosophers *use* rather than define them. From a theoretical viewpoint, operative concepts are not easily demarcated and thematized, thereby representing problematic notions that call for further research in the work of a philosopher. As such, questioning operative concepts does not mean to surpass their thinker. Similarly, Merleau-Ponty's emphasis on the limits of the suspension of the natural attitude is not meant to surpass or reject Husserlian phenomenology. In fact, Merleau-Ponty's phenomenology offers an example of critical phenomenology that centres on the possibilities of phenomenology as a *style* of thinking that is aware of the limits of Husserl's phenomenological method.

More specifically, on Merleau-Ponty's view, Husserlian phenomenology was not to be taken as a formal analysis of meaning that abstracts from the situated character of human experience. On the contrary, Husserlian phenomenology can be viewed as an attempt to articulate the structures of lived experience in order to better understand the reality of everyday life, in which we are always absorbed without necessarily reflecting on it. It is by recognizing how meaning is constituted at both subjective and intersubjective levels of experience that phenomenology provides the foundations for an ethical understanding of what it means to act and be a moral agent in the world. Merleau-Ponty ultimately suggests that the phenomenological tradition initiated by Husserl and developed in an existentialist direction (albeit in different ways) by Heidegger and Sartre, could be thought of as a 'style' or manner of thinking that aims to 'rediscover' our 'naive contact with the world' (Merleau-Ponty 2012, p. xxi). This includes the possibility of learning to see ordinary things anew, thereby awakening the self from unquestioned styles of being. Such a view entails that phenomenology is less an intellectualistic set of doctrines about the nature of consciousness, and more a practice of interrogating the horizon of subjective experience. In this respect, Merleau-Ponty invites the reader to think of phenomenology as a distinctive critical praxis that can be developed and transmitted as a body of knowledge that expands dialectically (that is, by engaging criticisms and opposite viewpoints) and historically (that is, by engaging its own intellectual and socio-political landscape). This is why Merleau-Ponty writes in the Preface to his *Phenomenology of the Perception* that only a hurried reader would stop at the different and often conflicting tendencies of phenomenology and declare it but a myth or a fad. His point is that phenomenology is in a process of continual development that advances through internal tensions and dialectical confrontations.

However, despite Merleau-Ponty's sympathetic critique of Husserl, as well as his confidence in the possibilities offered by phenomenology as a way of thinking, phenomenology is hardly a homogenous school of thought. Critical approaches to Husserlian phenomenology developed inside the phenomenological movement itself and among the theorists who were close to it, including Edith Stein, Max Scheler, Martin Heidegger, Alfred Schütz, Jean-Paul Sartre, Simone de Beauvoir, Frantz Fanon, Hannah Arendt, and Emmanuel Levinas, to name only a few phenomenologists, whom we address in this book. As we will see, while some of these critiques concern, for example, the role of empathy and the concept of the 'person', other critiques – specifically those born out of the existentialist turn – are more directly concerned with the role of phenomenology in describing and doing justice to the formation of social identities, including gender and race, as well as issues connected to socio-political experience and communal life.

This range of critical approaches to phenomenology indicates the extent to which phenomenology, as a tradition, has never been restricted to a single method or a unified critical stance concerning self, experience, and socio-political reality. As Merleau-Ponty reminds us, phenomenology is not accomplished through a static and immediate intuition of essences, nor is it confined to the works of one philosopher. Therefore, each critical assessment of the phenomenological tradition sheds light on different aspects of human and social experience that were either taken for granted or simply underdeveloped in previous strands of phenomenological research. In this context, the contemporary critical approach to phenomenology known as 'critical phenomenology' (to distinguish it from 'classical phenomenology') positions itself in a twofold manner with respect to the phenomenological tradition: as a critical appraisal of classical phenomenology and as a development of phenomenological discourse that centres on the critique of the presuppositions that surround the relations between power, embodiment, and social experience.

At stake for critical phenomenologists nowadays is the following worry: how can phenomenology be an analysis of the situated character of human experience that adequately tackles the relation between embodied experience, social identity, and socio-political norms? Can phenomenology describe not only the structures that are immanent to experience, but also the twofold relation between experience and those socio-political norms that affect and influence social identity, interpersonal experience, and social practices? Key concerns involve gender oppression and racialization, and how they affect self-awareness and social understanding, along with the normalizing and tacit practices that impinge on how sexuality, illness, and disability are thematized and experienced in everyday life.

As typical of phenomenological research, critical phenomenology is eminently interdisciplinary, bringing together classical phenomenology with feminist philosophy, philosophy of race, and queer and disability studies among other fields. By and large, critical phenomenologists draw especially on Merleau-Ponty, Frantz Fanon, and Simone de Beauvoir in order to advance investigations of embodiment, social identity, and political action. In this respect, critical phenomenology often questions, at least to some extent, Husserl's approach and its reliance on transcendental subjectivity.[6] For example, in one of her early descriptions of critical phenomenology, Lisa Guenther asks: 'How critical can "critical phenomenology" become, given its constitutive commitment to the first-person singular as an absolute starting point, prior to the "levels" of race, class, sex, and other dimensions of social subjectivity?' (Guenther 2013, p. xv). Guenther's view is that critical phenomenology needs to depart from a theoretical approach that prioritizes transcendental subjectivity and transcendental analysis over the analysis of social identities and their relation to socio-cultural practices and settings.

Guenther's concern is that a transcendental approach ends up thematizing gender, sex, race, and class as additive elements that are annexed to self, instead of regarding those categories as intrinsic to social identity and connected to socio-political experience through specific power relations (as involving race and gender oppression, but also normalizing ideologies about the lived body). On this front, Guenther's view is that normalizing practices and styles of behaviour are built into the fabric of our natural attitude to the world. As such, owing to phenomenology's commitment to investigate the fundamental structures of experience as they emerge in everyday life, phenomenological analysis is compelled to take into account the entanglement between power, body, and experience, as this emerges in everydayness. Such a relation between experience and socio-political structures appears to Guenther as 'quasi-transcendental' (Guenther 2020, p. 12) in the sense that, while not being a priori, it plays 'a constitutive role in shaping the meaning and manner of our experience' (Guenther 2020, p. 12). Furthermore, Guenther's reference to transcendental subjectivity as an 'absolute starting-point' underpins the worry that phenomenological discourse may not provide an adequate account of collective action and socially transformative practices.

Guenther's critique offers an important point of departure for discussing (1) the limits ascribed by some contemporary critical phenomenologists to classical-phenomenological analysis, especially Husserlian transcendental phenomenology; and (2) the type of critique to which critical phenomenologists refer. On the one hand, when it comes to the critique of transcendental analysis, Guenther's worry echoes the critique that Theodor Adorno originally raised against Husserl when he argued that Husserl's merit was that he vindicated the actuality of experience (that is, the subject-dependent character of lived experience) but at the greater cost of turning it into the transcendental system of an enclosed mind (Adorno 1977). Adorno's critique was that Husserl forsook an account of the material and historical conditions that affect human experience, privileging transcendental analysis over the critique of socio-cultural norms. For this reason, Adorno's evaluation is that Husserl's phenomenology would be indifferent to the socio-economic structures that condition historical reality, and whose acceptance cause the reproduction of the very power structures that inhere in ordinary experience. In a similar way, Guenther's concern is that Husserl's method privileges transcendental subjectivity at the expense of an engagement with social identity and power relations. While this line of criticism tends to overlook the role that history plays in transcendental phenomenology (see also 1.1.2), it is worth noting that contemporary critical phenomenology necessarily integrates various aspects of transcendental analysis.

To begin with, as transcendental subjectivity is an experiential reality that is rooted in embodied experience, it provides the basis for inquiring into the first-person character of experience as a universally valid character of experience that varies across individuals, bodies, and socio-cultural contexts. For example, as we will discuss in the next section, the first-person character of experience is crucial for highlighting the ownership of one's experience, especially in illness. Far from assimilating different subjectivities and experiences in a unique, neutral matrix, transcendental subjectivity highlights the need to make intelligible the validity of a subjective viewpoint. The concept of selfhood is indeed the prerequisite for thinking about individual and social identity. In this regard classical phenomenological analysis follows the footsteps of phenomenological psychopathology, seeking to uncover the intelligibility of different experiential senses of reality in a way that is liberatory for the subjectivities involved and relevant for the critique of medical practice.[7]

Second, the notion of a transcendental self that exists in isolation from others is foreign to the transcendental approach, as illustrated not only by classical-phenomenological arguments on empathy (see Chapter 3) but also by the analysis of communal life and political action (see Chapter 6). Furthermore, if the relation between socio-political structures and experience can be operative in a 'quasi-transcendental' way, as Guenther argues, then the arguments and analyses put forward by transcendental phenomenology are crucial for examining and identifying the dynamics of sedimentation that are involved in the acquisition of social practices and styles of being. This is how social norms and values can become 'second nature' and acted out unreflectively. From this point of view, transcendental phenomenology appears compatible with a critical approach that aims to better understand and situate socio-political phenomena.

On the other hand, Guenther's concern about the risk of producing compartmentalized analyses of sex, gender, race, and class by relying on an exclusive transcendental method of analysis should represent an important motive of reflection for transcendental phenomenology. The main preoccupation, in this case, is that the role played by sex, gender, race, sexuality, disability, and other similar aspects of personal and social identity, is not ancillary or secondary to self-awareness and social understanding. Similarly, communal life and political action need to be considered not only as enabling conditions of social experience but also in terms of a critique of institutionalized social practices. To this end, Guenther's view of critical phenomenology can be understood as a productive and dialectical expansion of the motives and concerns of classical and existential phenomenology. Specifically, critical phenomenology brings to light the wide spectrum of presuppositions that are part of the background horizon of the natural attitude, providing a new angle for integrating phenomenological analysis with the description of socio-political phenomena.

This brings us closer to the type of critique pursued by critical phenomenology, which is ostensibly tied to critical theory; that is, the critique of society and culture initiated in the 1930s by intellectuals who gathered around the Institute for Social Research in Frankfurt, including – among others – Theodor Adorno, Erich Fromm, Herbert Marcuse, Jürgen Habermas, and Axel Honneth. By and large, critical theory is a broadly Marxist tradition, which examines the challenges faced by individuals and groups under the capitalist system, including the analysis of ideology, the critique of social and economic exploitation, as well as the relation between the transformation and organization of labour with respect to social development.[8]

While there are notable and relevant affinities between critical phenomenology and critical theory that require further research (especially considering the works of Axel Honneth),[9] critical phenomenologists analyse social norms from the point of view of *how* those cultural values, norms, and representations find their way into individual consciousness and societal life. Differently stated, critical phenomenologists seek to understand how power structures affect perception, sensibility, and intersubjective experience, without necessarily using the normative lenses deployed by critical theorists, such as Marxism, psychoanalysis, or speech acts (despite the fact that critical phenomenology often shares with critical theory an interest in such research areas). Critical phenomenology is, in this sense, *descriptive*, in that it uncovers the naturalization and normalization of female subordination, gender oppression, and racialization. However, critical phenomenology also aspires to be *ameliorative*; that is, to improve the intelligibility of situated experience as well as to sustain collective practices of social critique.

In this regard, a number of critical phenomenologists draw on the works of Michel Foucault and Judith Butler. While Foucault examines how discourses – that is, bodies of knowledge that are accepted as true within a given society – inform self-experience and pre-reflective attitudes about the world (Foucault 1980, 1997), Butler's theory plays a key role in relation to gender theory, precariousness, and the power of public assembly. On their approach, meaning is not *constituted* or made intelligible through the subject's affective, intuitive, and discursive acts, but rather *produced* through social relations, discourses and power structures, which potentially influence how we perceive, understand, and regard others. In this context, critical phenomenology seeks to highlight how the self is not conditioned by power-relations as a passive medium, but also how the boundaries between self, other, and social norms are often liminal spaces that allow degrees of ambiguity.

As we can see, owing to this complex interrelation of aims and theories, critical phenomenology cannot be compartmentalized or reduced to a simple label or a single perspective. A number of difficulties in characterizing critical phenomenology thus need to be highlighted. On the one hand, critical phenomenology comprises scholarly work engaging with classical phenomenology. This means that in order to introduce the reader to contemporary debates in critical phenomenology it is necessary to illustrate the specific concepts and arguments developed by classical phenomenology so that we can trace their connections with contemporary critical-phenomenological analyses. An important upshot of this approach is that critical phenomenology helps to identify what is 'critical' (or has the potential to be so employed) about classical phenomenology. This shows that the conceptual repertoire of classical phenomenology represents an essential point of departure for analysis of interpersonal experience, corporeality, race, gender, social experience and political action. On the other hand, critical phenomenology cannot be neatly separated from feminist philosophy, critical race theory, and contemporary phenomenological research on perception, embodiment, illness, and sociality. This entails that critical phenomenology cannot be easily demarcated from the works conducted by a number of phenomenology scholars within and beyond the recent movement of critical phenomenology.

Finally, a further, albeit related, concern regards the very distinction between 'classical' and 'critical' phenomenology. As we mentioned, Merleau-Ponty, Beauvoir, and Fanon are the classics of the phenomenological and existential tradition to which the critical-phenomenological movement mostly refers. This suggests that these authors are already in some sense 'critical' phenomenologists, confirming the impossibility of neatly distinguishing classics of phenomenology and existentialism from critical phenomenology. To avoid ambiguities, in this book, we maintain the label of 'classical phenomenology' to refer to all the classics of the phenomenological and existential tradition (including Merleau-Ponty, Beauvoir, Fanon), while paying special attention to how Beauvoir and Fanon developed a critical phenomenology of gender and race (see Chapters 4 and 5 respectively).

On this basis, it appears that just as the phenomenological tradition did not present itself as a homogenous school of thought back in 1945, so too are contemporary critical approaches to phenomenology irreducible to a single orientation, stance, or evaluation. Accordingly, in this book we follow a pluralistic methodological approach that privileges the thematic connections of concepts and arguments in both classical and contemporary critical phenomenology. While we do not put aside the divergences between classical and critical phenomenology, we are also keen to highlight their convergences. Before doing so, in this chapter, we offer an overview of the major aspects that distinguish, from a methodological point of view, the types of critique raised by classical and critical phenomenology when it comes to the relation between embodiment, power, and experience.

1.1 Critical methodological approaches in classical phenomenology

1.1.1 The first-person viewpoint and the suspension of the natural attitude

The most relevant way in which classical phenomenology is, from the start, concerned with the concept of 'critique' involves the rejection of any reductionist approach to consciousness and experience. In his 1911 programmatic essay, 'Philosophy as Rigorous Science', Husserl describes phenomenology as a 'critique of reason' that resists both the 'naturaliza-tion of consciousness' and the 'naturalization of ideas'. Husserl's main targets were naturalism (the view that the standards of objectivity are those defined by natural sciences); psychologism (the view that logic and human cognition can be reduced to the empirical analysis of mental states), and historicism (the view that human nature, morality, and nature are shaped by historical context).[10] In this context, Husserl refers to the 'spell of the naturalistic attitude under which we all find ourselves' (Husserl 2002, p. 271) and that can be tempting when it comes to examining consciousness, owing to the fact that naturalistic assumptions about the mind are widely spread and accessible in culture. Yet Husserl resists a view of psychology that reduces the analysis of experience to the search for causal laws, physical properties, and mechanist models of explanation.

Husserl was interested in the project of a descriptive psychology as outlined by Franz Brentano, aiming to study the content of conscious experiences, its essential structures and relational patterns, including the origins and the laws by which experiential content is governed. In so doing, however, Husserl developed an original phenomenologi-cal approach, whose anti-reductive character is best expressed by his appraisal of what counts as a *phenomenon*. As Husserl puts it in the 1911 essay, a phenomenon 'is not a unity that could be experienced in several separate perceptions as individually identical, not even in perceptions by the same subject' (Husserl 2002, p. 269). Husserl rejects the equivalence between experiences and mental facts, as if the former could be observed from an external viewpoint and reduced to their basic components like physical things. While physical things in nature are objectively divisible into components, hence 'analysable' from without, the objects of psychology are *lived experiences*, which endure over time, hence they appear in a temporal flux. As such, experiences cannot be reduced to objectifiable or material units, since experiences vary not just from subject to subject (each of them embodying a unique viewpoint), but also within the same subject or ego, the bearer of the experience itself.

Think, for example, of how the same thing is experienced in different ways by the same subject. Upon receiving bad news, the taste of the cheesecake I was enjoying turns bitter in my mouth, while it is blissful when in good company and in a peaceful state of mind. The difference in this case, for Husserl, is not simply between two qualitatively distinct mental states, but rather between two different intentional relations to the same object. While the description I may provide in both situations can be analysed in terms of empirical correlations between the taste of the cheesecake at t^1 and the taste of the cheesecake at t^2, they do not account yet for the direct experience of the cheesecake that is given to me across that interval of time. Differently stated, Husserl is interested in describing that original and direct experience that is given to the self, and which is usually presupposed, or else conflated with the notion of mental state, when describing psychological phenomena. The risk of conflating the notion of selfhood with mental states is that of losing sight of the experiential quality of first-person experience.

Dan Zahavi speaks in this regard of the experiential self or minimal self (also called 'for-me-ness') as the most fundamental fact of phenomenal consciousness. This minimal self cannot be reduced to a social construct, because it does not exist either as a separate entity from the stream of consciousness or as a content that is distinct from the self who experiences it (Zahavi 2014). The experiential self is the sense of 'mineness' that distinguishes the taste of this apple or the representation of the apple I ate yesterday as *my own* perceptual and representational experience. On this view, the experiential self denotes the first-person perspective or point of view that is necessarily embedded in experiences on a pre-reflective level. Such a concept plays a key role when it comes to qualifying the sense of ownership that characterizes first-person experience, especially in psychopathology and illness. For instance, phenomenologists have shown that schizophrenic patients suffering from thought-insertion (where the patient reports having thoughts that appear 'inserted' in their minds by a third party or external force) are still aware that those thoughts are not in someone else's head but belong to their own stream of consciousness. As Zahavi and Kriegel put it:

> To deny that a patient suffering from thought insertion is completely bereft of a sense of ownership, or that such phenomena involve a complete effacement of for-me-ness, is not to deny that her overall sense of self is importantly different from ours. The clinician should recognize that such patients are subject to a kind of self-alienation or alienated

self-consciousness. But, as these very phrasings suggest, some dimension of self and self-consciousness is preserved even under those conditions; namely, for-me-ness proper. (Zahavi and Kriegel 2015, p. 43)

A phenomenological analysis of clinical data suggests that pathologies of self-awareness, such as those involving thought-insertion, fundamentally presuppose the capacity to refer certain experiences to oneself, despite the fact that patients have difficulties making those disturbances of experience an object of their attention. Unlike discursive or reflective self-consciousness, the sense of mineness is not expressed by conscious and discursive thought, as it pertains to all the range of experiences upon which we have some kind of epistemic authority. In this sense, for-me-ness represents a fundamental feature of egoic awareness in both psychopathological and non-psychopathological experience, providing the basis for more sophisticated forms of self-awareness.

To be sure, Zahavi and contemporary phenomenologists do not deny that concepts like for-me-ness can be 'elusive and slightly mysterious'. They deny, however, that getting rid of transcendental analysis would make the comprehension of consciousness and its experientable features less problematic, or even free from dogmatic assumptions about human experience. To uncover these fundamental structures of awareness, Husserl proposes a phenomenological analysis that examines the transcendental principles and operations that make the experience of an object (whether real or imaginary) fundamentally coherent *for* the experiencing self, even when the self in question may be hallucinating. In this context, Husserl is very clear that the study of intentionality requires a rigorous method.[11] Two fundamental methodological aspects involve the use of the epoché and the reduction. Performing a phenomenological investigation requires that 'we put the thing in question' (Husserl 1999, p. 38), namely that we suspend any value-judgement or assumption about the phenomenon that is under investigation, including assumptions borrowed from culture and science. The epoché, a concept that draws from the Ancient Greek Sceptics and that refers to the suspension of one's assent to a judgement, requires that one brackets any such assumptions in order to attend only to what is given in experience.

The use of the epoché is not to be confused with some form of radical scepticism, since the epoché is not about doubting reality or the validity of the natural sciences. Instead, the epoché represents an attempt to ground the analysis of experience in the absence of presuppositions, whether such assumptions come from sciences, religion, or other external sources of knowledge. In so doing, the epoché seeks to rule out the naiveté of what Husserl calls the natural attitude, namely the ordinary orientation to the world that characterizes everyday life (Husserl 2004, §§ 31–2). In the natural attitude, we normally take for granted various phenomena that present themselves to us, including the givenness of the surrounding world itself, until we make our experiences objects of reflection. For example, I am sitting at my desk writing this chapter and I am completely absorbed in the content I visualize on my screen. But what is common (or different) between experiencing my thought-processes and reading the words I write on the screen? How is thought experience different from perceiving, remembering, and expecting? Can we observe these phenomena in others or only in ourselves? Similarly, it is possible to wonder about experiences of valuing and willing. Are there degrees of valuing, for example when we appreciate the beauty of a work of art? On what basis do we give our assent or denial to specific actions and choices? How are our decisions connected to values? Are liking and loving the same phenomena or do they differ in important respects?

Thus, to bracket the natural attitude does not mean to detach ourselves from the world but rather to step back from our immersion in everyday life in order to attend to the structure and defining character of experience. To acquire knowledge of the structures and operations that inform experience without relying on unexamined assumptions is what Husserl called the 'phenomenological reduction' (Husserl 1999). In outlining his theory of the reduction, Husserl's objective was to explain how a distinct experience can be reduced to its constitutive content without introducing anything external to it. This means that phenomena are analysed and investigated *as* they appear to consciousness, while consciousness itself is regarded as an egoic pole of reference; that is to say, as the constant, though evolving, centre of experiences. To put it differently, Husserl believes that there cannot be any 'view from nowhere' when it comes to describing experience, because experience always belongs to someone, hence it is always oriented and situated within a horizon (that is, as bearing a distinct perspective on the world).

For example, the house that I see across my window appears to me within a perceptual field that includes all the appearances of the house I can access from my standpoint (e.g. the façade and the gateway), but also a range of other co-presentations that despite being unthematized or unseen belong to the objective constitution of the house (e.g. its back side, the courtyard, etc.). Although I do not perceive such sides directly, they are co-given in my perception of the house, as they build on memory and inform my expectations about the horizon of my experience. This is the reason why it comes as a surprise when our expectations in perceptual experiences are disappointed (as it happens, for example, when walking on a street, we see a façade without any back or sides to it, because we have entered, without realizing it, a construction site).

The phenomenological concept of horizon-consciousness refers to this contextual and spatiotemporal character of experience. A horizon is a field that expands dynamically, and includes both an inner horizon and an external horizon. An inner horizon corresponds to the temporal sequences of perceptual experiences I have of the house from various perspectives, whereas the external horizon comprises the general backdrop from which the house stands out, including, for example, the street and the neighbourhood. As the horizon situates a subjective viewpoint, it also includes my affective disposition towards the house (for instance, whether I find it safe or aesthetically pleasing) and my convictions (or positionality) about the place or the situation (for example, my evaluation of the worth of the house). On Husserl's view, a horizon includes an element of indeterminacy insofar as we are not consciously aware of all the elements that inform our waking life. While the focus of my attention is on the house, there remains a halo (or a 'fog', as Husserl puts in *Ideas I*, cf. Husserl 2004, p. 49) of dim awareness, including sensations, impulses, and memories of which we may be more or less aware. For example, while I am looking at the house, I am not reflectively aware of the range of associations between the house and former experiences of mine that are awakened by sounds, smells, and objects in my field of perception. Such a fringe of consciousness can be illustrated as an atmosphere (*Stimmung*) or an affective background that accompanies lived experience. In this respect, Husserl explores the reduction as a methodological tool in order to clarify the various manners of 'givenness' of an experienced object within distinct horizonal structures. In so doing, Husserl frequently cautions the reader to be 'sceptical, or rather critical' (Husserl 1999, p. 37) when carrying out the reduction, to avoid conflating phenomena with one's assumptions and presuppositions.

As we pointed out earlier, Merleau-Ponty famously objected in his Preface to the *Phenomenology of Perception* that the reduction cannot be completed, as we are always immersed in the standpoint of our everyday life of natural attitude, even when we take up the task of the phenomenological reduction. It follows that there is no way of extracting ourselves completely from an experiential horizon in order to view phenomena 'as they are in themselves'. However, Merleau-Ponty also maintains that phenomenology establishes a practice of reflective engagement with the content of experience, which cannot be understood in abstraction from its horizon. While from the perspective of natural sciences (which Husserl calls 'naturalistic') a person's perceptual background could be identified with physiological patterns of sense data, the phenomenological approach acknowledges that our experiential background stands in a dynamic and affective relation to the content of experience. Thus, perception is hardly a collection of sensory information that belongs to an impersonal viewpoint.

In this sense, to carry out the phenomenological reduction is less an attempt to ground phenomenology on static essences and more a continuous exercise in identifying the structures that *animate* experience across a domain of possible variations. Therefore, Husserl's transcendental method provides the foundation for a critical understanding of the genesis, structure, and modifications of experience in at least two main respects. First, in being committed to the description of first-person experience, classical phenomenology brings to light the sense of ownership of subjective experience, distinguishing it from a collection of empirical data. Second, classical phenomenology helps to recognize that the horizon of subjective experience is informed by a number of unexamined positions and assumptions that call for further critique and verification.

1.1.2 *The critique of historical tradition*

Phenomenological analysis brings to light the fact that the constitution of an individual's viewpoint is framed against a surrounding world (*Umwelt*) that includes other selves as well as the social and cultural practices. In *Being and Time* (1927), Heidegger regarded our everyday pragmatic dealing with the surrounding world as the defining feature of consciousness. Heidegger's point of departure is that things appear to us in light of the norms and rules that are embedded in contexts of everyday use and daily practice, which in turn define the purpose of the entities we deal with; that is, what those things are good for. Thus, a pen is good for writing, which is good for making books, which are good for filling libraries. On this view, the surrounding world appears to us as the realm of things that are 'ready-to-hand'. As such, we experience the world around us through the tools and instruments (what Heidegger calls 'equipment') we habitually employ, like hammers, pens, and laptops. Accordingly, the common world is discovered and experienced in terms of the various domains of our practical concern (i.e. using hammers for hammering, pens and laptops for writing). But what are the sources of the norms and rules we rely upon in our everyday experience? For example, pens and books are good for filling libraries, but whether books are good to promote learning cannot be determined by the technical rules involved in producing books and building libraries.

Heidegger's goal was to show that we are always situated in a totality of practical concerns (what he calls in *Being and Time* the 'the totality of involvements'), which, at times, becomes *an issue* for consciousness. When the totality of involvements fails to involve us effectively, as happens when things accidentally and unexpectedly break down or disappoint our expectations, our absorption in everydayness is likewise interrupted. Imagine going to the library to look for a philosophy book on the good life, and not finding it. Alternatively, perhaps you find the title you were looking for, but you are disappointed by its content, since it does not tell you what specific actions you need to take in order to lead the good life that is appropriate to you. According to Heidegger, the fundamental philosophical problem is about comprehending what is at stake for us in daily life. We cannot seek the answer about the kind of being we are by looking for recipes and instructions in the same way in which we deal with the world of equipment for everyday life. For this reason, Heidegger argues that, by questioning the sense of our own being, we are led to a remarkable 'relatedness backward or forward' (Heidegger 2001, p. 28); that is, to a mode of inquiry that goes back to the sources of signification of the norms and rules by which we abide in our quotidian life. This characteristic manner of inquiry, which moves from our natural comprehension of the world towards the origins of the meaning we rely on, characterizes the classical phenomenological critique of tradition. According to this procedure, phenomenologists seek to uncover the presuppositions and thought formations that are hidden in the practical contexts we inhabit. In doing so, however, they are necessarily compelled to take into account how historical traditions are constituted through the temporal stratification of cultural values and thought formations.

The relation between historical tradition, culture, and social life is encompassed by the concept of the 'life-world' (*Lebenswelt*) on which Husserl concentrates, particularly in his last works, including *The Crisis of European Sciences and Transcendental Phenomenology*, published in 1936. In these texts, Husserl delineates a theory of the life-world as the world of natural experience that is always experientially available to us, prior to any interest we may develop in looking at the world as an object of reflection and investigation. The life-world represents the 'biggest horizon', as it does not refer solely to a universe of entities, but to the sedimentation of historical and cultural values, thereby constituting the shared background of communal experience. Yet, even if the life-world represents the 'biggest horizon' of experiences, it is not *known* as such, as it is experienced in a naive and unsophisticated way as an unthematized background.[12] Think, for example, of the matter-of-fact truths that are part of our cultural background, such as the fact that matter is made of atoms and held together by causal laws and chemical reactions. Even if we may not be able to reproduce the demonstration of those scientific findings, their general content is part of our background knowledge, informing a certain cultural orientation. This indicates that scientific viewpoints and their related concepts flow into the life-world, entering the formation of culture as well as our interpretation of the natural world.

As the life-world is the terrain upon which subjective and collective orientations to the world arise, the thematization of the life-world provides the basis for understanding the origins of cultural formations as well as of historical traditions of thought. Yet, by taking the life-world as an object of inquiry and by questioning its fundamental assumptions, we find ourselves in a sort of circle (what philosopher Hans-Georg Gadamer calls the 'hermeneutic circle'). Understanding the past compels us to comprehend its development as this is actualized in the present, while the present requires a re-examination of the thought formations inherited from the past. Thus, phenomenological critique is not completely independent of its object of inquiry, and needs to proceed in a 'zigzag' manner (Husserl 1970, p. 58); that is, by offering relative clarifications on some aspects that help elucidate others. Both Husserl and Heidegger, then, elaborate on the meaning of tradition by way of interpretation (i.e. in a hermeneutical way), acknowledging that historical understanding is not a matter of asserting one point of view over another, but rather of interrogating the concepts of a historical past in a way that includes their relevance for the present. This means that the interrogation of the past can hardly be separated from the questions and issues that inform the present.

One of the most significant critiques of historical tradition begins with Husserl. In *The Crisis of European Sciences and Transcendental Phenomenology*, Husserl takes issue with the development of science in modern times. He argues that historical attempts to pursue the mathematization of nature; that is, to reduce nature to laws and principles based on mathematics, represented in fact an abstraction from the experienceable world of everyday life. Galileo was notably a forerunner in the seventeenth century of such a scientific approach. In particular, Galileo proved that all bodies accelerate at the same rate regardless of their size or mass. To this end, Galileo needed to conceive of bodies as behaving in the same way in the absence of obstacles that impede their motion, using mathematical models to determine the speed of bodies and their changes of motion.

Husserl characterizes Galileo's method as form of idealization due to its tendency to abstract from subjective qualities of perception in order to exclusively rely on quantitative and mathematical modelling. In this way, the natural praxis of ordinary experience is replaced by an anonymous and impersonal viewpoint whose position in space and time is defined by spatiotemporal coordinates. It is essential to stress that Husserl's critique is not against the progress of natural science brought about by Galileo. Instead, Husserl's critique addresses the generalization and extension of Galileo's scientific method from the analysis of motion to the understanding of the background of our ordinary experience. As Galileo's philosophical project was indeed meant to read the 'book of nature' through the lenses of mathematics, Husserl's critique concerns the impact of Galileo's method on the understanding of the life-world as an all-encompassing field of experience. His worry is that Galileo's approach would reduce the thematization of the life-world to a system of quantitative properties and physical mechanisms that abstracts from the position of the subject.

This was also a key concern for Heidegger, who regarded Galileo's method in a 1962 essay (well after the publication of Husserl's *Crisis*) as establishing a key paradigm shift in the conception of nature since Aristotle: 'Now nature is no longer an inner capacity of a body, determining its form of motion and its place. Nature is now the realm of the uniform space-time context of motion, which is outlined in the axiomatic project and in which alone bodies can be bodies as a part of it and anchored in it' (Heidegger 1993, p. 292). Heidegger contrasts the Aristotelian view of nature as a purposeful organization of living beings with the static and passive picture of nature that emerges from the mathematization of the physical world brought about by modern science. By looking at nature through the language of mathematics, modern science contributed to the formation of a collective mindset that regards nature as a realm for prediction, calculation, and manipulation. This entails forgetting the original philosophical interest that led scientists to investigate the laws of nature. Instead of inquiring into the lawfulness of natural phenomena and their correlation to human understanding, nature was to be regarded as co-extensive to the domain of technology. As a result of this, the mathematization of nature leads to a calculative approach towards reality, obscuring the comprehension of the actual 'being' of things.

While Heidegger's critique of historical tradition would eventually centre on the problem of the *concealment* of the question of being from the realm of everyday life, Husserl's concern was to bring to light the transcendental structure of the life-world, including its ties to subjective and intersubjective experience. Ultimately, Husserl sought to retrieve the life-world as a diversified and pluralistic horizon of sense for a community of subjects. For this reason, Husserl questions the traditions of thought that inform the life-world and that influence the way we thematize corporeality and lived experience. In this respect, it is worth noting that Husserl was aware that the mathematization of nature was a western cultural phenomenon that could not be universalized to all cultures. Despite this, Husserl's approach towards history appears characterized by a strong Eurocentric attitude, which has long been noted and criticized (Derrida 2003; Bernasconi and Cook 2003). For example, it has been pointed out that Husserl's references to Indian, Papuan, Chinese, and Bantu culture as well as to Gypsies tends to lock individuals and nations into their particularities. These are regarded as simply 'alien' and 'other' with respect to the development of European culture, which, for Husserl, was driven by the philosophical vocation initiated by the Ancient Greeks.[13]

At the same time, it is important to consider that Husserl's insistence on the transcendental constitution of the life-world was meant to counter biological explanations of human nature that were vigorously emerging in the intellectual landscape of Husserl's time (Moran 2011). Furthermore, in his letter to anthropologist Lévy-Bruhl in 1935, Husserl emphasizes how Lévy-Bruhl's ethnological and sociological insights proved crucial to phenomenology in order to 'empathize' with humanity in the effort to understand not simply humanity's 'world-representation' but rather the world that 'actually exists' for humanity itself (Husserl 2008, p. 3). Transcendental analysis, in other words, seeks to provide an access to the experiential character of human and social reality, and not an idealized and detached representation of history as a whole. This suggests, if not a revision of Husserl's approach to cultural pluralism, certainly an awareness of the problem of interpreting and analysing the life-world as a domain of social and cultural belonging, whose critique requires an encounter and ethical confrontation with different cultures.[14]

Therefore, while the emphasis on the Ancient Greek civilization as representing the origins of European culture is undeniable in a number of works in the classical-phenomenological tradition, it is important to point out that such an appraisal is part of a specific critique of the historical and cultural tradition. As such, phenomenological critique brings to the fore questions and arguments concerning the very possibility of a shared world (see Chapter 6).

1.1.3 The critique of alienation

Unlike the zigzag manner of inquiry that is distinctive of Husserl's and Heidegger's respective critiques of historical tradition, the existentialist approach to history and culture put forward by Sartre, Beauvoir, and Fanon features a dialectical method that is infused with elements of Marxist critique. Broadly speaking, a dialectical method consists in bringing together opposite and seemingly contradictory positions in order to overcome their opposition and reveal their reciprocal connection. This notion of dialectics is historically connected to nineteenth-century German philosopher G. W. F. Hegel, who employed a dialectical method to illustrate the development of reason across history. Overall, in Hegel, reason represents the essence of human nature, which recognizes itself as a power of self-determination by going through a historical process of self-alienation and self-estrangement. In this context, alienation means estrangement or becoming other than one is. The phenomenon of alienation is regarded by Hegel as a fundamental step towards the development of self-consciousness at both individual and collective levels. Indeed, from a dialectical viewpoint, self-consciousness is an achievement marked by conflicts and struggles, as epitomized by the master and servant struggle in Hegel's *Phenomenology of Spirit* (to which we return in Chapters 4 and 5), which served as a point of departure for Marxist readings of Hegel in France in the 1930s.[15]

Despite drawing on a dialectical method of analysis, Sartre, Beauvoir, and Fanon explicitly rejected Hegel's idealistic premises. While in the Hegelian philosophical project, the concept of alienation represents a critical moment of the development of reason that needs to be overcome, French Existentialists resisted the apparent closure of Hegel's idealism, as culminating in reason's absolute self-knowledge. In contrast to Hegel, they were interested in exploring the material implications of alienation and the challenges it posits in terms of racial alienation, gender oppression, and anti-colonial struggle. In this respect, they examined the relation between self-consciousness and history through the lenses of Marx's historical materialism. This entails the recognition that human subjectivity is placed not only in social and cultural networks that develop historically, but also situated in contexts that largely prevent individuals and groups from pursuing and achieving freedom as self-determination.

This type of analysis presents three main critical aspects when developed in a phenomenological sense: (1) the problem of examining the lived experience of oppression as this affects the first-person viewpoint of the subjectivities involved, without however reducing the self to the phenomenon of oppression. (2) The need to diagnose racism, sexism, and other forms of discrimination as occurring at the level of the 'natural attitude'; that is, as informing the taken-for-granted horizon of everyday life. Finally, there is (3) the problem of identifying the sources of oppression, racism, and sexism in socio-political terms, as an institutionalized and systemic phenomenon, not just as a subjective prejudice or attitude.

This set of problems emerges in Sartre's early diagnosis of antisemitism in his essay *Anti-Semite and the Jew: An Exploration of the Etiology of*

Hate (1946), where he attempts to describe the situation of the Jew in France in the years before and after the Second World War. Sartre presents the Jewish condition in terms of alienation, drawing attention to the ways in which Jewish people were racialized and discriminated against by antisemitic Frenchmen, and yet also regarded as aliens and outsiders by French democrats (Sartre 1995, pp. 46ff). Such a phenomenon revealed, for Sartre, the contradictory stance of democrats and the ambiguity of assimilation, as French democrats were eager to defend the project of Jewish assimilation but at the greater cost of asking Jewish subjects to deny their identity *as Jews*. By ignoring the social and religious identity of Jewish people, the proponents of assimilation were in fact asserting an 'essence' of Jewish subjectivity in which Jewish subjects could not possibly recognize themselves. In this context, Sartre illustrates the Jewish condition as being relentlessly conditioned by the objectifying power of the antisemitic gaze, that is to say, by the alienating power of antisemitic prejudice. Even Sartre, however, ultimately portrays the situation of the Jew as an 'over-determined' condition, divided between the antisemitic gaze and an undefined longing for assimilation. Indeed, the main problem of Sartre's analysis is that it fails to distinguish the lived experience of Jewish subjectivity from its socially constructed presentation. In so doing, Sartre ended up locking Jewish experience in the antisemitic gaze, failing to disentangle the former from the latter.[16]

While Sartre was aware of the limits of his analysis (Webber 2018, p. 130), and of his lack of engagement with Jewish identity, history, and religion, he brought to light the problems that are characteristic of a phenomenology of racialization, specifically the social construction of 'Jewishness', and the objectifying power of the antisemitic gaze. Drawing on Sartre, both Beauvoir and Fanon developed a phenomenology of gender and race that explore the social and cultural relevance of the sexist and racist gaze, describing how it operates in the natural attitude, and how it affects the self-perception of women and colonized people. At the same time, Beauvoir and Fanon draw attention to the dialectic between selfhood and social identity that takes place on a subjective level of experience. This means that a phenomenological exploration of gender and race does not reduce subjectivity to a social construct or to a passive medium upon which external forces are inscribed, but rather acknowledges the ambiguity of the human condition, and how gender and race, in different ways, contribute to the formation of a shared social and cultural identity.

In this context, the concept of ambiguity plays a pivotal role. Originally introduced by Merleau-Ponty and Beauvoir to challenge the dualism between mind and body posited by Cartesian philosophy (Silverman

1987; Weiss 2008a, 2008b, 2014), the concept of ambiguity reflects the view that concrete, lived experience is always situated in a contingent historical and socio-cultural context, which includes, among other aspects, language, culture, and upbringing. Thus, ambiguity refers to the impossibility of completely bracketing the contingent character of experience, including the social context, from the analysis of lived experience. Ambiguity is also related to bodily experience, for the body is, at the same time, a source of spontaneity that belongs to the self (as it allows freedom of movement, action, and expression) as well as the site of sedimentation of social and cultural meaning (particularly through gender and race). For Fanon and Beauvoir, the ambiguity of bodily experience is a central phenomenon of human existence, and it is also key to developing awareness and emancipation from alienating social-cultural constraints. As Beauvoir writes: 'to attain his truth, man must not attempt to dispel the ambiguity of his being but, on the contrary, accept the task of realizing it' (Beauvoir 2018, p. 12). Similarly, Fanon takes up a commitment to decolonize perception and imagination, gesturing to a new humanism that relies on a renewed understanding of the relations between body, identity, and emancipation, as we discuss in Chapter 5.

In this regard, it is interesting to note that in her *Ethics of Ambiguity* (1947), Beauvoir explicitly compares the existentialist approach to Husserl's phenomenological reduction:

> Existentialist conversion should rather be compared to Husserlian reduction: let man put his will to be 'in parentheses' and he will thereby be brought to the consciousness of his true condition. And just as phenomenological reduction prevents the errors of dogmatism by suspending all affirmation concerning the mode of reality of the external world, whose flesh and bone presence the reduction does not, however, contest, so existentialist conversion does not suppress my instincts, desires, plans, and passions. (Beauvoir 2018, p. 13)

For Beauvoir, the phenomenological reduction was meant to avoid both dogmatism and scepticism by bracketing our everyday attitude and letting us 'see' through our habitual orientation and ways of being. Thus, Beauvoir argues that the phenomenological method is not some kind of ivory tower that regards human existence from afar. On the contrary, the phenomenological method, in its classical formulation, helps us understand how we are situated in the world, without thereby abstracting from our desires, instincts, and feelings (and thus without forgetting that the subject is the living centre of such affective and volitional phenomena). Likewise, the 'existentialist conversion' leads one to discover and appropriate the meaning that is deposited in one's situation on the basis of the recognition that no value can be determined from the outside, but must instead be won by engaging one's intellect and cognition, and also perception, imagination, and desire. Such an approach is motivated by the fact that the possibility of error does not simply lie in the use of reason, but more deeply in the lack of authenticity of one's commitment, in one's 'incoherent sliding from one attitude to another' (Beauvoir 2018, pp. 34–5).

Since the projects disclosed by the existentialist conversion are structurally indeterminate and open-ended, Beauvoir does not commit to a normative ethics that would prescribe how one should act regardless of the circumstances. Instead, Beauvoir acknowledges the lack of coincidence between the projects one commits to and the contingent situation one lives in. In this sense, ambiguity is not only an ontological condition but also an ethical commitment to appropriate one's projects and to be responsible for them. While Beauvoir emphasizes the joyous character of such a process, this, however, does not alleviate the tension of having to make choices for which there cannot always be an absolute justification, and for which we remain nonetheless responsible (Weiss 2008, p. 32).

1.2 Contemporary critical phenomenology: key methodological approaches

As we have seen, classical phenomenology is first and foremost a descriptive and interpretative analysis of experience, and yet it also presents a diverse range of critical approaches when it comes to inquiring into the relation between subjectivity, embodiment, and social experience. Contemporary critical phenomenology not only inherits the practice of interrogation and inquiry that characterizes classical phenomenology, but also aims to deepen and develop further the problems that emerge in classical-phenomenological discourse, as we shall now see.

1.2.1 Between selfhood and social identity

As mentioned before, in classical phenomenology the concept of self or subjectivity is continuous with that of identity insofar as selfhood stands for the embodied viewpoint in relation to which meaning is constituted and through which the past is sedimented. More radically than other classical phenomenologists, French Existentialists developed a phenomenology of gender and race, reflecting on the ways in which visible markers of social identities, such as gender and race, inform personal awareness and are involved in alienating and unequal power relations. Drawing on both the Husserlian and post-Husserlian tradition, critical phenomenology thematizes social identity in non-essentialist terms; that is, as a relational and dialectical concept.

To begin with, social identity is not based on an essential set of characteristics (whether biological or metaphysical), nor is it a mere category used for classificatory purposes that has no reality or impact on lived experience. On the contrary, the concept of social identity refers to the positions that subjects occupy in embodied horizons of meaning and knowledge, comprising beliefs and communal values that are historically constituted and dynamically oriented to the future (Alcoff 2006). To account for this, Linda Martín Alcoff, in her work *Visible Identities: Gender, Race, and the Self* (2006), puts forward a theory of social identity whose relational character centres on a hermeneutic model of rationality. This means that social identity is based on interpretative meaning-making processes that are constitutive of one's history, background, and situation, in light of which individuals develop an understanding of their social and cultural position. More specifically, Alcoff maintains that social identities provide the self with 'plans of observation' or epistemic horizons to engage with and understand the issues of their surrounding world. Drawing on the phenomenological concept of 'horizon', which, as we saw earlier, admits degrees of indeterminacy, Alcoff argues that social identities articulate the field in which individuals are positioned within specific socio-cultural and historical contexts without depriving individuals of their agency and deliberative rationality. Different individuals can share with a social group a historical situatedness as well as historical experiences, which provide them with opportunities for knowledge and even vantage points for reflection. Yet their individual viewpoints are not absorbed by or identified with the claims that are characteristic of their social identity.

As Alcoff notices, 'two individuals may participate in the same event but have perceptual access to different aspects of that event' (Alcoff 2006, p. 43). Social identity is responsible for the cohesion of background knowledge but it does not *determine* individual epistemic judgement. A fully formed perspective requires the individual's engagement with the forms and principles that produce knowledge. Indeed, 'although meanings are made and remade, the "internal" agency of the individual to judge, to choose, or to act operates within and in relation to a specific horizon, and thus one is open to an indeterminacy but from a specifiable position' (Alcoff 2006, p. 43). Since social identity is subject-dependent and is characterized by flexibility and indeterminacy, the process of identity formation is always dynamic, and any attempt to reduce it to an essential or fixed set of characteristics or to a uniform description of behaviour would close off its open-ended character.

In this context, gender and race represent embodied horizons of meaning, which are imbued with cultural meaning and reproduced through habits. For Alcoff, both gender and race need to be explored in terms of how 'the body is lived, perceived in the world, presented, and experienced' (Alcoff 2006, p. 46). Thus, the phenomenology of race and gender help to understand the extent to which embodiment is contextually involved in the constitution of one's social identity.

From this point of view, the concepts of social identity and self are inseparable from each other. At least, Alcoff argues that, to the extent to which self and visible identities can be separated, such a separation is the result of a philosophical abstraction rather than an actual experiential phenomenon. This is not to claim that one's experiential self is entirely social or even constructed, but rather that the presentation of self – the way we appear to others in social contexts – is necessarily mediated by gender and race. As social identities refer to horizons of social meaning, they always depend on the engagement of self in acts of interpretation and social communication that institute wider networks of meaning and value. Furthermore, since a social identity is not a fixed or stable determination, its indeterminacy reveals the fact that alterity (or difference) is intrinsic to the notion of identity itself.

On this front, Alcoff's view is that alterity (i.e. what is 'other' with respect to self, such as other selves, culture, and society) is neither a negative element that is in need of recognition, nor an external power structure, as in Foucault. For Alcoff, one's relation to alterity is constitutive of self as an 'absorption, generation, and expansion'. As she puts it: 'the Other is internal to the self's substantive content, a part of its own horizon, and thus a part of its own identity' (Alcoff 2006, p. 45). Alcoff's view is that the cultural heritage that informs a subjective viewpoint is always expanding and evolving along with contextual social practices in which individuals are actively involved. It follows that any process of self-interpretation is also and at the same time a moment of critical re-appropriation and re-evaluation of contextual knowledge. Indeed, each self embodies a critical standpoint towards her sociocultural horizon by way of integration and transformation rather than negation or antithesis. An example of this is how the Holocaust represents a tragic fact that exists in every contemporary Jewish person's horizon but also of every Christian European's. On Alcoff's view, there will be a difference in the way these two groups relate to the history and narrative of the Holocaust, and thus a difference in the way the Holocaust shapes their sense of cultural identity. Specifically, such a difference involves:

[. . .] the one as knowing that he or she could have been the target of the Final Solution, and the other as knowing that this event occurred within the broad category of their culture. Each must react to or deal with this event in some way, but to say this does not presuppose any pre-given interpretation of the event or of its significance in forming a contemporary identity. (Alcoff 2000, p. 43).

This indicates that the concept of social identity calls for an analysis of one's relation to alterity as mediated by the stratified and diverse access to a common social and cultural background. Thus, while social identities cannot be transcended at will, as they are embedded in the horizon of one's experience, they cannot be reduced to 'cults of ethnicity' either (Alcoff, ibid.), as if they represented sheer political or partisans' interests.

1.2.2 Transactional bodies, narratives, and the critique of the natural attitude

In a number of critical-phenomenological accounts, narratives represent a fundamental means of accessing and describing lived experience. In so doing, critical phenomenologists depart from transcendental methods of analysis (such as the phenomenological reduction), privileging contingency over necessity in the analysis of social identity. This methodological shift is justified by the fact that social identities are not objective categories, but rather they are contextual and evolving over time. As Marian Ortega puts it:

> Preoccupied with questions of selfhood, subjectivity, and personal identity, philosophers have looked for general explanations over particular discussions describing selves as embodied and marked by race, sex, gender, ability, and other identities. [. . .] People of colour, immigrants, exiles, border dwellers, those at the margins, have paid attention to those particularities and have told their stories and described their struggles; they have offered gifts of words arising from their lived experiences. [. . .] Why not follow the so-called digressions to see where they lead, to see how they can transform our visions of ourselves and of philosophy itself? (Ortega 2016, p. 2)

To be sure, the use of narratives is not in contradiction with the tenets of classical phenomenology. In fact, the analysis of narrative and first-person reports is compatible with the phenomenological effort to bring to light the first-person perspective, especially in phenomenological psychopathology and phenomenology of illness (see especially Ratcliffe 2008, pp. 64ff). In a specific sense, however, critical phenomenologists rely on narratives to inquire into the constitution, change, and intersectional aspects of social identity, what Shannon Sullivan (2001) also calls the pragmatic 'transaction' between bodies and environment.

By and large, a pragmatic transaction refers to the practical interaction that occurs between bodies and the environment. In John Dewey's philosophical pragmatism, an example of transaction is habit, which functions as a form of adaptation of the organism to the environment (Dewey 1929, p. 282). While habits are natural responses of the body, they are also mediated by learning and social practices. A transactional view of inquiry regards knowledge and action in terms of processes, departing from causal models of explanation that presuppose a dualism between subject and object. Understood as a form of transaction, knowledge refers to the capacity of the mind to identify and re-construct the categories that structure reality through the subject's active interaction with what lies outside in space and time.

Drawing on Dewey, Sullivan argues that cultural meaning is deposited and transmitted through the lived body as a form of transaction with the social world. Transactional bodies are bodies that express meaning through language, gestures, and bodily practices that sediment over time, shaping new customs and shared social practices. The ambiguity of transaction, however, is that it involves habit, which is both transformative and adaptive. Social habits (including the habits that inform gender expression and behaviour) can sediment over time and break with existing social norms, but they may also become static and rigid unless they are sustained by the external environment in an active and mutual transaction of meaning. Thus, a pragmatic transaction involves individuals and groups along with institutions and cultural structures in educational processes that help individuals identify, understand, and enact transformative changes of habits.

To illustrate the dialectical character of transaction, Sullivan contrasts it with the melting pot metaphor that is often used in popular culture to describe the multicultural character of countries like the United States. Recalling how Dewey himself found the melting pot metaphor problematic, Sullivan points out that 'the melting pot is like a fondue into which cubes of different cheeses are thrown, with the end result being a complete dissolving of the individual cubes so that the fondue is made possible' (Sullivan 2001, p. 14). Sullivan notes that the melting pot metaphor has functioned in the United States to promote a view of cultural assimilation rather than integration, serving the interests of one group (whiteness) at the expense of others. As a corrective of this metaphor and as an illustration of transaction, she offers the metaphor of the stew:

> In a stew, the potatoes, onion, carrots, and spices neither melt into
> one another as do the individual ingredients of a fondue, nor do they
> remain isolated and separate, as do the ingredients of a tossed salad.
> Rather, as they are in the pot together, stew ingredients intermingle in
> such a way that each helps constitute what the others are. For example,
> and to oversimplify by focusing on two ingredients only, the flavors of
> the carrot and onion in a stew impact each other such that the carrot
> is no longer a carrot, but an onion-y carrot, and the onion is a carrot-
> y onion. A mutual interpenetration of the vegetables takes place by
> means of the intermingling of their flavors, making all of the vegetables
> something different from what they were before they were in the stew.
> This transformation does not mean that the vegetables have been col-
> lapsed into one another or into some sort of formless mush (unless the
> stew is overcooked). Rather, the carrot is still distinct from the onion
> and vice versa – an onion-y carrot is not the same as a carrot-y onion,
> after all – but at the same time that they are distinct, they permeate one
> another in a constitutive way. (Sullivan 2001, pp. 15–16)

The stew metaphor indicates that transaction is an active and ongoing relationship between subjects both in relation to themselves and
the cultural world. Sullivan acknowledges that the metaphor, like all
metaphors, may be flawed, as it conveys a sense of passivity (that of
the ingredients being passively impacted by one another), when in fact
the conceptual point of transaction is to indicate a relation sustained
by active connections in which no element or flavour takes over the
other. This means that social identities can be negotiated, challenged, and
transformed from within the course of individual experience thanks to
the active and ongoing exchange of meaning with others in the cultural
environment. At the same time, the stew metaphor indicates that cultural
identities are not chosen, the same way in which one does not choose
where one is born or the social groups one belongs to.

This is best illustrated by Gloria Anzaldúa's *La Frontera-Borderlands*,
where she reflects on her experience as an Indian, Chicana-Mexicana,
lesbian, and writer, coming to terms with multiple and overlapping
identities connected to her ethnicity, class, gender, and sexuality. For
Anzaldúa, each of her identities is lived through as a form of displacement in the social environment, in a way that makes it impossible for one
identity to take over the others, or even to be neatly and easily discernible
as a fixed set of dispositions and traits. This plural self is given voice and
substance through the act of writing, through which Anzaldúa explores
her *mestiza* (mixed) consciousness in terms of travelling across different
borders that are also different cultural worlds (upon which we return in
Chapter 5).

In this context, narratives are used to capture the pluralistic, contextual, and evolving character of multiple social identities. However, the use of narratives in critical phenomenology does not imply that narrativity is the source of the intelligibility of lived experience. Gail Weiss, for instance, rejects the equation between meaning and narrative intelligibility (Weiss 2003). The use of narratives in critical phenomenology refers to the need to reconfigure what is usually taken for granted when talking about the natural attitude. Since narratives bring to light how the body is situated across overlapping social horizons, first-person narrative accounts help to reveal the presuppositions of the social background, and how they are latent at the level of the natural attitude. For example, in *Queer Phenomenology*, Sara Ahmed emphasizes how the suspension of the natural attitude in classical phenomenology does not put out of play social and cultural presuppositions that remain operative in the background of lived experience. By way of example, she describes the experience of entering a dining room while on vacation in a resort with her partner:

> We enter the dining room, where we face many tables placed alongside each other. Table after table ready for action, waiting for bodies who arrive to take up their space, to be seated. In taking up space, I am taken back. I face what seems like a shocking image. In front of me, on the tables, couples are seated. Table after table, couple after couple, taking the same form: one man sitting by one woman around a 'round table', facing each other 'over' the table. Of course, I 'know' this image – it is a familiar one, after all. But I am shocked by the sheer force of regularity of that which is familiar: how each table presents the same form of sociality as the form of the heterosexual couple. How is it possible, with all that is possible, that the same form is repeated again and again? How does the openness of the future get closed down into so little in the present? (Ahmed 2006, p. 82)

The sheer regularity that pervades Ahmed's description is the regularity of heterosexuality as a regular pattern of behaviour and appearance in social spaces, which appear 'saturated', as it were, for queer subjects. Ahmed argues that the scene at the resort – heterosexual couples gathered around tables, embodying intergenerational and historical styles of behaviour – epitomizes a system of social reproduction that is implicit in the social background, where heterosexuality is taken to be the dominant or standard form of sexual orientation (see also Chapter 4). In this sense, a sense of familiarity and acquaintance arises, which includes specific presumptions and expectations of behaviour. Moreover, such familiarity with heterosexual patterns of behaviour influences how we orient towards the future, precluding an appreciation and understanding of the naturalness of different styles of sexual orientation. To what extent, then, can the phenomenological method help shed light on the set of assumptions that are operative in the natural attitude and that exert an indirect constraint over our natural stance towards the world?

In relation to this issue, Gail Weiss argues that it is not only essential to suspend the natural attitude, but also to de-naturalize the natural attitude itself. By de-naturalization, she refers to the fact that the natural attitude needs to be recognized as a complex and ever-evolving perspective, and not as a rigid and 'default' perspective:

> [The de-naturalization of the natural attitude] occurs when we begin to recognize that our natural attitudes are themselves complex, dynamic constructions, evolving and transforming over time, across space, and, most importantly, in response to specific social, cultural, and political encounters. We are not born with them and yet, once developed, our natural attitudes provide us with a 'default' perspective, or a taken-for-granted set of meanings, values, and norms that frame our expectations in any given situation. (Weiss 2016, p. 4)

It is noteworthy that Husserl did not aim to *change* the natural attitude, but only to suspend it. Therefore, Weiss argues that the goal of phenomenology should rather be to challenge 'the taken-for-granted assumptions that underpin or provide a foundation for the expectations associated with the natural attitude' (Weiss 2016, p. 11). Indeed, if the natural attitude is not a fixed and rigid structure, and if it can be altered, it is essential, from a critical-phenomenological point of view, not to accept it as a given fact. To this end, Weiss emphasizes the importance of heeding the analysis of those discordant or non-conforming experiences (which narratives bring to light) through which we recognize that a naive reliance on our natural attitude can fail us. This means that the unquestioned acceptance of the natural attitude can limit the comprehension and interpretation of the unfamiliar phenomena with which we are presented in everyday life.

Ahmed calls such a process 'visual economy: it involves ways of *seeing the difference* between familiar and strange others as they are (re)presented to the subject' (Ahmed 2000, p. 24). In a similar vein, Weiss argues that the failure of the natural attitude to render a coherent, stable, and familiar view of reality generates philosophical, political, and social questions through which it is possible to deepen self- and other-understanding.

1.2.3 Ameliorative critique

According to Weiss, Murphy, and Salamon in their introduction to *50 Concepts for a Critical Phenomenology*, critical phenomenology represents an 'ameliorative phenomenology' in that it seeks to improve theoretical analysis and conceptual frameworks along with collective action. Using Sally Haslanger's conception of ameliorative questions (Haslanger 2012), it can be argued that ameliorative projects involve the formulations of concepts and theories that expand our conceptual framework in order to also improve its practical applications. An ameliorative project is, therefore, inseparable from conceptual and descriptive analyses, which investigate how social categories, like gender and race, are used in specific ontological and epistemic domains that involve embodied, intersubjective, and social experience. In this respect, critical phenomenology helps to extend the range of descriptive analyses in which the concepts and arguments of classical and existential phenomenology can be employed, while also critically reflecting on the contexts in which such analyses are carried out. The most evident way in which critical phenomenology seeks to ameliorate classical-phenomenological discourse consists in drawing attention to the constitution of social identities and their intersectional character, bringing to light their intersection with power-based forms of oppression, such as racism and sexism. By expanding, integrating, and revisiting classical and existential phenomenological concepts and arguments, critical phenomenology ultimately enriches the relevance of phenomenological analysis itself.

Although the concept of *critical* phenomenology might sound purely negative, both in terms of pointing out the limits of classical phenomenology and of focusing on socio-political issues, such as oppression and injustice, the aim of critical phenomenology is ultimately a positive one: to build a more inclusive, accepting world that is better accommodating of difference and resistant with respect to oppression and discrimination (Guenther 2020, p. 16). This is connected to phenomenology's concern with political action in the form of communal action, activism, and solidarity (see especially Chapter 6). To quote from Arendt, 'it is out of solidarity that they [subjects] establish deliberately and, as it were, dispassionately a community of interest with the oppressed and the exploited' (Arendt 1972, p. 88). For Arendt, solidarity is the principle that inspires action, establishing a common dimension of belonging that is grounded on the recognition of plurality and uniqueness. Fundamental to Arendt's account is the idea that solidarity works by revising and expanding the way in which we think and act with one another in a world that we consider our own. To be driven by solidarity, for Arendt, means to institute a relational space that creates opportunities for action and thinking with others in a shared public sphere, while freeing individuals from social separateness and social invisibility. In a similar way, a critical-phenomenological account is inspired by the view that solidarity requires freeing individual experience from naturalized and normalizing presuppositions, which necessarily requires thinking through the meaning of plurality and uniqueness.

2

Corporeality

*Body awareness, body images,
and resistant bodies*

We must not say that our body is in space, nor for that matter in time.
It *inhabits* space and time.

Merleau-Ponty, *Phenomenology of Perception*

[. . .] The body continually transgresses all attempts to make it or the
narratives grounded upon it fully intelligible. And yet, the body can
never be dispensed with altogether, for the body is the omnipresent
horizon for all the narratives human beings tell (about it).

Gail Weiss, *Refiguring the Ordinary*

Phenomenology has always been at the forefront of research on embodied
experience. Embodiment, corporeality, or incarnation are the concepts
used by classical phenomenologists to describe the body as the centre of
subjective and intersubjective experience. By and large, phenomenologists maintain that the body is the condition of possibility for making
sense of our experiences, including the experiences of other people's
experiences. Not only are our feelings and sensations connected to the
body, but also our desires as well as our capacities for cognizing and
acting presuppose in different degrees the contribution of bodily capacities like sensitivity and motility. For this reason, the body cannot be
regarded as a purely physical thing that is mechanically conditioned by
external sensory inputs. Yet the involvement of the body in experience
can be ambiguous, given that the body is generally 'absent' or taken for
granted in ordinary experience, and it only comes to the fore when it is

no longer 'functional' or serving our purposes of movement and action.[1] Thus, the body's presence becomes conspicuous when it does not fit pre-existing normative expectations about bodily behaviour and appearance.

A phenomenological understanding of corporeality requires a pre-liminary understanding of three main dimensions of bodily experience: bodily awareness, the body seen by others, and the habitual body. Sensing one's body moving, feeling, and responding to environmental cues (what is also called *proprioceptive* awareness) reflects the body's characteristic spontaneity, which is based on sensibility and motility. To this end, phe-nomenologists stress that that sensibility and receptivity are not passive and inert capacities of the body. While a large part of European modern philosophy sensibility is often framed as the capacity *to be affected* by external stimuli, phenomenologists inquire into the layers of motivation in virtue of which the sentient body *responds* to the environment through affect (a term that broadly encompasses feelings, emotions, and moods), movement, and habit.

The phenomenology of embodiment, however, also draws atten-tion to how the body that is felt in first-person experience becomes an object or others. Specifically, the body becomes an object upon which other subjects cast a point of view that is in principle capable of objectifying and limiting bodily spontaneity. This offers important insights into the ambiguity of bodily experience in that it calls into ques-tion the relation between self-awareness and social experience. Such a connection can be further explored in light of the role played by habit in sustaining and facilitating the body's natural projection towards the outer world.

From a critical-phenomenological angle, these three dimensions of bodily experience help to identify how the body is entangled in networks of social meaning, upon which experiences of stigmatization, bodily alienation, and normalization are grounded. Indeed, as we will show, a critical-phenomenological approach is not only concerned with revealing the key structures of body awareness, but it also questions the rela-tion between body, experience, and power. In order to illustrate such issues and the trajectories of thought that inform them, in this chapter we proceed by first illustrating the critical aspects that inform the phe-nomenology of body in Husserl, Sartre, and Merleau-Ponty. We focus particularly on the concepts of double sensing, the distinction between body-subject and body-object, and the habitual body. We then show how such concepts play out in contemporary critical phenomenology with particular regard to experiences of objectification, stigmatization, and bodily alienation. In doing so, we also engage insights offered by contemporary phenomenology of illness, indicating its connection to critical-phenomenological discourse about bodily experience. We conclude by introducing the convergence between critical phenomenology of bodily experience and the philosophy of disability.

2.1 The transcendental-phenomenological critique of corporeal experience

One of the key tasks of the phenomenologist, as Husserl puts it, is to resist the naturalistic approach that reduces the body to an observable thing, as having an inner, inscrutable side (the soul or mind) standing against an external and physical counterpart (the materiality of the body). Taking issue with the tradition of modern European philosophy, including particularly Locke and Berkeley, Husserl raises the following concern:

> But I must not overlook, as does the psychology of 'data on a tablet of consciousness', that this 'tablet' has consciousness of itself as a tablet, is in the world, and has consciousness of the world: I am continually conscious of individual things in the world, as things that interest me, move me, disturb me, etc., but in doing this I always have consciousness of the world itself, as that in which I myself am, although it is not there as a thing, does not affect me as things do, is not, in a sense similar to things, an object of my dealings. (Husserl 1970, p. 251)

On Husserl's view, modern psychology fails to take into account the fact that the very object of its investigation, namely the mind, is not a passive receptacle of stimuli coming from without. Locke's identification of the mind with a blank tablet, for example, fails to acknowledge that the mind, even when regarded as a blank tablet, has in fact 'consciousness of itself as a tablet', as it is always capable of being filled with sensuous experience. Husserl refers to self-awareness as an intrinsic quality of self that is sensitive to the surrounding world and attuned to it on a sensuous and affective level. On this view, consciousness is continuously solicited by different things in the environment that awaken one's attention, desire, and feelings. The world represents the general backdrop against which such attunement takes place. For this reason, we do not experience the world around us as a thing but rather as a field, which is co-present in all our experiences despite not being thematized as such by consciousness.

Husserl distinguishes between a pre-reflective, unthematized consciousness, which accompanies our experience of objects in the outer world, and a reflective, thematic awareness that is explicitly oriented to objects of experience. This very distinction characterizes in a fundamental way bodily experience (Zahavi 2020, p. 107). Indeed, through self-perception, I experience my body as an unthematized, sentient reality (*Leib*) and only reflectively do I conceive of my body as a separate and objectifiable material entity (*Körper*). While the distinction between *Leib* and *Körper* is not captured by the English term 'body', Husserl emphasizes that both dimensions of corporeal existence are constitutive of our lived experience, though in different respects. For example, when we undergo a medical examination, we relate to our body as an external and physically distinct reality that lends itself to observation by others. Nonetheless, our lived experience takes place in and through a body that is implicitly and originally felt as our own. Husserl refers to the lived body (*Leib*) not only to highlight the role of embodiment in the analysis of lived experience, but also to emphasize the constitutive openness of the self towards alterity (Zahavi 2020). Alterity refers to experiences of outer objects and animate beings that are 'other' with respect to the self, as well as to the alterity that is implicit at the level of selfhood as an experiential, self-relating viewpoint.

This is best understood if we consider Husserl's concept of 'double sensing', which refers to the role of touch in our experience of spatiotemporal objects. When I see a sheet of paper, its front side occupies my visual horizon, and I am aware that the paper is at a relative distance from where I am. Touch sensations, on the other hand, yield the consistency, extension, and continuity of the sheet of paper, pointing to localized sensations on my fingertips. While the visual presentation of the sheet of paper allows breaks and interruptions (i.e. the sheet of paper appears as an external object me, and it has unseen sides), through touch the object fills space and directly resists my grasp, for instance because of its tactile roughness. While visual and tactile sensations normally interpenetrate in the perceptual apprehension of spatiotemporal objects, touch sensations more directly reveal the presence of self in experience. A relevant example of this phenomenon is that of the right hand touching the left hand. In touching my left hand, I am simultaneously perceiving the underlying features that belong to my left hand (e.g. smoothness, roughness, warmth) and the touch sensations that I can localize on my right hand. However, if I abstract from the touch sensations given through the right hand, the left hand appears to me as an object of outward perception, namely as a distinct and objectifiable reality.

Double sensing is paradigmatic of the two-fold manner in which the body is given to the self, namely 'as a sensed (bodily perceived) living body and as an outwardly perceived physical body of the outer world' (Stein 1964, p. 40). Differently stated, in the stream of experience, the body is simultaneously *sensing* and *sensed* as an object of perception. The concept of 'double sensing' reflects the characteristic openness of the self to the outer world, and it also indicates that we do not experience things and events from nowhere but always within a situated and embodied perspective. To this end, Husserl describes the lived body as the organ of experience, namely as the centre of interconnected areas of awareness, including the various aspects of seeing, hearing, touching, and moving, which contribute to the formation of a general kinaesthetic sense.

Kinaesthesia refers to postural awareness, including awareness of the movements of the parts of the body, such as muscles and joints. However, in Husserl's phenomenology, kinaesthesia has a deeper significance in that it brings to the fore the interconnected systems of motivations by means of which the body inhabits spatiality. For each movement of my body, whether I move my eyes, my head or my arms, there exists a simultaneous shift of orientation in relation to the objects surrounding me. For instance, when I walk, all things around me stand in a certain perspectival position. If I run, all things appear to be moving, or going past my body. Through my movements, I can set the rest of the surrounding world into motion or I can put it to rest by standing still (Husserl 1997, pp. 341–2). Yet I do not experience my head turning or my eyes moving, at least not in the sense that I am reflectively aware of each of my bodily movements as they occur in the muscles or joints. Rather, I experience certain perceptual possibilities as absent, while others become available or prominent to me (e.g. I cannot see what is behind my back, when I walk, but I am aware of the bumps on the road as well as of the noise signalling the presence of people around me).

It follows that the body cannot be perceived as an extrinsic entity separate from consciousness. On the contrary, the body represents the source of orientation within a spatiotemporal continuum, or, as Husserl argues in *Thing and Space*, a null-point in relation to which interconnected experiential fields are constituted. As Michela Summa remarks, Husserl's characterization of the lived body 'as a zero point fundamentally refers to the impossibility to take distance from my body as a whole, to move away from it or to get closer to it. [. . .] My lived-body is necessarily the locus where my subjective perspective is anchored' (Summa 2014, p. 262). Thus, for Husserl, the self is not an intellectual and abstract pole of reference, but rather a situated embodied being that moves in a hodological space (that is, comprising different spatial directions) to which the body remains sensitive even when standing still. Indeed, even when we do not move, we are still oriented in space towards the objects that surround us. In this regard, Husserl's attention to kinaesthetic awareness reveals the centrality of what Maxime Sheets-Johnstone defines our 'maternal tongue', namely movement (Sheets-Johnstone 2011, 2015), which is characteristic of animate bodies (both human and non-human) and is inseparable from the constitution of consciousness.

As Sheets-Johnstone points out, a whole history of learned movements is stratified upon the body (Sheets-Johnstone 2011, p. 129). Prior to learning how to speak and write, we are immersed in a realm of bodily gestures and movements (such as swallowing, crying, kicking, smiling, babbling, etc.), through which we gradually expand our repertoire of bodily possibilities ('I cans') in a naive and spontaneous way. According to Sheets-Johnstone, 'in these situations, we were precisely discovering our bodies, not controlling them. In attending to and exploring our primal animateness, and in thereby learning the myriad ways in which our bodily movement related us, and could relate us, to a surrounding world, we were apprentices, not would-be masters, of our bodies' (Sheets-Johnstone 2011, p. 129).

From this point of view, Husserl's phenomenology of embodiment can be read as a transcendental-phenomenological critique of corporeal existence (Paci 1972; Behnke 2010). At the heart of this critique is the view that the body is always involved in a dynamic relation to the environment through sensing and movement. By articulating the structure of corporeality in these terms, Husserl frees the body from the risks of fetishization, which occur when the body is regarded as a material and passive thing that is shaped by external powers, and that can be manipulated or objectified at will. If the lived body is primarily the organ of kinaesthetic experience, which is dynamically connected to the environment, then 'phenomenology teaches us that subjectivity is the possibility of freeing oneself from fetishization' (Paci 1972, p. 45). Paci emphasizes that at stake is a *possibility* because the lived body is first and foremost a system of potentialities and abilities that enables the self to present and manifest itself in the outer world, and to practically engage it. This is not to deny that the body can in fact be externally conditioned or subjected to coercion, but that even then there remains a fundamental capacity to relate to oneself as an experientially dynamic point of view, which provides the basis for feeling, thinking, and acting.

A helpful application of this insight is offered by Elizabeth Behnke's account of somatology (the investigation of lived corporeality in the Husserlian sense). Behnke takes into account the postural attitudes that characterize bodily responses to experiences of shame, such as cringing, withdrawing from others, and keeping one's shoulders hunched forward. Such stances are often symptomatic of a felt sense of inadequacy. While different social factors can impinge on and limit bodily self-awareness, Behnke argues that the social shaping of the body is never accomplished once and for all, but is rather part of an ongoing dynamic process that can be shifted and reverted by drawing on the kinaesthetic repertoire of the body. To this end, Behnke provides the example of a patient suffering from back problems because of his tendency to avoid bringing his posture to a full vertical alignment in fear of being perceived as threatening. At stake here is whether the patient can cultivate kinaesthetic awareness in order to realign his relation to the social environment. This is not realized by exerting an absolute domain over one's body or by following cultural norms that would define what bodily confidence should feel like. Kinaesthetic awareness is, instead, a continuous practice of bodily self-cultivation and self-adjusting, which includes degrees of reflective awareness and responsibility for the bodily stances we adopt.

On Behnke's view, 'if one individual transforms his or her style of making a body, the change reverberates throughout the local social fabric as well, and can introduce some strain in the status quo' (Behnke 2010, p. 245). This is not to say that it is possible to inaugurate new social standards by simply shifting one's postural stance or bodily presentation. On the contrary, Behnke's view entails the recovery of kinaesthetic awareness by repositioning oneself in space, instead of letting ourselves shrink into habitual and socially accepted patterns of expression and movement. It is indeed possible to recognize how one's body is 'sinking' and to reconsider the tacit standards against which our bodily possibilities are exercised. This points in the direction of a 'kinaesthetic responsibility' that is not based on projected external standards of bodily presentation. The kinaesthetic responsibility Behnke appeals to aims, instead, at reshaping and regaining one's own felt orientation in the world by initiating and getting used to new synergies of meaningful movements connecting the body to the social environment.

2.2 The existential-phenomenological critique of the body

2.2.1 The body-subject and the body-object

In the preceding section, we illustrated how the critique of corporeal existence, in a Husserlian sense, points towards kinaesthetic responsibility and awareness. Such a view gestures towards the reappropriation of one's body as a body-subject; that is, as a relational and dynamic centre of sensuous, affective, and perceptual experience. However, the experience of *being a bodily subject* is inextricably connected to the experience of being a *bodily object* for ourselves as well as for other subjects. To illustrate with an example: suppose that you are taking a stroll on a sunny day in the park, catching the smell of the leaves, the birds' singing, and the laughter of the children in the playfield. While you are enjoying your walk, you are not reflectively aware of the pace of your stroll or of the coordination of your bodily movements. These aspects do not enter the field of your attention, unless they become conspicuous in a relevant way. Imagine that you are suddenly greeted by a man seated on a bench. While you were not paying much attention to the man before his greeting, upon being welcomed by him your overall disposition to the surrounding environment shifts, taking a new distinctive quality; for example, if the greeting was offered in a cordial, friendly manner, you feel a sense of ease and familiarity. The relation between the gesture of the stranger and the disposition of the perceiver is a motivational connection that activates, on the part of the perceiver, positive associations, including feelings of trust and safety. However, if the greeting is accompanied by a sexist remark or by an intrusive gaze, that very experience signals an uncomfortable situation, one in which the perceiver is suddenly made aware of their bodily presentation, as their gender or any other visible aspect of their identity becomes conspicuous in a way that produces unease and even shame.

In this respect, bodily awareness signals the fact that I am both a subject of experience and an object for the perception that others have of me. When we are ashamed or embarrassed, we become painfully conscious of our body as a visible object for others. Similarly, during a clinical examination, the way in which the physician observes our body may have the effect of fixing us in the limb or bodily area that is under medical observation. From a phenomenological point of view, the relation between the body-subject and the body perceived and regarded as an object of perception is a major structural aspect of the lived body. While the experience of being a bodily object is intrinsic to the constitution of corporeality, it also seems to diminish and potentially compromise the field of possibilities afforded by corporeal expression. A body-object is, indeed, a body whose freedom of movement and kinaesthetic expression are potentially inhibited and limited.

Such a tension between the body-subject and the body-object is characteristic of Jean-Paul Sartre's existential phenomenology of the body, as presented in *Being and Nothingness* (1943). Like Husserl, Sartre maintains that the lived body is always situated in the world according to a certain orientation. Yet Sartre's existential turn brings to the fore the relation between body and world as an *ambiguous situation*. Ambiguity refers to the fact that the lived body is not only a dynamic and kinaesthetic centre of experience, but it is also situated in practical, cultural, and historical contexts, where to see is inseparable 'from being visible' to others (Sartre 2003, p. 341). To illustrate this double relation, Sartre distinguishes three dimensions of the lived body: the body-for-itself; the body-for-others; and the body-as-known-by-others.

To begin with, the body represents the 'point of view' onto the world, namely it stands for the incarnate perspective by means of which it is possible to have an experience in the first place. More specifically, the lived body is 'the point of view on which I can no longer take a point of view' (Sartre 2003, p. 353). Imagine being on top of a hill and enjoying that view. As Sartre puts it, 'this point of view on the point of view [of the hill] is my body. But I cannot take a point of view on my body without a reference to infinity' (Sartre 2003, p. 353). Sartre's idea is that there cannot be any experience without reference to a given perspective. We contemplate the landscape through the perspective provided by our bodily position and orientation, yet when we try to approach the experiential viewpoint through which such experience is given to us (namely, through our body), we dissolve the point of view itself. By reflecting on the role of the body as the medium of experience, one turns the body into an instrument or external object with respect to the self. Thus, on Sartre's view, the body is, at the same time, the viewpoint that opens up the world to me and the instrument through which I see myself situated in the world among other bodies and objects. However, unlike other instruments that are external to consciousness (think, for example, of a telescope), the body cannot be neatly separated and distinguished from consciousness. It follows that the body cannot have an access to itself *as* a point of view without withdrawing from itself, thereby foreclosing the apprehension of its first-person openness to the world. The circle that is thereby produced is the infinite pattern of self-relation that derives from the impossibility of escaping bodily consciousness.

Sartre calls this spontaneous dimension of the body 'the body for-itself'. As an experiential viewpoint that is open onto the world, the body is always projected outside itself towards the world (as Sartre says, the body 'transcends' and 'surpasses' itself). However, through the body, consciousness simultaneously experiences itself as a being situated in a given condition under certain circumstances, which in turn limit one's original spontaneity. This is what Sartre calls facticity, namely the unavoidability of contingency, such as the fact that I am born in a certain country or have a certain body. The lived body *exists* in the movement of projecting oneself beyond any fixed determination through feeling, thinking, and acting, while it constantly experiences the uncertainty of the given situation in which one is thrown. An existential situation, for Sartre, consists precisely in inhabiting such a tension between spontaneity and contingency.

Since the body-for-itself reveals the self-transcending character of the body but also the difficulty to thematize it as an object, the body-for-itself is an opaque dimension. Sartre argues that I am not usually aware of the body as a dimension of my existence unless the presence of my body is made apparent to me on an affective level, as it happens when my body is regarded by others as an object in virtue of its visibility, or in experiences of illness. Sartre considers illness a phenomenon that permeates bodily experience, having its own duration, affective qualities, and rhythm. In illness, the body is apprehended through pain, which colours one's daily life and habits. Pain permeates the surrounding world of the subject as a passive environment, for one can hardly make a movement or turn one's head without suffering. In a similar way, being exposed to the gaze of others reminds one of the facticity of one's body. As Sartre puts it:

> My *birth* as it conditions the way in which objects are revealed to me (objects of luxury or of basic necessity are more or less *accessible*, certain social realities appear to me as *forbidden*, there are barriers and obstacles in my hodological space); my *race* as it is indicated by the Other's attitude with regard to me (these attitudes are revealed as scornful or admiring, as trusting or distrusting); my *class* as it is disclosed by the revelation of the social community to which I belong inasmuch as the places which I frequent refer to it; my *nationality*; my physiological structures as instruments imply it by the very way in which they are revealed as resistant or docile and by their very coefficient of adversity; *my character*; *my past*, as everything which I have experienced is indicated as my point of view on the world by the world itself: all this insofar as I surpass it in the synthetic unity of my being-in-the-world is my body as the necessary condition of the existence of a world and as the contingent realization of this condition. (Sartre 2003, p. 352)

On Sartre's account, the lived body is always confronted with a situation that is partly informed by one's choices and decisions, but that is also to a large extent conditioned by historical, cultural, societal, and interpersonal factors. Such conditions determine the things we can afford to buy, the dispositions we develop towards others, the tools we can use, the places we frequent, and the ways in which we express ourselves and project towards the future.[2] On Sartre's view, the facticity of the body expresses the tension between the set of circumstances that relate to one's upbringing, bodily constitution, character, and social relations, and the individual project to affirm one's freedom as a value that is irreducible to external conditions. Such a tension becomes prominent when the body appears to others. In being with other people, our point of view implicitly registers features of their abilities, nationality, race, class, or age. Because of this, the transcending character of consciousness is somehow inter-rupted: we do not see individuals for-themselves but rather through their facticity. Similarly, others see me in a certain moment of my life or in light of my physical capacities or through the class to which I belong or in light of my race and nationality, and not as a free spontaneity to which those aspects belong as contingent and limited qualities. The body as object-for-other is the dimension of the body that captures this entanglement between freedom, bodily visibility, and social presentation. As Dolezal puts it, 'embodied social relations are constitutive of reflective self-consciousness and form part of the very fabric of our being. It is not as though action and perception come first and then self-presentation follows as some sort of second-order concern. Instead, they are entangled such that one cannot be said to precede the other' (Dolezal 2015, p. 47).

To be sure, the body as object-for-others is a dialectical dimension, for it involves a social interaction with others through which we learn about their character. However, according to Sartre, knowledge of someone's character is limited as long as this amounts to grasping a fixed set of char-acter traits instead of understanding others through the projects that they freely choose to pursue (Webber 2009). Through social encounters, the other may elude me because their bodily presentation, including the nar-ratives they may tell us, fixes them in a ready-made and limited version of who they are as individuals. Even the stories we tell about ourselves to others (about our past, nationality, job, and residence, for example) have the power to confine ourselves to contingent aspects of our existence. Because of this, we tend to relate to ourselves through the narratives we give and through the impact that such narratives have on others. This situation produces what Sartre calls the 'shock' (Sartre 2003, p. 375) of the social encounter: I am exposed to the look of the other, for whom I am an object, and I see myself through their eyes, hence I am no longer the lived and self-transcending movement I experience myself to be.

Sartre is very clear that the shock is unavoidable because it is intrinsic to the facticity of the body. In this sense, Sartre shows that the realization of one's freedom is a complex negotiation between bodily presentation and socio-cultural experience. Yet Sartre also casts a pessimistic view on the relation that holds together being-for-itself and being-for-others, as he thematizes the body as a sphere of vulnerability that exposes us to the risks of alienation. This occurs when we assume the other's point of view onto us, as exemplified by the third dimension of the body, that is, the body as it is apprehended and regarded from a perspective that is not my own (i.e. the body-as-known-by-others). At this level, one is self-conscious about one's body as others see it. In a way, this dimension of the body corresponds to the adoption, on the part of consciousness, of external values and criteria of evaluation in relation to which we regard our own body. Sartre compares this dimension of the body to the shift that occurs in illness when one's condition is diagnosed as a disease, that is, a state defined by a specific set of symptoms that are measured, compared, and assessed using fixed and standard criteria of evaluation. In this case, we regard ourselves in light of the diagnosis that we have received, and we comport according to the prescription provided by the physician. When this state becomes the ordinary and natural way of experiencing one's body, it produces alienation or estrangement, as the body's characteristic self-transcendence is reduced to an ensemble of anatomical and physiological features.

To be sure, Sartre's phenomenology of the body lacks the emphasis on motility and kinaesthetic awareness of Husserl's analysis of the lived body. Like Husserl, however, Sartre is concerned with the problem of the fetishization of the body, that is to say, with the risk of objectifying the body and reducing it to a passive and static dimension of experience. In this respect, Sartre's seemingly pessimistic picture of the lived body provides an account of the ambiguity of corporeal existence, revealing the impossibility of escaping one's facticity, and the necessity to come to terms with the radical contingency of the situation, including the latent possibility of alienation. A paradigmatic illustration of this set of issues is provided by Sartre's account of shame. In *Being and Nothingness*, Sartre offers the famous vignette of the man (Sartre himself) peeping through a keyhole, aiming to eavesdrop a conversation due to 'jealousy, curiosity, or vice' (Sartre 2003, pp. 282ff). Initially, Sartre maintains that he is completely unaware of his motives, as he is completely absorbed in the situation (Sartre 2003, p. 283). It is only when 'I hear footsteps in the hall', at the very thought that someone may be looking at me, that I apprehend myself in the situation I am in. However, this happens by seeing myself through the eyes of the other, as someone who is caught in a shameful action. As Sartre puts it:

> Shame is shame of *self*; it is the *recognition* of the fact that I *am* indeed that object which the Other is looking at and judging. I can be ashamed only as my freedom escapes me in order to become a *given* object. Thus originally the bond between my unreflective consciousness and my *Ego*, which is being looked at, is a bond not of knowing but of being. (Sartre 2003, p. 285)

Sartre's argument is that the presence (presumptive, imagined, or actual) of the other posits a limit to my freedom, causing that 'immediate shudder' (Sartre 2003, p. 246) that reveals my own facticity to myself. In this respect, the other's look represents the 'solidification and alienation of my own possibilities' (Sartre 2003, p. 287). Sartre is quite clear that alienation, in this context, does not correspond to reification or objectification but rather to self-estrangement: 'Strictly speaking, it is not that I perceive myself losing my freedom in order to become a *thing*, but my nature is – over there, outside my lived freedom – as a given attribute of this being which I am for the Other' (Sartre 2003, p. 286). The crux of Sartre's analysis is that the look of the other makes me suddenly aware of the set of facts that are true of me at that given moment (Webber 2009, p. 19), hence I am suddenly confronted with the factual realization of my existence as an object of reflection for myself as well as for others. Whether the gaze of the other is expressive of a negative or positive evaluation of my actions, I see myself through the eyes of others, thereby forsaking the sense of indeterminacy and transcendence that distinguishes the body for-itself.

It is worth noting that, for Sartre, the other does not have to be present in order to exert such an unsettling power onto the self. Think, for example, of how someone might feel ashamed at the thought of what a deceased parent or partner would think of what they are doing. As Alessandra Fussi argues, the *occasion* of shame does not have to be identified with the *cause* of shame (Fussi 2018, p. 32). Sartre emphasizes that in the phenomenon of the look I see myself regarded from a perspective that I cannot grasp, for the gaze situates me in the world according to a standpoint that is irreducibly external to mine. The intrusion of a third-person perspective in my own self-experience produces the estrangement of self, in the sense that I am suddenly caught in a tension between indeterminate, unreflective spontaneity and reflective self-awareness. This means that, for Sartre, bodily awareness exposes me to the possibility that I may appear different from what I experience myself to be.

In this regard, Sartre's analysis brings to the fore the relation between bodily self-awareness, shame, and social presentation. As Luna Dolezal stresses, the body as subject is constantly interacting with and negotiating 'the structures of the social, cultural and political fields. In attempting to master prevailing social codes and normative standards regarding body management, the subject is instructed by body shame' (Dolezal 2015, p. 99). Most notably, Dolezal draws attention to the 'politics of shame', that is, the set of cultural and social practices that use the phenomenon of shame to perpetuate social stigma, thereby generating objectification, marginalization, and social invisibility. As she writes:

> Historically, categories of 'inclusion/includability' and 'exclusion/excludability' have been determined in terms of 'pariah' groups focusing

on physical features that signify one's belonging to categories deter-mined by gender, race, sexuality and class. The idea is that at any given moment we know which group we belong to, because we either do or do not bear the physical feature associated with that group. Ensuring a sense of belonging, recognition and social inclusion becomes a constant quest to have the physical body 'pass' as 'normal,' or to achieve (in)visibility and recognition according to the standards of the dominant, or more powerful, social group. (Dolezal 2015, pp. 94–5)

Drawing on Sartre's phenomenology and bringing it into dialogue with social sciences (including the works of sociologists Norbert Elias and Erving Goffman) as well as Foucault, Dolezal points out that, histori-cally, social stigma arises by targeting gender, race, sexuality, and class as markers of the body that are laden with moral and social value. This strategy reveals at its core a Sartrean dynamic, whereby shame oper-ates on an affective level by isolating individuals from one another, and throwing them into a state of self-alienation. A notable literary example of this is Pecola, the main character of Toni Morrison's *The Bluest Eye*. As Dolezal remarks, Pecola is confronted not just with the racist judge-ment of her society, starting with the shopkeeper from whom she tries to buy candies, but also with the inability to return the objectifying gaze of racism due to her social disempowerment and invisibility.[3] Dolezal speaks, in this regard, of chronic shame, which pervades the experience of one's body and is used to manipulate and disadvantage marginalized people, including historically racialized groups, queer communities, and social (class-based) groups.

At the same time, Dolezal points out that shame plays an important role on a subjective level of experience in order to regulate and govern the mechanisms underlying the acquisition of social norms. Indeed, while body shame is politically relevant to uncover dynamics of social oppression and marginalization, shame also indicates how subjects gain awareness of themselves in front of others through their bodily presentations. More specifically, experiences of shame (or the possibil-ity thereof) reveal the self-evaluative structure of consciousness, that is, the emergence of the capacity to assess and evaluate one's actions (Dolezal 2015, p. 81). From this point of view, shame does not reduce the body to a passive medium on which social norms are inscribed, but rather signals a 'decisive change of perspective on oneself' (Zahavi 2014, p. 238) that is crucial for engendering more robust forms of self-consciousness about one's identity. However, a fundamental limit of Sartre's phenomenology of the body is the lack of consideration for the body's adaptability and flexibility, including the practices through which the lived body establishes a more positive and practical relation towards itself and the world.

2.2.2 Inhabiting the world through the habitual body

Sartre's emphasis on the alienating character of bodily experience was noted by his contemporaries, starting with Merleau-Ponty, who arguably had Sartre in mind when warning against the risks of the 'inhuman gaze' that observes the actions of others as if they were the actions of an insect (Merleau-Ponty 2012, p. 378). For Merleau-Ponty, bodily aliena- tion is the symptom of a disrupted communication between the body and the surrounding world rather than a latent possibility of the body, as in Sartre. Following Husserl, Merleau-Ponty's *Phenomenology of Perception* (1945) acknowledges the centrality of the body in experience and cognition, defining it as 'our primordial habit' and 'our anchorage in the world' (Merleau-Ponty 2012, pp. 93, 146). Like Husserl and Sartre, Merleau-Ponty rejects not only the dualism between mind and body, but also the reduction of the body to a physicalist thing that is inserted in space like an atomistic entity. To this end, Merleau-Ponty's arguments in the *Phenomenology of Perception* are presented in the form of a critique of the positions of intellectualism and empirical reductionism, which in different ways promote a dualism between mind and body. In so doing, Merleau-Ponty radicalizes Husserl's view of embodiment and departs from Sartre's approach, placing special emphasis on the actual engage- ment that takes place between the body and the environment. In so doing, Merleau-Ponty's analysis takes on an existential contour that is further enriched by his familiarity with empirical psychology and psychopathol- ogy. In this section, we concentrate on Merleau-Ponty's account of body schema and habitual body in his *Phenomenology of Perception*, showing how these concepts have been deployed in critical-phenomenological approaches to embodiment that inquire into the entanglement between corporeal experience and culture.

To begin with, Merleau-Ponty argues that the body inhabits the spatiotemporal world by being involved in it. Following Husserl, Merleau- Ponty argues that to be situated in space means to be oriented according to a certain perspective with respect to external objects. Yet each perspec- tival position is one of the multiple possibilities that become available to my body in a given situation. Merleau-Ponty speaks of the 'resistance' that external objects manifest towards the body (Merleau-Ponty 2012, p. 94) to account for the fact that, even when I am presented with visual profiles of an object, I am simultaneously engaging them on a motor and affective level. If I hold a mug with my right hand, I see only one side of it, but I trust that the hidden sides are not concealed from me and that they exist even if I cannot observe them in the present moment. Certainly, if I turn the mug around by the handle, I can see its hidden sides. Yet my expectation that the hidden sides of the mug are available to me while being hidden is not the result of inference or observation. My confidence derives from my acquaintance and familiarity with the physiognomy and resistance of the mug as a felt object of three-dimensional experience.

Similarly, when I take a walk in my neighbourhood, I am immediately oriented without having to recall or calculate the distance between my current location and my point of departure. This reflects the fact that the body does not act as an external medium between an inner side (the mind or consciousness) and the external world. Instead the body institutes a perceptual horizon within which external things are encountered, discovered, or recognized. It follows that the body cannot be reduced to a point in space, like the blue dot that signals my movements across space on the GPS. The movements of the blue dot on Google Maps depend on the external coordinates of an impersonal space that is observable from virtually any point of view. In contrast to this, the lived experience of the body is always situated in a perspectival horizon, hence it is confronted with the felt resistance of actual objects, which may evoke memories, present hostile occlusions or deviations, or be simply felt as familiar or unknown. As Merleau-Ponty puts it: 'When the word "here" is applied to my body, it does not designate a determinate position in relation to other positions or in relation to external coordinates. It designates the installation of the first coordinates, the anchoring of the active body in an object, and the situation of the body confronted with its tasks.' (Merleau-Ponty 2012, pp. 102–3).

These observations point to what Merleau-Ponty calls the 'permanence of the body', that is, the fact that the body is always present in experience like an inner background, against which things appear from a certain angle or perspective, as soliciting our bodily and affective response (be it the solicitation to grab the mug from a certain angle, or experiencing the aura of a city that awakens a web of associations and memories). Interestingly, Merleau-Ponty chooses the notion of 'permanence' rather than 'presence' to emphasize the fact that the body is not given as a medium or vehicle between consciousness and the world but rather inhabits space and *endures* in time. The body's relation to time is best illustrated by the notion of sedimentation. On Merleau-Ponty's view, the body bears the stratification (or sedimentation) of former experiences, which are re-enacted and taken up in the present whenever similar or appropriate circumstances occur. In this way, the body holds a 'mental panorama with its accentuated regions and its confused regions, a physiognomy of questions, and intellectual situations such as research, discovery, and certainty' (Merleau-Ponty 2012, p. 131). A mental panorama is the backdrop against which former experiences are sedimented with their distinct character and affective salience. As a result of this, the body's relation to the surrounding world is mediated by dispositions that are both subjective and context-dependent. There are indeed situations that appear familiar to us on a subjective level, soliciting a distinct set of stances and predispositions, including curiosity, wonder, and interest. For example, a logical quiz may predispose me with curiosity (if I have a knack for maths and logic) or unease (if I do not trust my abilities in maths), while visiting a new town activates a whole new way of learning about the foreign place, including subjective liking and disliking. In each case, we move within an affective and intellectual landscape that guides how we respond to the solicitations that are present in a given situation. At the same time, the body's past, along with unconscious and marginal experiences that fall outside body's awareness, generate the field of 'anonymity' that surrounds bodily experience.

It follows that, even though the notion of sedimentation may evoke a passive process of stratification (as the deposition of sediments in geology leads to the formation of rocks), the sedimentation of experiences Merleau-Ponty refers to is, instead, an active process of adaptation to the environment. On this view, past experiences are deposited in the body as a latent background that can constantly be reactivated in the course of experience. As Merleau-Ponty warns us:

> This word 'sedimentation' must not trick us: this contracted knowledge is not an inert mass at the foundation of our consciousness. For me, my apartment is not a series of strongly connected images. It only remains around me as my familiar domain if I still hold 'in my hands' or 'in my legs' its principal distances and directions, and only if a multitude of intentional threads run towards it from my body. Likewise, my acquired thoughts are not an absolute acquisition; they feed off my present thought at each moment; they offer me a sense, but this is a sense that I reflect back to them. (Merleau-Ponty 2012, p. 132)

Merleau-Ponty's argument is that the body is involved in a network of embodied communication with the outer world. This means that experiences are not stored somewhere in the mind, as an abstract deposit, but are rather part of the circuit of 'intentional threads' that connect the body to the world. To use Merleau-Ponty's example, my apartment is not to me a series of visual representations, but the familiar space I inhabit, whose spatial structure is held together by the movements I execute in it. My apartment is the familiar space in which I walk every day, knowing my way in it even when blindfolded or when the light is turned off. This form of acquaintance is not the product of reflection or inference, but rather the performance of the habitual body. I *know* my way to the bedroom without recalling, at each step, its distance from the living room, for I *sense* the lived distance between the two rooms, just like the typist finds his way on the keyboard without looking at the keys when he writes on his laptop. This is how the habitual body retains awareness of former experiences while also adjusting to new situations (as it happens when we move out and adapt, not without difficulty, to a new place).

To account for such phenomenon, Merleau-Ponty borrows from neurologist Jean Lhermitte the concept of body schema, which is the system of sensorimotor abilities, activities, and habits that function without the necessity of perceptual monitoring (Gallagher and Zahavi 2012, pp. 164ff). The body schema is a pre-reflective and non-objectifying form of body-awareness (Gallagher and Zahavi 2012, p. 165). Differently stated, the body schema builds on sensory-motor signals and motor expertise but also on prior background knowledge, providing a basis for the development of one's body image, as we will see in more detail in the next section. Importantly, the body schema provides a sense of bodily awareness in space by integrating different sensations and impressions in a plastic and flexible way. Unlike a blueprint, which is a sketch of bodily functions in abstraction from a lived situation, the body schema originates in the movements that the body takes up, adjusting itself dynamically to the circumstances.

On this view, the pre-reflective sense that I have of my body when I run is distinct from the bodily awareness I have when I am still. Yet, whether I run or stand still, my body-awareness runs continuously both temporally and spatially. This means that I experience myself as the same individual, even though I engage the surrounding world in multiple motor ways that enact what Merleau-Ponty calls 'motor intentionality', that is to say, our spontaneous motor directedness towards the environment. Furthermore, the body schema is not only context-dependent, but also subject-dependent, as it is sensitive to bodily alterations that may affect an individual's constitution and abilities. For example, the body schema of a blind person who uses a stick to walk adjusts itself spontaneously in order to integrate the awareness of the cane within the subject's posture and orientation. For this reason, Merleau-Ponty argues that the body schema is an *existential* capacity of the body that operates on a pre-reflective level of experience, which situates us in the world, projecting us towards certain opportunities for action and movement that are available in the environment. In so doing, we constantly integrate new learned movements, gestures, and bodily stances into our bodily stance.

In Merleau-Ponty's phenomenology, the concept of body schema helps to understand how motor capacities and overall affective experiences are directly involved in processes of meaning constitution and communication. This is best illustrated by Merleau-Ponty's analysis of the case of Schneider, a war veteran affected by brain injury and suffering from a mild form of visual agnosia, a disturbance of the organization and apprehension of purely visual presentations. According to the inquiry conducted by neurologists and psychiatrists Goldstein and Gelb (on which Merleau-Ponty draws), Schneider had difficulties organizing visual elements, like line segments, into a visual whole (*Gestalt*). When presented with an object, like a pen, Schneider would see patches of colour and lines that he would gradually connect together through inferential reasoning. His kinaesthetic awareness also appeared impacted. When asked to lift his leg or arm, he could perform this action only if allowed to see the limb in question. When his head, arm, or leg were touched, he could not say at what point he was touched, unless he was gradually prepared by the doctor to identify the spot in question. Nevertheless, Schneider could effortlessly perform habitual movements and actions that were familiar to him and context-dependent, like blowing his nose or lighting a candle with a match taken from his pocket.

According to Goldstein and Gelb, the case of Schneider reflected the inability to integrate two attitudes: the pointing attitude, which sustains the ability to perform abstract movements connected to visual presentations (such as localizing one's limb), and the grasping attitude, which is the ability to execute concrete or habitual movements, like blowing one's nose. On this basis, owing to his brain injury, Schneider manifested a split between cognitive and motor attitudes. Merleau-Ponty points out that the split of attitudes diagnosed by Goldstein and Gelb obscures the central difficulty manifested by Schneider, which was the ability to engage non-motor operations. In particular, Schneider's difficulty concerned the ability 'to give a motor sense to a verbal instruction' (Merleau-Ponty 2012, p. 142); that is, Schneider was unable to spontaneously activate his motor awareness in relation to abstract or constructed situations, like verbal instructions.

On this view, Schneider's case was the symptom of a disturbance of motor intentionality. Instead of introducing a dualism between different attitudes, as theorized by Goldstein and Gelb, Merleau-Ponty argues that Schneider's body schema seemed to lack its natural 'freedom', namely the natural sense of projection in the world that runs seamlessly across different situations, whether they involve familiar contexts or not. It follows that, for Merleau-Ponty, the disturbance of motor intentionality 'is not a question of either/or, rather it is a matter of degree' (Jensen 2009). Differently put, the body schema is prone to variations and alterations; it is not a construct that may or may not be given. In this regard, it is worth noting that Schneider could effortlessly perform habitual actions. This means that habit, far from being a mindless or mechanical operation, is instead an intelligent response of the body schema, which alters, transforms, and expands our interaction with the world. If the lived body anchors us in the world, it is precisely by means of the intelligence and flexibility afforded by habit.

Merleau-Ponty's phenomenology of habitual body plays a key role in critical-phenomenological approaches to corporeality, particularly with regard to the so-called 'intelligence' of habit we have just mentioned. To begin with, Merleau-Ponty's description of the habitual body suggests that the body is not mechanically conditioned by external rules but sensitive to the meaning sedimented in its past as well as to environmental cues. As such, the body does not passively incorporate attitudes and styles of behaviour, for it is capable of distinguishing between familiar and unfamiliar gestures, movements, and orientations, even when the norms that infuse them have not been subjected to assessment or conscious reflection. To this end, Merleau-Ponty argues that bodily gestures and expressions are grasped without the aid of representation. I understand the gesture of my friend across the street, who signals me his intention of not following me. I do not see his gesture and the movement of his hand as two separated phenomena. Rather, I grasp the meaning conveyed by his gesture as intrinsic to the movement of his hand. As Merleau-Ponty says: 'I see my partner's resistance, and my impatient gesture emerges from this situation, without any interposed thought' (Merleau-Ponty 2012, p. 113). As the understanding of another's gesture arises through the situation, it necessarily taps into the cultural background upon which one always leans in order to appropriately understand bodily forms of expression in everyday situations.

For this reason, misunderstandings due to cultural misinterpretation are quite common. Shannon Sullivan points out a number of situations that arise in multicultural contexts, where certain gestures and stances may appear dichotomous or ambiguous, like squeezing a friend's arm as an expression of friendship, which can be misunderstood as a sexual approach (Sullivan 2001, pp. 73ff). In this regard, Sullivan observes that Merleau-Ponty fails to acknowledge this aspect of communication, as he privileges the emergence of sense and signification out of an unquestioned similarity between the pre-reflective experiences of different bodies, without considering their histories or the impact of societal and cultural elements on them. The risk of Merleau-Ponty's approach, according to Sullivan, is that he underestimates the fact that, often, I inhabit a familiar world 'because I can see nothing but my own intention in another's behaviour' (Sullivan 2001, p. 73).

To be sure, grasping the sense of another's gesture is not an infallible process, but rather part of a kinaesthetic dynamic that is necessarily ambiguous as well as open to corrections and revisions. At the same time, however, such an ambiguity compels us to question the extent to which the cultural horizon, which for Merleau-Ponty is sedimented in experience, enters the process of meaning constitution that is carried out by the lived body, and that is potentially held in one's 'mental landscape'. To put it differently, the question is whether the characteristic spontaneity by means of which the body projects itself in the world is also informed by cultural and societal paradigms. This problem has to do with the adoption, on the part of the body schema, of cultural habits, including racializing styles of perceiving others, but also bodily posture, gesture, and orientation. This is what Helen Ngo calls 'racist habits'; namely bodily responses that are internalized in one's body register to the point of being scarcely noticed by the subject that manifests them, like clutching one's purse in the presence of a Black man (recounted in Yancy 2017, on which Ngo's analysis relies and upon which we will return in Chapter 5) or using derogatory expressions as colloquial or slang.

In this regard, Merleau-Ponty's account of habitual body shows that societal and cultural practices can be unreflectively adopted and taken up in one's bodily stance. Yet this is a reversible process. The receptivity of habit indicates that a bodily stance is, in principle, capable of being shifted and appropriated by the self. Drawing on Merleau-Ponty, Ngo stresses that the two fundamental components of habit, namely orientation and projection or possibility, are always in a productive tension at the level of habitual action, suggesting that habit is not only receptive but also active in the process of *holding* a certain stance (Ngo 2017). To this end, Ngo establishes a parallel with the Chinese martial art *Wushu*, whereby the practitioner does not simply maintain a certain position for the sake of training, but prepares herself for the next movement of strike. In this regard, Ngo notes that 'in Chinese the word for stance, 步, can also be translated into English as 'step'. Holding is not only active, it also enables and prepares us for movement' (Ngo 2017, p. 40).

This means that the sedimentation of contextual knowledge is not an inert process that unfolds without the subject being cognizant of it. Since the habitual body launches the body forward while re-enacting contextual knowledge, the performance of the habitual body implies degrees of awareness and the capacity to recognize and shift the course of one's orientation. For this reason, there is room for assigning some responsibility to bodily stances and racist habits that are unchallenged and uninterrogated (Ngo 2017, p. 42). This is particularly relevant because it indicates that at stake in the case of racist habits are not simply discursive and social practices that shape collective habits (what sociologist Pierre Bourdieu called *habitus*), but also individual embodied stances.[4]

In this regard, Lee (2014) argues that Merleau-Ponty's emphasis on the stratification of the past that informs the cultural horizon we inhabit outlines a type of responsibility that is not restricted to the actions we undertake as moral agents but also as partaking in a common horizon that is sustained and informed by bodily gestures and practices. On Lee's view, we are responsible for the horizon we inhabit, and that we contribute to shaping, regulating, and maintaining through our lived experience. As Lee writes, our actions do not originate 'in spurts of isolated moments but as a continuum, built into the minutia of choices' (Lee 2014, p. 244). Such a view of responsibility draws on Merleau-Ponty's account of embodiment in that, as long as the body is actively involved in acts of understanding and communication, our bodily behaviour and ethical decision-making cannot be neatly detached from the environing world in which we live. Thus, Merleau-Ponty's view of habitual body and embodiment paves the way for integrating responsibility and moral agency in terms of bodily accountability, though this is an aspect that is still relatively underdeveloped in the literature.

It appears then that two main critical themes are interwoven with Merleau-Ponty's phenomenology of the body. First of all, Merleau-Ponty's phenomenology develops further the transcendental-phenomenological critique of corporeal existence. In this regard, Merleau-Ponty shows in what sense the body cannot be reduced to an atomistic thing observed from an impersonal viewpoint by shedding light on the 'permanence' of the body in experience. In contributing to such a critique, Merleau-Ponty places special emphasis on the active role played by the body in responding and adapting to the surrounding environment, thereby entering processes of meaning constitution and communication. On this basis, critical phenomenologists argue that the lived body positions us in the world in a way that holds us accountable for our corporeal and un-reflected styles of behaviour.[5]

At the same time, Merleau-Ponty acknowledges that we must 'rupture our familiarity' with the world as we know it in order to identify the noetic structures that operate at its foundation (Merleau-Ponty 2012, p. xxvii). On this view, Merleau-Ponty's phenomenology draws attention to the process of sedimentation as a phenomenon that need to be deciphered, reconstructed, and understood in its genesis and development on both a subjective and a collective level of experience. On this basis, it is possible, from a classical-phenomenological viewpoint, to identify the type of habits and social norms that are operative in the natural attitude. From a critical-phenomenological perspective, however, the fact that the lived body is always involved in existing cultural and societal networks posits the need not only to suspend the familiarity of the surrounding world as the coherent and stable backdrop of everyday life, but also to identify and break with the unquestioned norms that disrupt and hinder bodily flexibility and spontaneity. To this end, as we shall see in the next sections, the phenomenological critique of corporeal existence can be integrated by the phenomenological critique of the body images that alienate the body from itself.

2.3 Resistant bodies: body images, illness, and disability

2.3.1 Body images and bodily alienation

As we pointed out earlier, the body schema provides the basis for the formation of body image. However, the body schema differs from the body image in that the former is not objectifying and non-representational. The body image, by contrast, provides a map of one's body that is constantly updated in the course of the experience by the body schema. This means that we have a certain representation of our limbs and overall appearance, including our size, height, and morphology. We are also aware of the changes occurring in our limbs and general appearance as we age, become ill, or undergo various types of bodily changes, surgery, or medical interventions. Gallagher and Zahavi identify three main intentional elements that are inherent in the structure of the body image:

(1) A subject's *perceptual* experience of his/her own body.
(2) A subject's *conceptual* understanding (including folk and/or scientific knowledge) of the body in general.
(3) A subject's *emotional* attitude toward his or her own body. (Gallagher and Zahavi 2012, p. 164)

While the body image originates and develops through one's perceptual experience, it also changes dramatically in the course of our life as we learn to relate to ourselves on both a conceptual and an affective level. Thus, the body image undergoes continuous transformations, some of which are especially prominent in adolescence, as the body goes through various transformations in puberty. The body image significantly evolves and changes also in illness and in the course of organic psychophysical changes, and in this respect, it displays a peculiar interplay with the body schema. Merleau-Ponty's discussion of the phantom limb in his *Phenomenology of Perception* offers one of the key classical-phenomenological insights into the development and transformation of one's body image.

In the experience of the phantom limb, the patient typically reports sensations of pain associated to the missing limb. Drawing on the 1935 analysis of psychiatrist Paul F. Schilder, Merleau-Ponty argues that the phenomenon of the phantom limb can be understood as an affective situation that involves the re-organization of the body schema and re-acquaintance with one's body. Most notably Merleau-Ponty argues that, when the organism receives a certain stimulation, the body is not thereby causally conditioned to execute a movement like a piece of wood that bends when it is hit by the hammer. On the contrary, 'the organism's function in the reception of stimuli is, so to speak, to 'understand' a certain form of stimulation. [. . .] The brain becomes the place of an 'articulation' that intervenes even before the cortical stage and that blurs [. . .] the relations between the stimulus and the organism' (Merleau-Ponty 2012, p. 77). Merleau-Ponty's position is eminently anti-behaviouristic:[6] the body's relation to the stimulations coming from the outside are taken up by the organism in an active way rather than being passively or mechanically produced. The body's orientation and the movements that the body can afford reorganize and adjust themselves dynamically according to a kinaesthetic plan that is to a great extent dependent on affective factors as well as on the individual's life situation. On this view, the phantom limb reflects the adjustment of the body to a new situation, one that requires the absence of a limb we used to rely on, and that is now absent, like a friend who passed away.

The parallel between the phantom limb and the lost friend is introduced by Merleau-Ponty to account for the fact that the phantom limb is not a memory or a recollection of the past; it is not an 'image' either, in the sense of a sheer representation of the limb we used to have. On the contrary, the phantom limb is the trace of the affective and sensory connection to a form of life (that is to say, a postural model and a sense of orientation informed by one's sensations, perceptions, and emotions) that is no longer available. For this reason, Merleau-Ponty speaks of the phantom limb in terms of an 'organic repression' of the past. This means that the phantom limb reflects an alteration of the body schema that the individual is reluctant to accept yet; hence it is repressed whenever one counts on the use of the lost limb to perform a certain movement. The pain is, in this case, connected to the difficulty of facing the alteration of one's body image, which is concomitant with the alteration of the body schema.

From this point of view, the body image plays a mediating role between the kinaesthetic and motor orientation of the body and the localization of sensations in different parts of the body. The body image provides a map to distinguish between one's body and the environment, but also between movements of the limbs and the rest of the body (Grosz 1994, p. 84). At the same time, Merleau-Ponty's reference to the notion of 'organic repression' is reminiscent of Freudian psychoanalysis, on which Schilder relied to illustrate the relation between body image and different types of psychological conditions. In this respect, the body image is impacted not just by illness and bodily alterations, but also by interpersonal and social experience. Schilder, for example, emphasized that:

> [. . .] There is, from the very beginning, a very close connection between the body images of ourselves, and the body images of others. We take parts of the body images of others into others, and push parts of our body images into others. We may push our own body images completely into others, or in some way there may be a continuous interplay between the body images of ourselves and the persons around us. This interplay may be an interplay of parts or of wholes. (Schilder 1999, p. 235)

As Schilder points out, one's body image is influenced by our projection into the body images of other people, with whom we may not necessarily identify, but on which we nonetheless draw to forge a holistic representation of our own body. This is a phenomenon that has often been associated to how infants develop awareness of their bodies. The same process is, however, exacerbated in the case of social neurosis, where patients are obsessively concerned with their body image, as they monitor any perceived 'abnormality' in their appearance by contrast to the bodily presentation of others (Schilder 1999, p. 302). In discussing this phenomenon, Schilder emphasizes that the body image is connected to the subject's anatomy and libidinal impulses[7] as well as to one's history and socio-cultural environment.

According to Weiss, both Schilder and Merleau-Ponty regard the body image as a dynamic structure that is continually 'constructed, destructed, and reconstructed in response to changes within one's body, other people's bodies, and/or the situation as a whole' (Weiss 1999, p. 17). As the case of the phantom limbs indicates, the body image responds to subtle psychological and physiological changes and, since it is largely pre-reflective, it is difficult to thematize. As a result of this, a *multiplicity* of body images constellates bodily experience. Indeed, as admitted by

Schilder, 'we have an almost unlimited number of body images' (Schilder 1999, p. 67). Even 'the amputated person tries in a more or less playful manner to find which one [which body image] he can use' (Schilder, ibid.).

As the body image is not static and reflects the changes that occur in one's life, the multiplicity of body images is a symptom of the multiple plans for movements that the body builds up in responding to environmental clues and physiological changes. In so doing, however, the body also picks contextual, societal, and cultural solicitations that exert a large influence in the shaping of the body image as well as of self-perception. Such an aspect, that Schilder scarcely considers, despite noting the weight of culture and interpersonal experience, is notable in the feminist critique of the socially shaped body. Such critique points out the manipulation of the women's body images to make them fit socially conditioned standards of beauty and attractiveness (which we further discuss in Chapter 4).

From a phenomenological point of view, the phenomenon of body images posits two main important issues. On the one hand, the recognition of the multiplicity of body images calls into question the dichotomy between 'the normal' and 'the pathological' in relation to distorted body images. Far from looking for the integration of one's body images into a unitary and fixed model, it is instead essential to recognize the multiple dimensions of the lived body, which 'jointly compose our multidimensional experience of ourselves' (Legrand 2015, p. 94). On the other hand, the distortion of body images due to the normalizing effect of widespread cultural assumptions draws attention to the unreflective adoption of societal and cultural standards in the formation of one's body image. In this regard, the body appears vulnerable to dynamics of self-alienation that are rooted in the adoption of a third-person stance towards oneself, as in the Sartrean third dimension of the body. Rather than enabling a feeling of familiarity and ease, the body is regarded from a third-person perspective, due to the attempt to take control of one's body image.

To further illustrate this, it is helpful to consider, by way of example, phenomenological analyses of anorexia nervosa, an eating disorder affecting women and men, whose symptoms include excessive weight loss, food starvation, and disturbances of body image. The relation between eating disorders and cultural models of femininity has not gone unnoticed, especially in feminist philosophy (Bordo 1993). More recently, Dorothée Legrand has widely and extensively examined anorexia from a phenomenological angle, emphasizing the flaws of the widespread conception of the anorexic as a person who seeks the destruction of her body to meet impossible standards of slimness. For the anorexic does not act like a disembodied subject but rather as an embodied self who paradoxically seeks the preservation of her body by destroying the body perceived as a manipulable object by others. At stake, according to Legrand, is the attempt to free the body from the Sartrean dimension of the body known-by-others.

On Legrand's view, starving one's body is a ritualized process that aims to reinforce one's experience of self-control within and against the pressure of external conditioning. Paradoxically, while anorexic patients progressively lose control over their body as anorexia progresses (due to the debilitating effects of starvation), they nonetheless attempt to separate their bodies from the feminine, highly sexualized standards of western society (Legrand 2010). In so doing, 'this body is also built as a self-contained system, as the patient drastically controls all that penetrates it, thereby diminishing its vulnerability to invasion and corruption from the outside' (Legrand 2010, p. 196). To be sure, such a process is a vicious cycle that ultimately makes the anorexic body more similar to the object of sexual desire idealized by western society. However, in doing so, the anorexic subject reveals a deeper struggle, which is less about achieving ideals of perfection through comparing one's body to standardized body images, and more about emancipating oneself from the objectifying gaze of the other. As Legrand points out, such a view has remarkable consequences for clinical practice, as the purpose of therapy should not be to restore a 'correct' body image, but rather to overcome the polarization between body-subject and body-object in order to enhance bodily ownership and improve interpersonal relationships.[8]

From a critical-phenomenological point of view, disturbances of the body image reflect the paradox highlighted by Legrand, but also a deep connection to culturally constructed phenomena of disgust, shame, and abjection. As Slatman and Yaron argue, 'from a phenomenological perspective, embodied self-experience and embodied agency is at once an *individual* and a *social* affair' (Slatman and Yaron 2014, p. 223). This has to do, in particular, with the transformation of the body in a self-enclosed system that seeks to avoid contamination or intrusion from the outside, as it was pointed out earlier. Such a resistance towards the hegemony of a particular cultural body, whether this is internalized or rejected by the anorexic, highlights a tendency to create and pursue clear-cut boundaries between the inside and the outside, the clear and the unclear, the proper and the improper. From a psychoanalytic point of view, the creation of boundaries is essential to individuate the self, just like the fear of contamination is necessary to protect the integrity of one's body.

However, when the creation of boundaries is laden with moral value, such boundaries enclose the body in a fixed dichotomy between the inside and the outside, revealing a special terror for the perceived *corruption* of one's body. Philosopher and psychoanalyst Julia Kristeva, for example, notices the connection between abjection and the need to expel and reject aspects of one's corporeality for the sake of achieving a sense of rebirth against a perceived contamination. This produces the 'revolt' directed at a threat that seems 'to emanate from an exorbitant outside or inside' (Kristeva 1982, p. 1). By crystallizing and demarcating the body from the outside, the abject body manifests a difficulty to cope with the multiplicity of body images that constellate the experience of corporeality, which is characterized not only by localized stimuli, sensations, and feelings, but also by 'abhorrent' bodily parts and features (i.e. body fluids, sexual organs, fat, etc.). For this reason, Weiss argues that distinguishing between spontaneously projected body images and distorted body images is 'a much more difficult task that one may at first suppose' (Weiss 1999, p. 50).

According to Weiss, anorexia manifests the rejection of the potential 'destabilization' brought about by abject body images in order to pursue the rigor of an 'excessive coherence' (Weiss 1999), namely the coherence brought about by the repudiation of the multiple body images we intrinsically possess. On this view, at stake in particular forms of bodily alienation is not only the conflict between body image and the reifying gaze of the other, but also the 'agonistic relationship' that one establishes with one's own body. Weiss' argument is that the Sartrean tension between the body-for-itself and the body seen by others can be found in both anorexic and non-anorexic experience. Indeed, as we saw earlier, Sartre's view of the body highlights a dynamic relation between self and other that is constitutive of bodily experience, though it can be exploited to produce self-estrangement and stigmatization. By the same token, according to Weiss, the enormous social pressure put on the body cannot univocally account for bodily alienation. The root of anorexia could also be found in the struggle of the body to make sense of one's constitutive multiplicity.

By taking into account the way in which 'aberrant body images' are constituted and how they are at odds with individual and societal expectations, Weiss encourages a corporeal response that accepts the continuous transitions we make from one body image to another (Weiss 1999, p. 53). This process involves the re-appropriation of one's natural 'body turbulence', which can only be achieved through 'a medical, cultural, and philosophical commitment to multiply our aesthetic body ideals' (Weiss 1999, p. 56).

2.3.2 Normality versus normalization

As it emerged from our previous discussion, classical phenomenological discourse is filled with references to clinical cases and pathologies, including the phantom limb, agnosia, visual impairment, and hallucinations. Historically, phenomenology has contributed in important ways to psychopathological research by re-assessing and analysing phenomena of physical and mental illness. As Spiegelberg put it in his seminal historical introduction to the role of phenomenology in psychology and psychiatry, 'the real measure of phenomenological "presence" is its active role in ongoing research' (Spiegelberg 1965, p. xxxv). This is confirmed nowadays by the growing body of research in phenomenological psychopathology as well as by the fruitful dialogue established between phenomenology and psychopathology and psychotherapy.[9] While phenomenological psychopathology is indebted especially to the works of Karl Jaspers, a number of phenomenological psychopathologists (including, among others, Eugène Minkowski, Ludwig Binswanger, and Henri Ey) drew on classical phenomenology to challenge standardized methods in medical practice and psychological counselling. Among other aspects, they were interested in exploring the alteration of natural time in psychopathological experience, aiming to uncover the experiential viewpoint of the patient in her existential milieu. To a large extent, such insights are indebted to Martin Heidegger's existentialist analysis, and particularly to Heidegger's view of lived time as the disclosure of one's affective disposition towards reality.

For Heidegger, our experience of time is laden with affective qualities that are revealed by our moods. For example, when we are sluggish or bored, things and situations seem 'blue', as if they are tinged with an ineffable and uninspiring tone. This is not a physical property of the things we deal with, but rather the result of our affective projection onto them. When we are in a mood, even the most familiar things manifest themselves to us with a different tonality, as it were. For example, when in a cheerful disposition, the sound of my colleague typing on the keyboard does not affect me in the least, but rather reminds me joyfully of the passing of time, which is going to bring me closer to the meeting with the person I love, to the class I am excited to teach, or to the phone call I have been waiting for. But, when we are in a gloomy mood, one in which the present does not motivate and the future does not entice, the same noise affects me otherwise as distracting and annoying. In this respect, it is important to notice that, while moods influence our relation to the world, they do not coincide with a perceptual state. What changes from one mood to another is not the content of the given experience, but its practical significance or relevance, which in turn affects my overall disposition to reality. To this end, Heidegger is quite clear that moods are not mental states, as they arise out of one's practical involvement in a situation, hence they are intrinsically relational.[10] On Heidegger's view, we are always in a mood, whether we are aware of it or not, as moods are part of our sense of reality (Heidegger 2001, p. 175).

The sense of reality underpins the sense of belonging to a world that is normally taken for granted in the natural attitude. According to Matthew Ratcliffe, an altered sense of reality is not to be equated with an impaired condition. Since the sense of reality unfolds and changes over time, any ruptures or fragmentation of the flow of experience reflects a variation in the kind of patterns of relevance that structure our orientation in the world. The sense of reality is therefore characterized by fragility and vulnerability (Ratcliffe 2008). Understanding the sense of reality has important implications for both phenomenology of illness and contemporary critical phenomenology in that it brings to light the embodied perspective of the self, specifically in the clinical encounter, as pointed out by S. Kay Toombs.

On Toombs' view, the physician tends to adopt a naturalistic attitude that 'reifies the illness and conceives of it as an objective entity – a disease state, [. . .] as a pathological fact' (Toombs 1992, p. 14). In this respect, Toombs' reflections bring to mind Sartre's analogy between the body-as-known-by-others and disease. At stake is the reduction of the lived body to an ensemble of physiological and neurological properties. Husserl himself was aware of the fact that, when I communicate my experiences of illness to others, 'then I become for them an interesting *pathological* object, and they call my actuality, so beautifully manifest to me, the hallucination of someone who up to this point in time has been mentally ill' (Husserl 1989, p. 85). The struggle to communicate one's experience is an aspect that is well illustrated by Toombs' narrative.

According to Toombs, while the physician inhabits a temporal order that counts as 'normal' and ordinary, as it is measured by the clock, the patient lives in the extended temporality of illness, where minutes seem like hours, and hours like days. The lived time of the patient differs from the 'natural time' of the clinician, who relies on an objective time-scale in order to establish the patient's condition and its symptoms. Thus, physician and patient eventually refer to 'the temporality of illness and the disease state according to two different and incommensurable time dimensions' (Toombs 1992, p. 15). As a result of this, the patient finds herself unable to communicate her condition to the clinician, who in turn risks seeing in the patient nothing but the symptoms of a disease.

As Albert B. Robillard writes in his memoir, recounting his life with

ALS (Amyotrophic Lateral Sclerosis), the struggle to communicate with nurses and clinicians on the part of the patient does not only highlight a duality in terms of how time is lived (an objective time-scale versus a subjective one), but it also calls into question the institutionalization and naturalization of one of the many orders and structures of embodied communication:

> The institutionalized, naturalized, socially consensual order of conversation has a rhythm, a time order, that assumes an intersubjective coordination of physical human bodies. Having a body that could not inhabit this time order breached the normalized conversational environment every time I tried to talk. Yet, as I learned from the local nurses, a few people demonstrate that the normal time order is but one among many time orders and structures for communication. (Robillard 1999, p. 63)

The clash between the 'naturalized' time of the clinician, as partaking in the 'normal timeframe' of time as a continuous sequence of distinct units, and the lived time of the patient is symptomatic of the rupture of what counts as 'normal' or 'ordinary' in the experience of illness. To breach the natural order of objective time, as Robillard writes, is to affirm that a different experience of time is not only possible but also already existent, though it represents a deviation from the representation of time as a quantitatively measurable reality. This resonates with the classical-phenomenological critique of reductionist and mechanistic approaches to bodily experience, as it brings to light the experience of temporality as duration, which unfolds through the first-person perspective of the body.

   In this context, it is important to note that variations of time experiences are consistent with the classical-phenomenological view of 'normal experiences'. For example, Husserl speaks of the significance of the 'normal' perceptual conditions through which ordinary experiences are given to consciousness (such as, the condition of optimal illumination for seeing colours). Such conditions are distinguished from 'abnormal conditions' that represent deviations from the 'normal' sensuous conditions of experience (Husserl 1989, §18). However, by normality, Husserl does not mean an objective standard for natural experience (Steinbock 1995; Wehrle 2019). On the contrary, he refers to optimal regularities that obtain between consciousness and the circumstances, which vary not just across individuals, due to their different psychophysical constitution, but also within the same individual, without thereby corresponding to a norm of what should count as standard experience or behaviour. Thus, the struggle of communication that is experienced in illness is the struggle to identify and communicate what the optimal conditions of one's experience are, which in turn allows the recognition of different types of normal experiences.

On this front, contemporary phenomenology of illness represents a critical application of phenomenological discourse in at least two main ways: on the one hand, as we have seen, phenomenologists offer a conceptual framework to rethink the patient–clinician relationship. This includes insights into the differences that structure clinical encounters, which can be extended to practices of communication aiming to reduce progressively the felt distance between patient and clinician. Such a distance is produced by the clinician's reliance on a third-person viewpoint regarding the patient's lived experience. On the other hand, the phenomenology of illness provides a conceptual and fine-grained repertoire for the thematization and analysis of the sense of reality that is distinctive of illness. In so doing, phenomenologists challenge the normalization of descriptive accounts of the lived body, highlighting the distinctive experiential qualities of illness without thereby downplaying its symptoms and physiological conditions.

For example, while the sense of reality varies across different types of illness, it is possible to describe the fundamental phenomenological qualities that underpin the ordinary experience of reality in illness. In illness, the world ceases to be practically relevant, meaning not just that certain projects cannot be afforded, but also that they cannot exert any pull or solicitation. In this sense, the characteristic bodily projection in the outer world that classical phenomenologists ascribe to the lived body appears closed down. With regard to such bodily orientation, Ratcliffe speaks of 'existential feelings', distinguishing them from both emotions and bodily feelings in order to capture the irreducibility of existential feelings to the overarching stability and homogeneity of other feelings and emotions (Ratcliffe 2008).

For Ratcliffe, existential feelings underpin the ways in which we are situated in the world, hence they cannot be suspended or put aside, not even in the phenomenological *epoché*. Existential feelings have a bodily character, and yet they do not fit ordinary classifications of emotions in that they structure all experiences in terms of an underlying sense of belonging to the world. In this respect, existential feelings are subject to a number of fluctuations and shifting positions according to the evolving character of the subject's natural experience. On this view, existential feelings provide existential orientations, namely they shape and give salience to a number of practical possibilities in the world. It follows that existential feelings are not a variety of feelings but are intrinsic to the constitution of the sense of reality, having a deeper reach than the Husserlian notion of natural attitude. Indeed, while Ratcliffe acknowledges that the natural attitude, as conceived by Husserl, is not a self-evident and universal stance but a form of 'opening onto the world', he also argues that it fails to capture the alterations and existential changes that affect the sense of reality, namely the changeable and shifting stance to the world that is intrinsic to embodied experience.

Havi Carel's phenomenology of illness provides a helpful application of these insights, particularly with regard to the reconfiguration of bodily certainty or bodily doubt that accompanies existential feelings. Bodily certainty denotes the field of possibility and openness that characterizes familiar or routine actions and movements. Ordinary actions that are performed effortlessly and even mindlessly reflect a tacit confidence in the skills and abilities that project us in the world. This is what Carel calls a 'tacit feeling of trust, familiarity, and normalcy' (Carel 2016, p. 92). The experience of illness, by contrast, reveals how bodily doubt affects not simply one's reflective evaluation of one's skills but operates at the very level of motor intentionality. Broadly speaking, bodily doubt is a feeling of helplessness, distrust, and isolation, having different degrees that vary in duration, intensity, and specificity. In this regard, for example, episodic instances of bodily doubt (e.g. having an infection or the flu) are notably different from chronic forms of bodily doubt that are experienced in Parkinson's disease. Furthermore, bodily doubt can be all-pervasive or related to specific actions (e.g. taking the stairs).

The important phenomenological quality of bodily doubt is that it may occur unexpectedly, interrupting one's ordinary engagement with the environment by 'replacing immersion with suspension'. This means that bodily doubt interrupts one's natural and spontaneous involvement in the world, thereby affecting bodily confidence even when one's condition can be communicated and shared. As Carel puts it, bodily doubt '*necessarily* prompts the ill person to critically renegotiate her participation in the shared world of public norms' (Carel 2016, p. 98). Illness does not call into question the practical intelligibility of the surrounding world and the demands that impinge on the self, but rather the very possibility of dealing with the world in a temporally continuous and coherent fashion. In this respect, bodily doubt brings to light not only the vulnerability of the lived body, but also the injustice brought about by healthcare in not attending to the needs and experiences of the patient.

More specifically, Carel refers to the failures of healthcare to appropriately tackle and take seriously the testimonies of patients. On Carel's view, such a phenomenon manifests itself as a form of epistemic injustice (to which we will return in more detail in Chapter 6), which occurs when individuals are denied recognition as competent knowers or epistemic agents. In the case of healthcare, epistemic injustice occurs in two main ways: on the one hand, patients' testimonies are not given epistemic consideration because of their specific physical or mental condition, which automatically deprives them of their epistemic abilities as cognitive agents. A typical example of this is that of patients with a chronic condition, who know their condition well and have a good grasp of the knowledge and medical information surrounding it, and yet their needs, questions, and concerns are routinely disregarded or not given any attention by clinicians. On the other hand, patients may be heard and considered, but judged inarticulate or irrelevant because of their difficulties in communicating with the clinician. This situation is often connected to the lack of training, on the parts of clinicians, to appreciate the specific form of articulacy patients rely on to express themselves (Carel 2016, p. 188). As Robillard reports in his memoir: 'I am afflicted with a neuromuscular disease, and I cannot talk or communicate in anything approaching the social consensus of "real time". When I could not communicate, I had no participation in my care or the way I was regarded and the way I came to view myself' (Robillard 1999, p. 50).

The 'institutionalizing power' of healthcare to which Carel refers is particularly relevant for disability studies. Like chronic illness, disability is typically processed through the lens of medicalization, resulting in ableism, that is, the set of beliefs, practices, and policies that produce normative expectations about individuals and their abilities. Disability is often presented in negative terms, as a lack of normal skills or as a marginal position due to the physical constraints that affect the exercise of one's abilities and capacities. As Robillard notes, in the perception of others, one typically surmises a full range of bodily abilities and instrumentalities that can be employed to act, move, and produce things in a seemingly effortlessly way. However, 'the sight of the paralyzed, the crippled, the lame is a sharp denial of this commonsense, reciprocal knowledge' (Robillard 1999, p. 72). That the taken-for-granted knowledge about individuals is vitiated by ableist assumptions that are diffused in society and sustained by material structures, including services, healthcare, and infrastructure, represents, from a critical-phenomenological perspective, the normalization and institutionalization of ableism.

As sociologist Erving Goffman pointed out in his classic essay *Stigma* (1963), the stigmatization of individuals and groups perceived as deviant, non-conforming, or unfit operates at the level of individual and collective perspectives, casting people apart through prejudice and thereby acting as an instrument of social control by enforcing, through the process of stigmatization (and the attendant inducement of shame), conformity to certain norms and values. From this point of view, there exists an important connection between affect and politics, as existential feelings can be connected to situated, historical conditions that produce durable feelings of anxiety, shame, and disconnection. For example, in *The Cultural Politics of Emotion*, Ahmed draws attention to the ways in which marginalized groups and individuals learn to live 'with the effects and affects' of heterosexism and homophobia, as involving pain, shame, depression, anxiety, and fear (Ahmed 2014, p. 154).

In this context, Robert McRuer notices the correlation between definitions of able-bodiedness and the capacity to exert physical labour, which typically represents a value or an asset in the neo-liberal market. On his view, the compulsory nature of able-bodiedness is historically connected to the emergence of the industrial capitalist system, where one is free to sell one's labour, implying that one is free to have a body only to the extent that one uses it for work and productivity. As McRuer puts it, 'compulsory able-bodiedness functions by covering over, with the appearance of choice, a system in which there actually is no choice' (McRuer 2006, p. 8).

According to McRuer (2006), able-bodiness is in many ways even more naturalized in contemporary culture than heterosexuality, as the normalization of heterosexuality and the consequent marginalization of queerness presuppose the able body at its foundations. To this end, McRuer speaks of 'crip theory' to conceptualize and thematize the 'spectre of disability' that is characteristic of able-bodied heterosexuality. 'Crip theory' is meant to provide a critical space where 'certain nondisabled claims to be crip are more imaginable', such as being at the same time queer, immigrant worker, homosexual, and with multiple sclerosis. McRuer's 'crip theory' is based on the history of activism, social struggles, performances, artistic productions, and personal stories of 'coming out crip' that resist the compulsory imaginary of able-bodiedness and its inability to conceive of queer and crip practices, relations, and domesticity.

While disability is often framed as 'a threat to unquestioned versions of normalcy', to the point that disabled people become a problem to and for the world conceived as 'normal' (Titchkosky and Michalko 2012), McRuer questions the institutional and socio-economical settings that sustain such a view. At stake in this case is not just the understanding of what counts as 'normal' with respect to one's individual and subjective experience, but the intersection between body, institutions, and social practices, which together reinforce a system that conceives of disability as a problem in need of a solution rather than 'a *life* to be lived in the natural attitude' (Titchkosky and Michalko 2012).

A key upshot of the relation between phenomenology, embodiment, and disability studies is therefore the possibility of an experiential horizon that resists the objectification and normalization of illness and disability. As we have seen throughout this chapter, the phenomenology of body is inseparable from interpersonal experience, as bodily self-awareness is connected to how we apprehend ourselves as embodied beings as well as how we negotiate our bodily presentation by experiencing others and being experienced by them. Furthermore, interpersonal experience is fundamental for achieving mutual understanding and building up bonds informed by a deep and fine-grained comprehension of the situated character of embodied experience. To this end, we now turn to the phenomenology of intersubjectivity to explore further the relation between corporeality and interpersonal experience.

3

Intersubjectivity

Empathy, being-with others,
and the ethics of sensibility

By empathy with differently composed personal structures we become
clear on what we are not.

Edith Stein

We are fully dependent on each other for the possibility of being
understood and without this understanding we are not intelligible, we
don't make sense, we are not solid, visible, integrated, we are lacking.

María Lugones

Intersubjectivity (from the Latin *inter*, 'between', and *subiectivē*, 'subjective') is a key concept in phenomenology, as it refers to the experience
of other selves as a necessary condition of possibility for self-awareness.
Can there be self-awareness independently from the experience of other
minded beings? In what ways, if any, is the experience I have of myself
drawn on my perception and understanding of the states and behaviour
of other subjects?

It is important to stress that, from a classical-phenomenological point
of view, the set of issues surrounding intersubjectivity is not concerned
with demonstrating whether or not other selves exist (the so-called
'problem of other minds'). Quite to the contrary, a phenomenology of
intersubjectivity interrogates *how* we perceive, understand, and relate to
foreign experiences, that is, experiences that are distinct from our own.
In doing so, the phenomenology of intersubjectivity provides the basis for
investigating the basis of our natural stance towards others.

In this chapter, we illustrate the key aspects of the phenomenology of intersubjectivity that inform the relation between self and other as well as the problems of relating to and understanding experiences situated in multiple socio-cultural worlds. As such, the concepts and arguments that we explore in this chapter provide the backdrop for situating the phenomenology of gender and race in the next two chapters, as well as the analysis of social and political experience in the final chapter. Throughout this book, we encourage our reader not to regard the key concepts of this book (corporeality, intersubjectivity, gender, race, social experience and political action) as separate from each other but, rather, to bear in mind their reciprocal connections and implications.

When it comes to illustrating the key aspects of interpersonal experience, there are two main related areas of inquiry. On the one hand, as we mentioned, the phenomenology of intersubjectivity investigates how we perceive and understand others' experiences, an aspect that ties the notion of intersubjectivity to empathy. Recognizing others as fellow human beings is what classical phenomenologists typically call empathy or *Einfühlung* ('feeling into another'). As we will see, in Husserl, Stein, and Scheler, empathy is a perceptual-like phenomenon, involving not only the capacity to recognize other embodied beings as such (as opposed to inanimate things), but also the capacity to grasp and respond to their states and feelings as meaningful expressions that belong to unique personal standpoints.

On the other hand, intersubjectivity presupposes a surrounding world as the general background in which encounters with others take place. As noted by Husserl in his manuscripts of the second book of his *Ideas Pertaining to a Pure Phenomenology and to a Phenomenological Philosophy* (published posthumously in 1952), in our everyday life we take our subjective experience to be given only to us, as part of an egoic framework, when in fact such experience takes place within and against the backdrop of an intersubjective world that is often taken for granted (Husserl 1989, p. 203). While it is in principle possible to think of ourselves as separated from the world around us, as if we led private lives that are independent from the lives of others, the 'relations of mutual understanding' that structure the common world (such as empathy, affection, language, social practices) do not thereby cease to operate in how we understand reality and perceive ourselves situated in it.

It follows that, while experience is tied to a unique first-person standpoint, it is not thereby private in terms of its constitution and communicability. In this way, the phenomenology of intersubjectivity brings to light issues pertaining to empathy and its possibility, paving the way to existential analyses concerning what it means *to be with others* in a world of practical purposes and concerns. As Heidegger points out, in our ordinary experience we do not encounter 'free-floating' subjects against whom we stand as solitary individuals. On the contrary, we experience others *environmentally*, that is within contexts that are structured by our practical goals and interests. Therefore, from an existential-phenomenological angle, the concept of intersubjectivity brings up questions about the ontological character of our *being*-with others. This means distinguishing the *being* of the entities we are involved with, but also interrogating the nature of our involvement with the world and the norms we abide by in everyday life.

In inheriting and taking up these fundamental directions of the phenomenological approach, critical phenomenology pays special attention to the different ways in which the world resurfaces in the self-and-other relation, not just as an ontological reality or cultural milieu, but also as a taken-for-granted background that is still operative in the way we perceive and understand others. On this basis, a critical phenomenology of intersubjectivity draws attention to how we *learn* to see and recognize others within *and against* the socio-cultural world we inhabit. As we will see, this type of phenomenological investigation is closely connected to Heidegger's concern with (in)authenticity, but also to Merleau-Ponty's ontology of the flesh and Levinas' account of being-*for* the other.

We proceed by illustrating the premises of classical-phenomenological theories of intersubjectivity, focusing on two main axes: the role of empathy as a source of knowledge of other embodied selves, and the ambiguous relation between self, other, and the world. Both axes are constitutive of a phenomenological critique of intersubjective experience in both classical and critical phenomenology. For each argument, we illustrate its meaning and key aspects in classical phenomenological accounts, before pointing out their relevance for critical phenomenology, and the respective differences that arise between these two phenomenological approaches. In particular, we show how critical phenomenology shifts the analysis of intersubjective experience towards an account of intercorporeality and moral responsiveness.

3.1 At the roots of intersubjective experience: the problem of empathy

3.1.1 The self–other distinction

Husserl's engagement with the nature and possibility of empathy (*Einfühlung*) was stimulated by Theodor Lipps' pioneering investigations on the same topic, which sparked an important debate at the beginning of the past century among early phenomenologists, including Max Scheler and Edith Stein.[1] Common to Lipps and classical phenomenologists is the view that empathy represents a *sui generis* source of knowledge of other minds, insofar as it does not depend on inferential thinking or analogy. On Lipps' account, empathy is an affective and immediate response to another's state, which shares significant aspects with perceptual experience. Empathy occurs spontaneously in hearing the cry of a child or in seeing the glowing smile of a friend, as it is motivated by the affective and sensory qualities of another's expression, gesture, or behaviour. What makes empathy a distinctive experience of other minds is the fact that we feel *drawn* to another's experience, participating – on an affective and sensuous level – in their state.

Originally used in the context of aesthetics, the German term *Einfühlung*, translated into English in 1909 by Edward Titchener as 'empathy', was used to characterize the subjective transposition of the spectator into a work of art. As a philosopher and a trained psychologist, Lipps was acutely aware that the term 'empathy' could be ambiguous, as there can be different forms of empathy depending on whether we feel transposed into, say, a work of art, or whether we respond to the human expression of a fellow human being. On a general level, Lipps argues that empathy is the activity whereby we transpose ourselves into a given object, and we animate it – as it were – through our perceptual and representational experience. For example, when we observe an object, like a spinning ball, we follow out its trajectory, projecting onto it an impression of tension and force that draws on our own self-experience of movement. Lipps maintains therefore that we empathize with objects when we synthetize their different appearances by projecting onto them a sense of vitality that certain objects activate in us.

In the case of empathy towards human beings, Lipps argues that we find ourselves drawn to imitating or replicating certain movements or gestures we see in the other. In this regard, Lipps speaks of an instinct of empathy, which awakens in the perceiver the disposition to feel or reproduce those movements or gestures we see in another because we have gone through them in the past. If I am familiar with a gesture that expresses sadness and I see that gesture in another person, then, Lipps argues, I instinctively re-enact my former experience of sadness. On Lipps' view, two impulses operate simultaneously in the empathic experience: an impulse towards expression, which is the bodily response we spontaneously enact towards others' states, and an impulse towards imitation, insofar as we tend to replicate those states and expressions that we observe in others.

An illustration of this is the experience of watching a funambulist. Consider, for example, Philippe Petit's famous performance on the tight-rope connecting the Twin Towers in New York in 1974. People watching the scene (in real time as well as on screen) empathized (in Lippsian words) with Petit by inwardly reproducing the motions of his body on the tightrope. In evoking such movements, the spectators instinctively experienced the feelings and bodily reactions they would have if they were to walk at a high distance from the ground. Due to the instinctual character of empathy, Lipps is very clear that empathy has nothing to do with mental comparing or inferential analogy, since empathy occurs only when something is immediately *felt* in one's own experience. Yet, when empathy is fully realized, Lipps maintains that there is a certain 'fusion' between the perceiver and the object perceived (Lipps 1909).

Lipps' theory of empathy as a form of instinctive imitation of the movements we observe in another (also known today as motor mimicry) was criticized by classical phenomenologists for the lack of an adequate distinction between self and other. If empathy entirely consists in being transposed into another's experience, how can empathy be a source of knowledge of other minds? Are we not, after all, projecting our own experiences onto others, thereby losing sight of what makes a 'foreign experience' different from our own? Max Scheler believed that Lipps' theory was 'approximately correct' when it comes to investigating pat-terns of crowd-psychology, but that it failed to account for the nature of our experience of other selves (Scheler 2017, p. 220). In a similar vein, in her 1917 doctoral dissertation *On the Problem of Empathy* (completed under the supervision of Edmund Husserl), Stein questions Lipps' argument:

> I do not actually go through his [the acrobat's] motions but *quasi* [almost]. Lipps also stresses, to be sure, that I do not outwardly go through his motions. But neither is what 'inwardly' corresponds to the movements of the body, the experience that 'I move', primordial; it is non-primordial for me. (Stein 1964, p. 16)

Stein stresses that, when watching the acrobat, not only we do not need to imitate his outer movements in order to relate to the acrobat's state, but even the sensations and feelings that we feel inwardly (such as fear or vertigo) represent a *response* to the acrobat's performance. Such a bodily response is 'non-primordial', meaning that it is motivated by the perception of the acrobat's motion rather than being originally enacted through the sensations of our own body movements. As such, there cannot be any fusion between our state and the acrobat's, as each experience belongs to a distinct and different centre of sensorimotor awareness. If anything, in feeling transposed into another's experience, we 'forget' that there is a difference between our embodied position and theirs. Yet this indicates that empathy is less the experience of a subject identifying herself with the intentional object of perception than an act of 'self-forgetfulness', whereby one feels led in a certain direction by a foreign experience. Nonetheless, there remains between self and other a fundamental distinction owing to differences of bodily constitution, temporal awareness, and spatial orientation that are intrinsic to each embodied viewpoint.

By and large, phenomenologists like Scheler, Stein, and Husserl repudiate the view of empathy as imitation and projection (which is captured by the common expression of 'putting oneself in another's shoes'), as they regard empathy as the basic experience of intersubjective life. On their view, empathy brings us closer to a foreign experience in different degrees of awareness, though classical phenomenologists offer different arguments and methodologies to justify this.

For Husserl, *Einfühlung* requires a transcendental justification. On his view, empathy plays a fundamental role in illuminating the very possibility of perceiving and relating to other fellow living beings.[2] In this respect, the Fifth Meditation included in the *Cartesian Meditations*, a text based on a series of conferences held by Husserl in Paris in 1929, provides a key angle for understanding the spontaneity of empathy in contrast to Lipps' theory of instincts. In these lectures, Husserl attempts to provide a transcendental theory of intersubjective experience; that is, an account of the intentional structures that are constitutive of our basic awareness of other embodied beings. In so doing, Husserl departs from the Cartesian approach to which his very lectures are dedicated. Descartes' 1641 *Meditations on First Philosophy* raised the metaphysical problem as to whether other selves exist in the world. Descartes' analysis is an inquiry into the foundations of knowledge that proceeds by extending the method of radical doubt to all our perceptions, beliefs, and acquired knowledge. In so doing, Descartes establishes his own existence as a thinking being as the basic truth upon which all knowledge is built, prior to inquiring into the possibility of the existence of other subjects.

For Husserl, Descartes' error was to take for granted that indubitability amounts to truth, when in fact all knowledge and experience can only provide a presumption of certainty that is in need of phenomenological critique and analysis. Furthermore, while Descartes presents the thinking ego, or 'I', as a self-subsisting entity, in principle separate from other thinking beings, Husserl argues that each self is necessarily connected to another subject or *alter ego*. This method builds on a particular form of *epoché* in that, within such an attitude, the experience of others is reduced to its fundamental intentional structure. Such an approach consists in bracketing the characteristics that pertain to mundane experience in order to attend to the ways in which the other affects the ego. The *alter ego* encountered in this way is understood as a centre of intentional activity, namely as an animate or embodied alterity.[3]

On Husserl's view, the transcendental reduction shows that not even by abstracting from the existence of others would we cease to be 'experienceable by everyone'. Even though in our natural attitude we find ourselves surrounded and even limited by other selves, we are, in fact, transcendentally interconnected. This fundamental quality would not be lost 'even if a universal plague had left only me' (Husserl 1960, p. 93). As shown in the previous chapter, the lived body represents a centre of sensorimotor responsiveness, through which I am simultaneously aware of myself and others. Unlike physical objects, the experience of another self affects me as the manifestation of a living being that is essentially similar to me and yet irreducible to myself. From a transcendental point of view, the justification of this relational phenomenon is explored through the concept of 'pairing', which refers to the analogy that structures self-perception in relation to the presentation of another lived body (*Leib*). Husserl describes pairing as a 'living mutual awakening' (Husserl 1960, p. 113), whereby I simultaneously perceive and recognize another self as a fellow embodied being without having to entertain any thought or inferential process about it. Such recognition is based neither on motor instinct (as in Lipps) nor on projection (in the sense of inferential reasoning) but rather on a pre-reflective transfer of sense from my own self-experience to the lived body of another. What kind of transfer is this?

Husserl speaks of 'analogizing apperception' and 'apperceptive transfer' to indicate that the transfer in question is the result of the activation of pre-reflective syntheses of association, whereby the perception of the foreign lived body resonates with my own self-experience. As my body 'awakens' to the other, I co-perceive them to be as sentient and receptive as I am. Thus, the other lived body is not to be deduced from my own existence. On this view, empathy represents a pre-reflective directedness to other-minded beings, who mirror my own being and whose situated experiences are irreducible to my self-experience. Such a structural, transcendental similarity between self and other provides the basis for relating to and exploring another's lived experience. In this sense, empathy is actualized in the stream of experience, that is, in the natural encounter with other embodied beings (including animals).

According to this view, through empathy we do not simply grasp features of outer behaviour but rather apprehend the expressive unity of mind and body, e.g. we 'see' the anger in the raised brow of a colleague (and also the pain in the cat's paw), and the shame in the blushing of our friend. It follows that we cannot separate off the perception of a person's state from their experiential horizon. Indeed, empathy gives access to the horizon inhabited by another self, which we can approach in various degrees of understanding and participation. In this regard, Stein emphasizes that empathy is a quasi-perceptual experience that is realized gradually, and that is infused with multiple tendencies. For instance, I empathize with a friend who has received joyous news, while I am filled with grief over a bereavement. In this case, consciousness is split between two states that may obstruct each other but also flow into another. Stein's argument is that being pulled towards two different experiences at once does not make empathy a stance of either adherence to or rejection of the foreign experience (as Lipps argued). On the contrary, empathy is characterized by a flow of tendencies that colours an underlying directedness to another's experience. Elisa Aaltola defines such a flow in terms of 'embodied resonation', whereby the affective response that characterizes empathy is not just a movement outward, namely, towards the other, but also equally inward, 'towards one's affective landscape' (Aaltola 2014, p. 252). As she puts it:

> Empathy indeed has interruptive power, which forces one to change in the face of what one witnesses, to become (at least momentarily) fluid through responding to the experiences of others. Thereby, one is exposed to the fear, suffering or joy of the other individual, together with one's own response (such as grief) to these states; and this exposure incorporates the possibility that one may have to re-examine one's own approach to the world, and one's very constitution. (Aaltola 2014, p. 252)

Empathy has a critical potential in so far as it reveals our stance towards another's state, making it a potential object of inquiry. In this context, it is worth noting that, while embodiment is a necessary condition for empathy, the latter is implemented by non-perceptual conditions. For example, Stein makes it clear that empathy implies the capacity to understand emotions and feelings by becoming attuned to the content that is 'hidden' or not available to outer perception:

> I not only know what is expressed through facial expressions and gestures, but also what is hidden behind them. Perhaps I see that someone makes a sad face but is not really sad. I may also hear someone make an indiscreet remark and blush. Then I not only understand the remark and see shame in the blush, but I also discern that he knows his remark is indiscreet and is ashamed of himself for having made it. Neither this motivation nor the judgment about his remark is expressed by any 'sensory appearance'. (Stein 1964, p. 6)

Stein argues that empathy involves an attunement to the situation in which interpersonal experience takes place. This entails grasping contextual hints and other non-perceptual aspects of the experience, enacting a form of social sensitivity that is attentive to the motives of the other's state and expression. In this sense, it is possible to draw on personal experience to better grasp the affective tonality of another's situation. For example, acknowledging that one is blushing because she is embarrassed by the remark made by another typically requires contextual awareness on the part of the empathizer, including first-person acquaintance with the ambivalence and awkwardness of social behaviour.

This goes in the direction of what Ratcliffe has called 'radical empathy' (Ratcliffe 2012), that is, a stance of receptivity to others' states that incorporates an experiential insight into their sense of reality, even when the affective changes they go through are radically different from our own. Since all of us are familiar with experiential shifts that are often difficult to describe (from jetlag and hangover to emotional distress and heartbreak), we can rely on such a reservoir of meaning to interpret the experiential viewpoint of another. Crucial to radical empathy is the actual interaction with people, using sensitivity and imagination as a way of connecting to their possible experiences, and not to project onto them our own beliefs, expectations, and desires. Similarly, in Stein, empathy enables sensitivity towards different ways of being. As Aaltola remarks, through affective empathy one moves gradually further 'away from the initial moment of resonation', 'forming responses to that moment, the other individual, and even one's own attitude' (Aaltola 2014, p. 252). From this point of view, empathy represents a form of responsiveness to others' states and emotions that allows one to de-centre her perspective, and to better understand not only others but also oneself.

3.1.2 Understanding persons

In the preceding section, we emphasized that in classical phenomenology, particularly in Husserl and Stein, empathy provides a ground for experiencing other selves as *minded beings*. In what way, however, does empathy also allow an *understanding* of others as *persons*, that is, as having personal character and moral worth? For classical phenomenologists like Husserl, Stein, and Scheler, the 'problem of empathy' consists precisely in reconciling these two fundamental aspects of intersubjective experience, namely its immediate, perceptual-like character with the hermeneutic capacity of understanding other subjects and appropriately responding to their states and expressions in the socio-cultural world.

Already in his 1912 essay, 'The Idols of Self-Knowledge', Max Scheler stresses that 'when we become aware of a "man", the first thing we see is his social self' (Scheler 1973b, p. 92). By social self, Scheler refers to the fact that we never experience individuals 'pure and simple', but always clothed with the social image that they project around themselves and according to which they fashion their conduct to conform with social expectations and standards. As the values we assimilate through society and culture change historically, we end up seeing ourselves through the eyes of a public opinion that is, in itself, unstable and changeable. In Scheler's words: 'the individual sees himself, inwardly and outwardly, through the eyes of the onlooker, and everything he experiences, feels, judges, and wills is only a *consequence* of, a reaction to, the alleged "picture" which he offers to the onlooker' (Scheler 1973b, p. 93). To this end, Scheler's phenomenological approach is an emancipation from the illusions that obscure perception (such as taking the social self for the inner core of the person) in order to learn to see individuals for who they are and not through their social projection.

As Scheler points out, we don't perceive physical bodies and then spiritual qualities, but rather spiritual embodied unities; that is, persons. Scheler maintains that each person is a unique being as a carrier of values that are instantiated through acts of feeling, valuing, and willing. For Scheler, values are manifold and varied, and they are latent in our experience of objects and other persons. As such, values are grasped and recognized in the course of experience, yet they also express ethical imperatives that are independent from experience, that is, a priori. On this view, values are ranked in different categories depending on the strength, duration, depth, and reach in which they are experienced.

In this regard, for Scheler, affective responses to others are characterized by sensitivity to values across different levels of experience. This means that, in experiencing others, we become attuned not simply to their states and expressions, but also to the relation between their feelings and emotions and different value-orientations. Thus, it is possible to empathize with the bodily feelings of other people, as they are expressive of the values of pleasure and displeasure (for example, a person's satisfaction with a good meal or their discomfort with a cold). However, we can also empathize with someone's pleasure in evil. In this respect, Scheler is sceptical of the use of the term *Einfühlung,* which – on his view – was an expression vitiated by Lipps' notion of projection. Instead, Scheler argues that emotional understanding requires attunement to the spiritual realm, namely, to the domain of moral values, such as beauty, fairness, and truth, that are revealed through our emotions. On his view, there cannot be any genuine fellow-feeling that is not based upon spiritual love, which grasps the essential qualities of another person. Indeed, for Scheler, it is love that helps us discern the character of another person and see through the shell of their social self.

By anchoring intersubjective experience on the realm of values, Scheler does not insist on the transcendental distinction between self and other in the same way as Husserl and Stein do. Indeed, in the second edition of his *The Nature of Sympathy,* he refers to an 'undifferentiated stream of consciousness' from which we gradually learn to distinguish ourselves from others (Scheler 2017, p. 251). This is not to deny that there are indeed differences between self- and other-experience.[4] Nor does Scheler argue that the character of a person is transparent, for empathic understanding is gradual and may not fully capture the intrinsic and essential core of another being. Rather, Scheler's idea is that we cannot separate the experience of other persons from the metaphysics of values, which manifest themselves to us through sentience and affectivity.

While Husserl and Stein agree with Scheler that empathy is grounded in the expressive unity brought about by the lived body, they tend to depart from his metaphysical account. In this regard, they provide a theory of interpersonal understanding that centres on the egoic stance through which persons are motivated to understand one another as well as to explore their differences and value-commitments, while also acknowledging each other as worthy of respect. This view lies at the heart of Stein's dissertation as well as of the second volume of Husserl's *Ideas II,* a collation of manuscripts written between 1908 and 1928 and published posthumously – thanks, among others, to the editorial work of Stein. Particularly in *Ideas II,* Husserl's classic distinction between the body as a material or physical reality (*Körper*) and the lived body (*Leib*) as an egoic centre of orientation is developed on account of the two main attitudes that are available to consciousness towards reality: the naturalistic and the personalistic attitude.

While in the natural attitude we tend not to question the realm of nature or our existence, through a shift of perspective it is possible to hold a value-oriented stance towards the world around us. For example, one can regard nature as a material domain, involving living and non-living entities, which are characterized by extension, duration, and qualitative change (strict sense). Yet it is also possible to regard nature as the domain of living beings, who exist as subjects of feelings and volitions (broad sense). Husserl characterizes the attitude oriented to nature in the strict sense as the naturalistic attitude, while the attitude that is concerned with the psychophysical reality of the subject is the personalistic attitude.

It is noteworthy that these two attitudes highlight two different ways of conceiving the body. From the point of view of the naturalistic attitude, the body is a material reality that is subject to external causal powers (*Körper*). As such, the naturalistic attitude is typical of the scientist or the physician when they regard their patients exclusively as bodies affected by a disease that is qualitatively and quantitatively determinable. Yet Husserl's argument is not meant to criticize the naturalistic position *per se*. We always fall back onto the naturalistic attitude in order to analyse and investigate natural phenomena in terms of causal relations. In doing so, we implicitly assume that we belong to a community of subjects whose bodies are structurally similar, that is, subject to the same physical laws.

Unlike the naturalistic attitude, the personalistic attitude regards the body as a lived experience (*Leib*), which is connected to a moral and practical orientation. Specifically, the personalistic attitude is the overall stance that considers other selves as bearers of styles of behaviour, as having character and value-oriented agency. In this attitude, which is inspired by respect for the worth of individual persons, one attends to the affective qualities of another's environing world in different degrees of fulfilment, striving to comprehend the motives and dispositions that guide their character and behaviour. As *Ideas II* states, 'I secure these motivations [i.e. the motives that guide another's character and experiences] by placing myself in his [i.e. the other] situation, his level of education, his development as a youth, etc. and to do so *I must needs share in that situation*' (Husserl 1989, p. 287).

Sharing the situation of others does not mean projecting oneself onto others or speaking for them, but rather comprehending how they are positioned in their respective world-horizon, including the values they abide by. For this reason, already in her dissertation, Stein emphasizes that empathy is not realized in single acts or experiences, but rather requires a gradual explication of the motives of the other's expression in the effort to understand them. In the course of such a practice, one also discovers the values that inform one's orientation by affinity or contrast with the values of others (Stein 1964, p. 105). In so doing, empathy reveals a critical valence insofar as it allows for the disclosure and critical comprehension of one's attitude in relation to the attitudes and values of other subjects. This is probably one aspect of Stein's phenomenology that still needs to be more widely appreciated and explored, especially from a critical-phenomenological angle.

3.1.3 Understanding others within and against the social background

Classical phenomenologists like Husserl and Stein stress that recognizing other selves as persons, and knowing them as such, builds on an attitude that is informed by sensitivity to others' embodied ways of being. This requires a shift of orientation from the natural attitude in which we are usually absorbed towards the personalistic attitude. While in the natural attitude we may be aware of other people as limiting our actions or freedom of movement, the personalistic attitude builds on the recognition that an other self can never be secondary or derived from the experiencing ego. Yet, even when we take up the personalistic stance described by Husserl and Stein, we do not thereby abandon the domain of the natural attitude in which we always live. This is an aspect that phenomenologist Aron Gurwitsch pointed out as problematic in his *Human Encounters in the Social World* (1977), where he wonders whether, notwithstanding the roles of empathy and the personalistic attitude, we remain absorbed, in our natural attitude, in a practical world that determines the sense of the encounter with the other. In a way, to be able to understand one another, an implicit grasp or understanding of the world in which we are situated is also presupposed.

It is at this level that critical phenomenology radicalizes classical phenomenology by interrogating the social and cultural structures that are co-perceived in everyday experience. This concern bears important implications for the analysis of empathy as a form of interpersonal understanding in that it brings to the fore the role that the social and cultural world plays as a general background of intersubjective experience. From a critical-phenomenological point of view, the social background is operative in at least two fundamental senses. On the one hand, the social background represents the general backdrop against which intersubjective encounters take place, which is animated by specific attentional patterns. For example, for each subject, the horizon is structured as to include a foreground and a background. What makes certain things stand out while others remain in the background? Do the things that are part of the background '*sustain* a certain direction, in other words, to keep attention on what is faced' rather than what is relegated, marginalized, or simply hidden (Ahmed 2006, p. 20)? This is connected to the concept of 'visual economy' we pointed out in Chapter 1, that is to say, with the need to contextualize the difference between what appears familiar to us and what seems strange, odd, or queer, because it does not fit habitual patterns or expectations. On the other hand, the social background is connected to how we thematize the *visibility* of the subjects we encounter.

As pointed out in Chapter 1, the suspension of the assumptions ingrained in our natural attitude is the preliminary task of Husserl's phenomenology. Yet such a suspension should also facilitate the identification and critique of those structures that are co-present in how we interpret the contexts and situations of human encounters. To this end, Weiss argues that we should not replace hegemonic patterns of interpretation with counter-ideologies, but rather avail ourselves of the phenomenological method in order to critically re-examine the structure of the horizon itself. This consists in pursuing 'an awareness of the horizon and the structuring role it plays in everyday perception so that one can render it visible to/for others. By rendering the horizon visible [. . .] one also transforms the horizon itself, making it the critical figure rather than the uncritical ground of one's discourse' (Weiss 2008a, p. 107). Weiss' idea is that phenomenological analysis plays a key role precisely when it reveals the horizonal structures that operate in the natural attitude. In other words, the phenomenological method may become a hermeneutic device when used for revealing to others the overlapping schemes of interpretation that operate in our perceptual fields. From this point of view, critical phenomenology reconsiders the relation between self, other, and the background through the concept of ambiguity, revisiting in important ways the worldly character of being-with others as well as the ethical valence of sensibility, as we shall illustrate in the next sections.

3.2 Being-with others and (in)authenticity

3.2.1. The ambiguity of being-with others

That intersubjectivity can be an ambiguous concept was made clear by existential phenomenologists in the first half of the twentieth century, especially by Martin Heidegger's and Jean-Paul Sartre's early works. Both Heidegger and Sartre, in different ways, describe human existence in terms of being thrown into a world of practical concerns and intersubjective relations that are often characterized by inauthenticity and ambiguity. Despite this, for both of them, selfhood is inseparable from the interpersonal character of human existence, and it is precisely because of such interdependence that Heidegger's and Sartre's early works anticipate the concerns critical-phenomenological discourse.

In *Being and Time* (1927), Heidegger endorses a critical revision of the basic concepts of philosophy and science, arguing that 'the level which a science has reached is determined by how far it is *capable* of a crisis in its basic concepts' (Heidegger 2001, p. 29). The productive crisis that Heidegger envisages for philosophy consists in deepening the understanding of philosophical concepts by disclosing their hidden source of truth against the entrenched habits of psychologism and naturalism. Like Husserl two decades earlier, Heidegger rejects psychologism, seeking to identify the authentic foundations of meaning and truth. However, Heidegger's critique addresses the whole tradition of European philosophy, including classical phenomenology in the form taught and presented by Husserl.[5]

According to Heidegger, who served as Husserl's assistant, Husserl's investigations fail to take into account the ontological character of experience. By this, Heidegger means that phenomenology falls back into psychologism when it presents itself as a discipline concerned with the analysis of the intentional structures of experience as these are given to the self. In order to do justice to the nature of phenomena, for Heidegger, phenomenology should instead disclose the ontological grounds of appearances in terms of their relation to being (*Sein*). Being is the universal that pertains to every entity, but not in the sense of a predicate. For Heidegger, being is rather '*the transcendens pure and simple*' (Heidegger 2001, p. 62). The notion of 'transcendens' recalls the medieval doctrine of transcendentals, according to which being, as a universal, runs through all categories (such as quality, quantity, relation, possibility, necessity etc.), and yet it is always beyond and above 'every entity and every possible character which an entity may possess' (ibid.). On this view, for Heidegger, being is not to be found in the entities of the world as a substance or an essence. Instead, being is constitutive of the various manners in which entities exist in the world, that is, of how they manifest themselves.

As Heidegger puts it, 'Whenever one cognises anything or makes an assertion, whenever one comports oneself towards entities, even towards oneself, some use is made of "Being"; and this expression is held to be intelligible "without further ado", just as everyone understands "The sky is blue", "I am merry", and the like'. But here we have an average kind of intelligibility, which merely demonstrates that this is unintelligible' (Heidegger 2001, p. 23). Heidegger's idea is that being manifests itself through the ways in which entities comport to one another, including their states, actions, beliefs, skills, etc. This fundamental, existential sense of being is, however, forgotten in the everyday linguistic use of 'being'. Through language, it is possible to distinguish between being as a predicate or copula ('the sky is blue') and as an existential verb ('I exist'), without thereby uncovering the ultimate sense of being that runs through all forms of linguistic meaning as well as of practical involvement with the world. For this reason, Heidegger claims that the authentic question of being is the central question of philosophy.

To this end, Heidegger draws a distinction between an 'ontological' analysis, which is concerned with the fundamental structures of human existence, and an 'ontic' description, which is concerned with the entities we encounter in the world. While ontological analysis seeks to uncover the a priori existential structures (*existentials*) that make possible meaningful encounters with other entities, an ontic analysis involves the factual dimensions of individuated beings, including the particular ontological domain to which entities belong (e.g. biology, anthropology, law, etc.). However, neither type of analysis is exclusive. Indeed, one cannot do one without the other. As Freeman argues:

> [. . .] There is no ontic without the ontological – since the latter is the condition for the possibility of the former; nor is there the ontological without the ontic – for that would commit Heidegger to the position that there is such a thing as Being in-itself, or Being qua Being, whereas *Being and Time* precisely sets out to refute this position. (Freeman 2011, p. 369)

According to Heidegger, the analysis of human existence should proceed from what is most familiar to us, starting with our basic involvement with the entities that we routinely encounter in our everyday life (what Husserl would have called the natural attitude). In so doing, Heidegger shows that ontological analysis necessarily provides the foundation for all ontic domains, for facts about entities in the world (e.g. material things, biological beings, persons, actions, laws, etc.) presuppose an implicit and taken-for-granted understanding of what it means to be-in-the-world. In this sense, Heidegger does not establish a dualism between the ontic and the ontological domain, as he seeks to reveal their necessary co-implication. This is also consistent with Heidegger's effort to avoid both the objectification (in Heidegger's language, 'onticization') and the idealization of being, in order to uncover its relational and self-disclosing nature (as the being of the world, ourselves, and the entities we encounter). On this view, phenomenology becomes a universal hermeneutical ontology, namely an interpretative analysis of the ontological possibilities and conditions of human existence. This type of inquiry proceeds by letting the being of the entities we encounter in the world manifest itself according to its different manners and modes of existence, without imposing onto them the categories of a sense-bestowing consciousness (which, for Heidegger, was Husserl's main flaw).

To this end, Heidegger chooses the term Dasein (literally meaning 'being-there' or 'being-here') to refer to those entities for whom their own being is an issue. That is, Dasein captures 'that entity which in each case I myself am' (Heidegger 2001, p. 80). At a first glance, it may sound odd that Heidegger uses a spatial expression to refer to human existence. In fact, Heidegger connects the concept of human existence with a continuous quest for self-comprehension. For this reason, in his 1929–30 lectures on *The Fundamental Concepts of Metaphysics*, Heidegger draws attention to the notion of homesickness that the Romantic poet Novalis famously attributed to philosophy as 'the urge to be at home everywhere' (Heidegger 1995, p. 5). Musing on Novalis' fragment, Heidegger notes that 'our very being is this "restlessness" to become what we are and to find meaning without abandoning our finitude or deceiving ourselves about it, but by safeguarding it' (Heidegger 1995, p. 6). Accordingly, Dasein captures the finitude of human existence in its striving to comprehend itself *as* this very being that is capable of comprehension, but that also finds itself dispersed in the world.

Furthermore, Heidegger's choice of the term Dasein reflects what McMullin calls Heidegger's 'protest' against the modern conception of selfhood and any attempt to reify it as an object of naturalistic investigation (McMullin 2013, p. 15). Unlike rocks, tools, and other inanimate objects, Dasein is *in-the-world* in a characteristic temporal manner, namely as a finite being, or as a being-towards-death. For this reason, the being of Dasein is irreducible to the being of objects that are simply available (ready-to-hand) or present-at-hand, like the water in the glass that satisfies my thirst or the broken hammer in my toolbox that must be repaired. Yet Dasein also manifests itself first and foremost through its engagement with the things that one encounters in the world. Being-in-the-world, as one of the basic existential structures of Dasein, is a way of dwelling or inhabiting the surrounding environment in a practical manner.

For Heidegger, this entails partaking in practical networks of meaning and signification, which prescribe what counts as correct or standard in everyday situations, like picking up a pen for writing or using a knife to peel an apple. It is only when the taken-for-granted structure of such networks is interrupted or otherwise obstructed (as it happens when I cannot find my knife or my hammer breaks) that Dasein's absorption in the world is interrupted, and its understanding is thereby awakened to other possibilities. It follows that human existence manifests itself as a being-thrown in the world that is projected towards the future while being immersed in the concerns of the present. The totality of such temporal dimensions articulates Heidegger's concept of 'care' (*Sorge*).

In Heidegger's ontology, care coincides with the being of Dasein, hence it cannot be reduced either to a quality of human experience or to a personalistic attitude. This is part of Heidegger's strategy to centre phenomenological analysis on the ontology of lived experience rather than on the relation between self and other, as in Husserl and Stein. For Heidegger, subjectivity cannot be thematized in terms of a theoretical or cognitive relationship to intentional objects, but rather in terms of its inherent possibilities to deal or cope with the world, as 'a capability-of-being that has been handed over to itself and has always already projected itself onto possibilities' (Dahlstrom 2013, p. 172). From this point of view, Husserl's attempt to develop an egoic phenomenology as the pre-condition for the analysis of alterity and intersubjectivity is regarded by Heidegger as a regress to an ontic description of being, namely to a positivistic account of experience that fails to describe our involvement in the world.

For Heidegger, intersubjectivity does not proceed from a self who is affectively and perceptually *directed to* others, for the ontological state of Dasein is that of dwelling or inhabiting a world (being-in-the-world) that is always shared with entities who are themselves Dasein. As Heidegger puts it, 'by "Others" we do not mean everyone else but me – those over against whom the "I" stands out. They are rather those from whom, for the most part, one does not distinguish oneself – those among whom one is too' (Heidegger 2001, p. 154). In this sense, Heidegger's goal is to prove, *contra* Husserl, that the concept of intersubjectivity does not require the transcendental justification of the presentation of other selves to the ego. On Heidegger's view, we do not encounter others as standing around, as distinct and thematic objects of perceptual apprehension, but rather as always 'at work', that is, involved in those practical networks of meaning that inform our way of being-in-the-world. This is what Heidegger calls being-with, which is an essential feature of existence. Being-with captures the way in which Dasein is always surrounded by and engaging with things-at-hand as well as other subjects (whether these are present or perceived or not). This does not mean that other subjects can be mistaken for things, but that others share the environing world that Dasein inhabits, including its practical and social rules. The difference between inanimate things and subjects manifests itself in the different quality of Dasein's comportment towards them. While Dasein's relation to things is informed by concern, its relation to other selves is characterized by solicitude.

With regard to this, Heidegger maintains that it is possible to be solicitous by way of sustaining others, namely, by helping them realize their possibilities and become transparent to themselves, hence to achieve self-awareness. However, it is also possible to be solicitous in the opposite way, that is, by denying others' autonomy and by treating them as objects that lack motivation and understanding of their own. Given that the essence of Dasein is to be absorbed in practical domains by way of concern and solicitude, Dasein's understanding of being turns out to be inseparable from a basic understanding of others. As Heidegger puts it, '[. . .] because Dasein's being is being-with, its understanding of being already implies the understanding of others. This understanding, like any understanding, is not an acquaintance derived from knowledge about them, but a primordially existential kind of being, which, more than anything else, makes such knowledge and acquaintance possible' (Heidegger 2001, p. 161).

Heidegger's argument is that being-with others provides the ground for both authentic and inauthentic forms of interpersonal interactions both towards ourselves and others. Since Dasein is constantly immersed in a world that is also practical and social, human existence is always exposed to the possibility of getting lost in the world, in the sense of passively complying with the unquestioned patterns of behaviour that constellate being-with. On Heidegger's view, to live inauthentically means to let oneself be deprived of one's fundamental 'answerability' (Heidegger 2001, p. 165). Inauthentic existence is marked by the inability to make decisions as well as to take ownership and responsibility for one's actions and choices. It is, in short, the refusal or inability to be 'answerable' for who one is and what one does. In this respect, Heidegger refers to the anonymous 'They' (*das Man*) as the major source of inauthenticity into which Dasein may fall. On Heidegger's view, the 'They' (*das Man*) is neither a universal subject nor a plurality of subjects (like a mass) hovering above individuals. It is rather an impersonal power that is generated by the passive acquiescence with unexamined norms, thereby inducing Dasein to forsake the possibility of exercising moral responsibility.

In a way, for Heidegger, the impersonality of the 'They' belongs to the constitution of human existence in that it is inscribed in the network of meaning of everydayness. In our everyday life, we take part in a number of situations and contexts whose rules and norms are always sustained by the anonymity of the 'They'. To enact authenticity, however, is not to break with the continuity and pragmatic certainty of everydayness, but, rather, to appropriate one's existence without letting external norms prescribe the form of interpretation of one's being. When Dasein fails to do so, the 'They' disburdens Dasein of its being (Heidegger 2001,

p. 165), meaning that Dasein fails to take responsibility for its choices and – rather than choosing to be oneself and to heed the call of one's conscience – passively conforms to common sense.

However, it would be misleading to assume that the 'They' has an exclusively negative connotation. Critical-phenomenological readings of Heidegger's phenomenology emphasize, for example, that the immersion in the reality of *das Man* is not intrinsically inauthentic but rather indicative of the ambiguous relationality of Dasein. With regard to this, for example, Nancy Holland draws attention to the fact that the realm of the *das Man* is the sphere in which Dasein, as Heidegger says, 'lives proximally and for the most part' in a way that goes beyond social conformity (Holland 2001). Holland refers, by way of example, to the psychoanalytic concept of 'scripts', namely relational patterns of self-defeating behaviour that require the involvement of other players (such as the Oedipus script that mandates the antagonism between sons and paternal authority, or the Cinderella script that entails the antagonism between daughters and stepmothers). Holland argues that such patterns are often assimilated through the family but also and more fundamentally via the social context. For Holland, such scripts function like the 'They' in that they provide schemes of interpretation for dealing with others.

However, precisely because social roles are enacted in living out scripts that are socially and culturally transmitted, 'to live entirely outside the they-self, to make up one's own meanings in every case, would be one definition of madness' (Holland 2001, p. 133). Holland gestures to the challenges of negotiating one's social role within and against the matrix of a certain social script. In this way, Holland casts doubts on the possibility of achieving authenticity as a durable state. On her reading, authenticity is best understood as a temporary condition that is not immune to failures and self-deception. This makes Heidegger's view of inauthenticity a precondition for a radical understanding of the way in which individuals can be complicit with the structures of their own oppression by accepting and perpetuating social roles, scripts, or, as Heidegger would say, 'idle talk'.

'Idle talk' is 'the possibility of understanding everything without previously making the thing one's own' (Heidegger 2001, p. 213). Like gossiping, idle talk is a way of passing off information as coming from someone else without having knowledge of the grounds or sources of those contents. In this sense, idle talk is worse than misinformation in that it closes off the opportunity for authentic communication that is still available when we seek to understand and connect to what others say. Since idle talk discourages inquiry and comprehension, it precludes actual interpreting and understanding, contributing to forging a stubborn sense of reality that is passively shared. In this respect, Holland argues that once we understand where the power of the idle talk lies, and the extent to which we are involved in it, 'we can better understand why legal/judicial remedies and individual good intentions are never enough to eradicate them' (Holland 2020, p. 318).

Heidegger's concern with the ambiguity of being-with others plays a key role in Sartre's early account of intersubjective experience. As we saw in Chapter 2, for Sartre, the facticity of human existence consists in being thrown into a situation that we seek to transcend by committing to specific projects. Following Heidegger, Sartre argues that ambiguity is intrinsic to interpersonal experience. Being-with others reveals the possibility of self-deception but also the fragility and vulnerability of one's existential projects, which Sartre calls bad faith.

This concept is best illustrated by Sartre's play *No Exit* (*Huis Clos*), in which three characters (Garcin, Inez, and Estelle), each of them responsible in different ways for some type of cruelty, are locked up in the afterlife in a room, having to bear each other's gaze for eternity. Unlike Inez, who is the only character in the play that is remarkably unaffected by guilt or fear,[6] Garcin and Estelle are tormented by the thought of what others may be thinking of them. Overwhelmed by the fear of such judgement, Garcin and Estelle seek in vain validation from each other as well as from Inez. Their effort is to affirm a positive image of themselves, although, ironically, they cannot look at themselves in a mirror. As Estelle admits, looking back on her former life:

> I've six big mirrors in my bedroom. There they are. I can see them. But they don't see me. They're reflecting the carpet, the settee, the window but how empty it is, a glass in which I'm absent! When I talked to people I always made sure there was one near by in which I could see myself. I watched myself talking. And somehow it kept me alert, seeing myself as the others saw me. (Sartre 1989, p. 19)

The obsession with the visibility provided by the mirror is, in itself, a symptom of the anguish of inauthenticity. Though the play portrays the acute discomfort and uneasiness that characterize self-deception and bad faith, the play at the same time reveals the impossibility of escaping another's point of view. For Sartre, the polarization between being-for-oneself and being-for-others is latent in interpersonal experience, informing the way we think of ourselves and our position in the world among others. Nonetheless, according to Sartre, the opposite of bad faith is not good faith, or else some form of sincerity, but instead a 'critical relationship to evidence. [. . .] Bad faith works if one can lie to oneself. To do so requires eliminating one's relationship to what makes lies appear as lie: evidence' (Gordon 2020, p. 19).

Evidence, for Sartre, is not an apodictic certainty or an intuitive access to essences, but rather a way of coming to terms with one's own existence, including the projects and values we commit to. Unlike Scheler, Sartre argues that values have no existence in themselves, but only insofar as 'they appear before the regard of reflection' (Sartre 2003, p. 119). For Sartre, values are subjective as they inform the projects we pursue, hence they reveal the quality of one's commitment to a given project. It follows that we become aware of the values we abide by through the patterns of our actions and projects, and we are responsible for how we take them up in front of others. On this view, bad faith consists in failing to realize such a possibility for self-reflection and relinquishing the opportunity to explore our relation to reality, even when this involves acknowledging one's inauthentic way of being.

In this regard, according to Lewis Gordon, the opposite of bad faith can be either *ignorant* good faith (when one admits the possibility of being in bad faith, as a potential threat to one's beliefs) or *authentic* good faith, which entails a commitment to not shy away from the evidence of inauthenticity, making the choice to treat that evidence in a way that is appropriate and conducive to truth (Gordon 1999, p. 56). In this respect, authentic good faith requires a commitment to accept the anguish connected to bad faith, and to strive for the truth. From this point of view, while Sartre's account seems to cast a negative light on interpersonal experience, his approach, like that of Heidegger, calls for a critical reassessment of what it means to be authentic among others. More specifically, Sartre's and Heidegger's early works offer a way to rethink intersubjectivity in light of the ambiguity of the roles that we happen to play in the social world.

However, while both Heidegger and Sartre establish a connection between the ambiguity of intersubjectivity and the call for responsibility, they are less explicit about those conditions of human facticity that cannot be transcended or that cannot be neatly confined to the Heideggerian 'They'. This includes, for example, gender roles and the ascription of cultural traits that are operative in interpersonal experience even when the individuals that are supposed to 'play' those parts reject them or do not identify with them. Such cases involve not only cultural and gender scripts (e.g. the ascription of 'femininity/masculinity' as standards of female/male behaviour or cultural stereotypes based on one's ethnicity and nationality), but also situations where one is entangled in a web of multiple social and cultural identities that are partly endorsed and partly played out of necessity. In such cases, to entirely strip individuals of their social roles risks falsifying the reality of social experiences and neglecting the context-dependent character of a situation. From this point of view, being-with others in the world turns out to be a critical way of navigating different cultural worlds. From a critical-phenomenological angle, this aspect is addressed by the concept of world-travelling, which in a way, integrates the concept of being-with others, while also pointing to a critical-phenomenological sense of interpersonal understanding, as we shall now see.

3.2.2 Being-with others as world-travelling

An important illustration of the ambiguity of being-with others in critical phenomenology can be found in María Lugones' account of world-travelling, which plays a pivotal role in Latinx phenomenology (see also Chapter 5). Originally introduced in her 1987 paper '"World"-travelling, and Loving Perception' (Lugones 1987) and then revisited in her 2003 book *Pilgrimages,* the concept of world-travelling brings to light the liminal space that lies at the borders of different social and cultural realities. Such places of pilgrimage or liminality, as Lugones calls them, are the places inhabited by women who write 'from the other side' with a sense of 'anger, pain, urgency, a sense of being trapped, pounding the walls with a speech that hurts my own ears' (Lugones 2003, p. 169).

World-travelling is the practice of moving across social worlds that are not only extremely different from one another, but that also stand in reciprocal tension. On Lugones' view, the world does not have to be experienced through a dominant or uniform socio-cultural dimension, because it includes multiple and shifting socio-cultural positions. One example is being Hispanic in the United States, which does not correspond to any of the dominant Anglo ways of depicting Hispanic communities in the United States. The world can also be lived through within a stereotype that is socially imposed, or as Lugones puts it, 'it may be that I understand the construction, but do not hold it of myself. I may not accept it as an account of myself, a construction of myself. And yet, I may be animating such a construction' (Lugones 2003, p. 220).

In her analysis, Lugones draws on her own experience of inhabiting what feminist philosopher Marilyn Frye calls 'the arrogant eye' (Frye 1983). Like Heidegger's account of inauthentic solicitude, the arrogant eye is 'the kind of vision that interprets the rock one trips on as hostile, the bolt one cannot loosen as stubborn, the woman who made meatloaf when he wanted spaghetti as "bad" (though he didn't say what he wanted). The arrogant perceiver does not countenance the possibility that the Other is independent, indifferent' (Frye 1983, p. 67). The arrogant eye denies freedom to the other person, as woman is exclusively regarded as a pleasing object. In this respect, the arrogant eye provides a classical illustration of an objectifying and sexist style of perception, which is, however, according to Lugones, not exclusive of men. Quite to the contrary, 'women who are perceived arrogantly can, in turn, perceive other women arrogantly' (Lugones 2003). It is not simply that women may fall prey to the same arrogant stance that distinguishes the sexist man. Lugones considers the case of women who fail to connect to other women's experiences because they fear identification with their visible and embodied oppression. This lack of understanding has important political consequences when it is connected to the problem of creating shared bonds of solidarity among women. For example, Lugones regards the lack of understanding between women of colour and white women as the central aspect of failed coalitions between women. As long as women see one another exclusively in terms of the dominant differences that shape social narratives (e.g. as beings that are exclusively oppressed or exclusively privileged), fragmentation and distrust will prevail.

To this end, Lugones offers her own antagonistic relationship with her mother as an example of such issue, describing the difficulties she experienced in relating to her mother's situation. This had to do with Lugones' fear of identifying with her mother's condition; that is, the condition of a Latina in a patriarchal world. To the extent that she regarded her mother as oppressed, Lugones resisted the possibility of gaining insight into her mother's world, for fear of sharing the feeling of being the victim of a system of disempowerment. In a way, Lugones' resistance is connected to the problem of empathizing with others without projecting onto them our own feelings, beliefs, and assumptions. As we discussed at the beginning of this chapter when surveying the problem of empathy in classical phenomenology, empathic attunement to another's lived situation does not require identification with their experience. On the contrary, empathy implies the capacity to discern another's experiential horizon as belonging to a self who is worthy of attention for her own sake. In a similar way, Lugones argues that interpersonal understanding cannot be grounded on projection, but rather requires world-travelling, which is the practice of exploring others' social and cultural identities in their specific milieu. This entails comprehending how other people are situated in their cultural worlds in ways that may not align with either our expectations or with the norms of the cultural world from which we regard them. Thus, world-travelling involves the recognition that social identities are complex and ambiguous negotiations between personal characters and attitudes and the socio-cultural worlds one inhabits.

Through world-travelling, it is possible to identify salient features of others' ways of being that stand against the social background, and that may not have been apparent or relevant until then due to consolidated patterns of interacting with and interpreting others' styles of being. Lugones' example is that of travelling in her mother's world and discovering her against the dominant social background; that is, not as an oppressed woman of the patriarchal world, but rather as a resourceful and resilient subject that would engage her social context in a personal and creative manner. Lugones thus describes how she gradually re-learned 'to see' her mother as a self-determining agent rather than the pliable victim she was afraid of identifying herself with. Indeed, the key feature of world-travelling is that we travel worlds, not social narratives. This allows the multiple identities and projects of the people we encounter to come to the fore in their individuality, without projecting onto them our fears and expectations. In this way, world-travelling represents a way of practising empathy, understood as a stance of sensitivity to multiple and even challenging ways of being. While Lugones' argument is not immune to criticism, especially when it comes to reconciling world-travelling and political solidarity,[7] it does provide a fruitful way to engage from a different angle interpersonal and empathic understanding.

Related to this, it is worth noting that world-travelling entails the recognition that each of us lives across multiple social realities. As Lugones puts it, to be a world-traveller means 'to have the distinct experience of being different in different "worlds" and of having the capacity to remember other "worlds" and ourselves in them' (Lugones 2003, p. 221). By tapping into the multiple cultural worlds we inhabit, we develop a better ability to connect to others on the basis of the experiences and memories we have gained in one of the different realities we partake in, including the contexts we dislike or in which we feel ill at ease. To this end, Lugones insists that world-travelling has to be practised in a playful way, namely with a stance of openness to the world-realities we engage with, without an agonistic stance or assumption of possessing or mastering such worlds.

3.3 Intercorporeality and the ethics of sensibility

As we have seen so far, classical and critical approaches to intersubjectivity draw attention to the connection between intersubjectivity and the socio-cultural background that informs interpersonal experience. Experiencing others means not just being acquainted with their embodied presentation, but also acknowledging their being situated in a socio-cultural milieu that resurfaces in the encounter itself, potentially affecting how people are perceived and understood. This calls into question the role of perception as the capacity to witness others' experiences and to attend critically to their situation. In this respect, an important trajectory of critical phenomenology emphasizes the ethical role of sensibility, shifting responsibility towards vision, perception, and attentiveness.[8] Such explorations are informed to a great extent by Maurice Merleau-Ponty's late ontology (especially *The Visible and the Invisible*) and Emmanuel Levinas' account of alterity, as we shall now illustrate.

3.3.1 From intercorporeality to critical-ethical vision

Maurice Merleau-Ponty is the French phenomenologist who, more than any other twentieth-century classical phenomenologist, took upon himself the task of deepening the embodied character of intersubjective experience. As we saw in Chapter 2, Merleau-Ponty argues that the body yields a unique and personal perspective onto the world. The permanence of one's body consists in an open communication with the world, as a latent horizon that is 'ceaselessly present prior to all determining thought' (Merleau-Ponty 2012, p. 95). In this regard, Merleau-Ponty emphasizes the 'ambiguity' and 'marginal presentation' of the body in self-perception, specifically through touch. As we saw in Chapter 2, the right hand touching the left hand is simultaneously subject and object. In this regard, Merleau-Ponty points out that the hand touching the other hand performs a carnal reflection, as it were, of the body onto itself, in that the body is simultaneously grasped as a distinct intentional object but not as separate from the experiencing self. As Merleau-Ponty puts it, the body is 'neither tangible nor visible insofar as it is what sees and touches' (Merleau-Ponty 2012, p. 94).

This ambiguity of the body is eventually developed by Merleau-Ponty in a more radical and ontological fashion in his late writings, particularly in the unfinished manuscript *The Visible and the Invisible*. Merleau-Ponty appeals to the 'enigma' of the body as this simultaneously sees and is seen, 'touches itself touching, it is visible and sensitive for itself' (Merleau-Ponty 1964). Such reflexivity (or reversibility, as Merleau-Ponty calls it) of bodily experience is illustrative of the carnal reality of experience, which can hardly be reduced to the duality of perceiver and perceived in that it simultaneously involves self- and other-experience.

In *The Visible and the Invisible*, the encounter with another embodied being is described by Merleau-Ponty as the coming-to-be of an apparently 'private world', which gradually discloses itself though gestures, tone, and affective responses, thereby entering the 'fabric of my own being' (Merleau-Ponty 1968, p. 11). The communication between different incarnate worldviews is thematized by Merleau-Ponty as intercorporeal-ity, that is, in terms of contact between two or more incarnate horizons having a common 'natal bond' to the being of the world, which is in itself carnal. By and large, Merleau-Ponty's goal in these writings is to recast perception in ontological terms in order to bring to light the corporeal condition that underlies all lived experiences, and which he identifies with the flesh of things. By flesh, Merleau-Ponty does not mean either mind, or matter, or substance, but rather the generative principle of the totality of being (*natura naturans*), which shares the same nature of the beings that are generated (*natura naturata*). As he puts it in 'Eye and Mind', the body is a thing among things 'caught in the fabric of the world', and 'the world is made of the same stuff as the body' (Merleau-Ponty, 1964, p. 163).

More specifically, the carnal reality of being is made intelligible through the body, which acts as a prism that is at once receptive and opaque. The body is receptive insofar as it responds to the solicitations of the surrounding world, internalizing and appropriating them through habituality (as we saw in Chapter 2). However, the body is also opaque in that it does not grasp itself in its affective experiences, hence it does not reveal itself as the source of the meaning of being. It is in virtue of the carnal bond between being and the body that perception grasps diversity and multiplicity, and that a range of different experiences are simultane-ously given to the senses, despite being reflectively thematized in isolation from one another. To illustrate this aspect, Merleau-Ponty refers to the visibility of a cube, which can be grasped in a series of profiles and from different perspectives. However, just because the cube is visible from a certain angle and has a hidden side does not mean that its visibility is exhausted by binocular vision. While a certain cohesion of the visible may prevail at a given moment when I look at a side of the cube, the actual grasp of the different sides of the cube is achieved in a dynamic and sensuous process of touching the other sides. Merleau-Ponty goes so far as to claim that 'every visible is cut out in the tangible', and that 'since the same body sees and touches, visible and tangible belong to the same world' (Merleau-Ponty 1968, p. 134). His argument is that, from an ontological point of view, the visible and the tangible form a folding system (chiasm) so that the spatiotemporal distance that holds visible things apart from one another is in fact an ontological plenitude, filled by the flesh of the things.

However, Merleau-Ponty also argues that the reversibility between the seer and the seen (e.g. to be seen is to be a seer, and to be a seer is to be seen) is not a closed circle. The hidden side of the cube radiates even without a seer, and I never see myself as others see me. As such, reversibility is never really complete or fulfilled in any ultimate synthesis. Instead, reversibility represents a circuit that contracts the body in single acts of apprehension, while remaining open and receptive to the invisible field that sustains it. On this view, the invisible is not to be reduced to the non-visible (i.e. as the reality that cannot be seen with the eyes or that is hidden), but rather needs to be thought as the very condition of the possibility of the visible. That is, invisibility does not result from an absence, but structures the very possibility of seeing. Ultimately, Merleau-Ponty rejects the dualism between perceiver and perceived, identifying being with the flesh of the body, and refiguring perception as the encroachment of the body upon the world.

Merleau-Ponty's view of intercorporeality allows a reconsideration of the ambiguity of the body and that of being-with others in terms of affective communication. As Kelly Oliver points out, 'for Merleau-Ponty, the anonymity of vision makes relationships possible without subjects dominating their objects' (Oliver 2008, p. 135). If the flesh of the world holds together the commonality of carnal experience, it allows for a deeper communication between self and other. Indeed, at stake in Merleau-Ponty's ontology is no longer the classical duality between self and other but rather their ontological continuity, which grounds affective forms of responding and attending to others' experiences. Two notable illustrations and applications of this concept in critical phenomenology can be found in Kerry Oliver's account of witnessing and Alia Al-Saji's view of hesitation.

Oliver utilizes Merleau-Ponty's account of intercorporeality in order to ground the phenomenology of bearing witness to one's experience. To be able to articulate one's experience and to tell it is the primary way in which we bestow meaning upon our experiences by making a demand of answerability of others. As Oliver puts it: 'we make sense of our experience and our own agency by telling our experiences to others; even if we don't literally describe our experiences to another person, we give them meaning by thinking them to ourselves as we might tell them to another' (Oliver 2008, p. 147). This presumptive or imaginary other represents, for Oliver, the 'inner witness' (borrowed from psychoanalyst Dori Laub) or 'addressable other' that bears testimony to our existence. Oliver's view is modelled upon Merleau-Ponty's ontology of intercorporeality in that the dialogical model of address and response is first acquired in inter-subjective embodied experience. The structure of dialogue represents, for Oliver, the precondition for exercising agency as historically situated individuals (who are positioned among other situated subjects) as well as for holding ourselves accountable in front of ourselves and others (what Oliver – following Levinas, as we shall see – calls the responsibility of subjectivity, which is logically and ethically prior to individual, historical positions).

The disintegration of the inner witness occurs when individuals are confronted with the tragic challenge of bearing witness to what is beyond recognition or else 'unspeakable', as happens to genocide survivors as well as to survivors of extreme violence and oppression. Witnessing has here the double sense of testifying to something we experienced first-hand (as eye-witnesses) and bearing witness to something that seemingly eludes the expectation of answerability from others. The tension here is between bearing witness to what one has experienced, and bearing wit-ness to the profound alteration and disruption of one's sense of reality. In such cases, the juridical sense of eye-witnessing fails to heed the silence of survivors, and risks objectifying their experiences by reducing them to the inability to speak or communicate.

However, as in Merleau-Ponty's ontology the invisible is not the opposite of the visible, similarly Oliver argues that the unspeakable is not the opposite of eye-witnessing, but rather sustains it. This means that the testimonies of genocide survivors are ontologically grounded in the carnal continuity between self and other, which sustains the demand of answerability and responsibility that is intrinsic to moral subjectiv-ity. Differently stated, the testimonies of survivors are not located on a different ontological plane, despite being the result of severe trauma. Merleau-Ponty's view of the flesh suggests that, from an ontological point of view, heeding others' testimonies is in fact a possibility rooted in the carnal bonds that connect us to one another, on the basis of which we are in principle capable of attending to the narratives of genocide's survival. However, whether testimonies are listened to and given moral attention is an ethical demand that cannot be entirely based on Merleau-Ponty's ontology of the flesh, for this involves the use and exercise of moral awareness. In this respect, while Oliver refers to Merleau-Ponty's anti-dualism between subject and object to articulate, from an onto-logical perspective, the structure of witnessing, she also makes clear that witnessing requires the integration of an ethical justification, one that is based on Levinas' phenomenology, as we shall see in the next section.

While the concept of intercorporeality provides the ontological ground for witnessing, it is also relevant to inquire into the affective and ethical dimensions of perception. At stake in this case is the possibil-ity of altering habituated styles of regarding others through encrusted presuppositions and prejudice. In this respect, Alia Al-Saji has brought to light the role played by hesitation in interrupting habits of perception, drawing particularly on Henri Bergson's account of *durée* as well as on Merleau-Ponty's ontology. On Al-Saji's view, hesitation operates by revealing the limits of the field of vision in the course of the perceptual experience itself. As a bodily affect, hesitation signals the interruption of a habitual performance, hence it delays the course of habitual action, but it also gives time to the body to anticipate its next movements, hence to recognize its present style of moving as this unfolds in time. In Al-Saji's words, 'hesitation creates an opening in habits and makes them visible for themselves and within the world' (Al-Saji 2009, p. 380). Using Merleau-Ponty's ontological framework, Al-Saji describes hesitation as the 'blind spot in vision' that allows the visibility of what is invisible to us, namely our perceptual orientation towards others. On this view, hesitation enables us to track social positions and to make perceptual orientations potential objects of critical self-awareness. While Al-Saji is very clear that hesitation does not suffice to overcome objectifying styles of seeing, she nonetheless maintains that hesitation is necessary for the transformation of the visual field. This is less an alteration of the intentionality of the 'I-can' (that is, of motor agency) than an affective shift that takes place at the heart of one's affective disposition. From this point of view, hesitation is the symptom of a perceptual and affective shift that is critical for *un-learning* to perceive and recognize other subjects. This, however, also involves a critical confrontation with one's conceptual maps and frames of reference that habitual actions take for granted, and that hesitation crystallizes and makes visible to self.

In this context, Al-Saji points out that such a type of critical-ethical vision is awakened by co-living with 'othered' subjects (as in transracial families and marriages); that is, by sharing with them (through love, parenting, or close friendship) contexts of domesticity and habituality that undermine the positions of external observers. This is, for example, the case of transracial families where white parents learn to see *with their* kids the discomfort and affective disruption brought about by racialization. In this way, the very positionality between self and other is recast through affective bonds, where 'the other is not an object in the perceptual field, but a magnetizing centre, or counterweight, whose very style of being, way of seeing, and memory inflect that field. To see with others is hence to find one's perceptual and affective map to be redrawn through the force of attachments to others' (Al Saji 2014, p. 161).

3.3.2 Being-for the other: the ethics of sensibility

The connection between sensibility and ethical seeing we have just outlined is indicative of the ethical implications of intersubjective experience, when this is regarded in terms of *responsiveness* to the other. To be responsive to another presupposes not just an ontological bond between self and other but also an ethical dimension, whereby I am simultaneously held responsible *for* the other by being-with-them. In the tradition of classical phenomenology, this thesis is central to Emmanuel Levinas' phenomenology of sensibility, which informs a number of critical-phenomenological approaches to self- and other-experience.

A former student of Husserl and also of Heidegger, Levinas calls attention not simply to the primacy of affective and embodied experience, but also to the vulnerability of carnal experience and its ethical implications. In so doing, Levinas departs critically from both his former mentors, offering a critical phenomenology of sensibility, especially in *Totality and Infinity: An Essay on Exteriority* (originally published in 1961) as well as in *Otherwise than Being, or Beyond Essence* (first published in 1974). By and large, Levinas contends that the concept of intentionality fails to do justice to the concept of ethical responsiveness to the other. Levinas moves from the assumption that, as incarnated beings, we are ethically sensitive not only to the lived experiences of others but also to their dignity and moral value. In this respect, Levinas aims for a transformation of the transcendental subject into an ethical subject that is keen to take up responsibility *for* the other as coming *from* the other person *qua* another (Bernet 2000).

In *Totality and Infinity: An Essay on Exteriority*, Levinas proceeds by arguing, against Husserl, that 'sensibility is of the order of enjoyment, not of the order of experience' (Levinas 1969, p. 137). Levinas' provocative claim is that sensibility, as a form of enjoyment, is intrinsic to all states, experiences, and activities, including thinking, living, eating, sleeping, and feeling. Enjoyment 'nourishes that activity and makes it possible. Enjoyment explains why we bother at all: we bother to live, to think, and to act, because we enjoy it and suffer from it' (Diprose 2002, p. 133). On Levinas' approach, carnality represents both the ground and the motivation for experience and the constitution of meaning. To this end, Levinas' methodology breaks with all types of mediations or classical distinctions between self and other, passivity and activity, or sensibility and spontaneity. His style, as noted by Waldenfels (2002), is characterized by a hyperbolic paradoxical language that blurs the difference between thinking and sensuous experience.

Such an approach marks a significant difference from both Husserl and Heidegger. As we saw before, Husserl's phenomenology is attentive to the epistemic and affective forms that constitute sensibility, including kinaesthesis and tactility, which operate at a pre-reflective level of self- and other-awareness. In this respect, Husserl regards sensibility in transcendental terms in the effort to overcome the limits of Kant's transcendental approach (Summa 2014). While recognizing that Husserl's greatest contribution to philosophy is the discovery of 'subjectivity as a source of significations' (Levinas 1991, p. 65), Levinas contends that in Husserl's phenomenology there remains a constant analogy between sensation and representation, which reduces sensibility to a theoretical construal of the self. Differently put, Levinas' concern is that Husserlian phenomenology prioritizes epistemic intelligibility over sentience to the point that 'the affective remains an information' (Levinas 1991, p. 66).

In contrast to Husserl's approach, Levinas argues that sensibility needs to be recast in terms of ontological openness, as the possibility of giving oneself to the other that is exemplified by the maternal body, and not as a tendency intrinsic to a theoretical drive, as in Husserl or even in Heidegger. Against Heidegger, Levinas maintains that the ontological quality of sensibility cannot be equated to the manifestation of being or else to any grounding ontological principle. For Levinas, Heidegger's ontological project of describing existence by disclosing the being of the entities in the world still posits the existence of a primary ontological principle (being). In fact, Levinas contends, the very possibility of having access to such an ontological principle presupposes sensibility. In forsaking both the concepts of intentionality and being as guiding threads for the analysis of lived experience, Levinas reconfigures the relation between sensibility and signification in terms of exposure to the Other, who is, however, 'not reducible to exposure to another's gaze' (Levinas 1991, p. 72). For Levinas, the ontological structure of sensibility is permeated by alterity, a point that was already implied by Husserl's and Merleau-Ponty's phenomenology of touch. Yet Levinas contends that sensibility cannot be framed in terms of self- and other-relation, as the exposure to the other has a characteristic moral quality that precedes the differentiation between self and other.

To illustrate this, it is important to note that, from Levinas' point of view, the proximity of the other is not regarded as a *position* situated in space and time, but rather as an encounter that animates sensibility without requiring the mediation of intuition or representation. Levinas' idea is that the face of the other is not an image that is first represented, deciphered, and interpreted, but rather a call that, like a divine command, summons the interlocutor to enact with sincerity those very acts of perception and interpretation. Levinas thus elevates the face-to-face encounter to the fundamental event explored by 'first philosophy' (understood by Levinas as ethics), reconfiguring the proximity of the other as an ethical demand that precedes any representation.[9]

From an ethical point of view, the Other, whether capitalized or not, is the other self who awakens and shocks the ego out of its 'sameness'. This means that the self is called out of its private, personal life and compelled to attend to others' experiences, as Oliver argues by referring to ethical subjectivity as being prior to socio-cultural positions. Yet, while Oliver's account of witnessing brings together Levinas' ethics and Merleau-Ponty's ontology, it is important to stress the difference between these respective frameworks. From Levinas' point of view, Merleau-Ponty's ontology of the flesh still implies a correlation (albeit dynamic and not formal) between seeing and being seen. In contrast to this, Levinas emphasizes that the meaning generated by sentience or sensibility is an immersion in life without reference to any other relationship or position.

More specifically, according to Levinas, three moments are constitutive of sensibility: enjoyment, contact as vulnerability, and proximity. Enjoyment represents the actual fulfilment of sensuous experience. Levinas' idea is that the ontological exposure to the other requires a subject who originally enjoys self-sufficiency and satisfaction. Only in this way can there be a giving to the other, a 'tearing away of the mouthful of bread from the mouth that tastes in full enjoyment' (Levinas 1991, p. 74). On Levinas' view, the emergence of self is not governed by a dialectical relation between selfhood and otherhood, as in Sartre's phenomenology, which would involve alienation and differentiation as constitutive moments. Instead, enjoyment reflects the fact that life is originally experienced as plenitude and fulfilment. As Guenther puts it: 'As a child born into the world, I do not spring up fully formed, nor do I begin in a state of indistinction or fusion with my surroundings; rather, I begin by enjoying and living from the open-ended surplus of "good things" in the element. Levinas emphasizes the sense in which the born self emerges *ex nihilo*, such that the child is 'not simply caused or issued forth from the father [or mother], but is absolutely other than him [or her]' (Guenther 2006, p. 59). Guenther draws attention to the fact that enjoyment refers to our natural and spontaneous immersion in the materiality of life, as informed by the hospitality of the maternal body, which precedes the coming-to-be of self.

The second element of sensibility, contact, refers to the emergence of sense through incarnation. As Levinas puts it, 'incarnation is not a transcendental operation of a subject that is situated in the midst of the world it represents to itself; the sensible experience of the body is already and from the start incarnate. The sensible – maternity, vulnerability, apprehension – binds the node of incarnation into a plot larger than the apperception of self' (Levinas 1991, 76). As we have pointed out, for Levinas, the constitution of meaning does not occur through intentional acts, whether perception, imagination, or cognition. Such an approach,

which Levinas associates with Husserl's methodology, risks reifying subjectivity, losing sight of a more fundamental aspect of sensibility, namely
its involvement in corporeal and maternal gestures of hospitality. This is
what Levinas calls the condition of vulnerability as exposure and contact,
which generates meaningful experience through acts of care, such as
nourishing, clothing, and lodging. On Levinas' view, such bonds do not
posit an intentional, intuitive *content*, but rather constitute the *matter*,
that is, the substance of intersubjective relations.

Levinas ultimately argues that the sensible binds to a 'plot larger
than the apperception of self', that is to say, sensibility as contact and
vulnerability is intrinsically constituted by intersubjective nexuses,
made intelligible by affective and carnal – not intuitive or reflective
– relations. On this view, meaning is constituted as a being-*for*-the-
other, namely as a vocation and commitment, and not as an intentional
directedness of consciousness towards alterity. It follows that being-for-
the-other is also a traumatic, disquieting, and challenging experience,
which Levinas calls 'obsession by the other'. To be obsessed means to
be persecuted, to sacrifice oneself in order to bear responsibility for
another, just like the mother is, at the same time, a symbol of hospitality
whose body is taken hostage by the children. Yet Levinas extends this
insight to the relationship that is established with the neighbour. To
be-for-another is a disturbance of the self, who finds herself displaced,
unsettled, and ordered by the face of the Other, who is not a part of the
horizon like any other intentional object, but is inscribed in the very skin
of the self.

On Levinas' view, despite my presumption of rational autonomy and
individual agency, the Other compels me to attend to them independently of my subjective standing towards them. An example of this is
the injunction not to kill, which for Levinas is absolutely signified by the
face of the Other. This is due to the fact that the face of the Other is the
incarnation of a sensuous bond that is experienced prior to intuition, as
rooted in the vulnerability of the flesh. Thus the Other may as well be
given to me in the present, but they also belong to a different temporal or
spatial order, for the signification of the face is not a perceptual content
but a more primitive and carnal intimation. In this sense, proximity,
in Levinas, includes the weight of trans-historical and trans-cultural
responsibility, which is absolute in that it binds me to the past that
precedes my birth, as well as to the open and unpredictable possibilities
of the future towards which my own being and that of the Other are
thrown.

To be sure, Levinas' approach has been criticized for offering a view of
moral obligation that centres on a secularized view of divine command,

requiring self-sacrifice as an absolute norm without further distinctions and specifications (Bernet 2000; Butler 2015, pp. 99–122). Feminist philosophers have also questioned Levinas' emphasis on the feminine as generosity and absolute responsibility. However, Levinas' account of vulnerability also provides a way of reconsidering the role of hospitality in terms of cross-cultural dialogue (Kearney and Semonovitch 2011) and environmental philosophy (Edelglass et al. 2012). Furthermore, from a critical-phenomenological point of view, Lisa Guenther has drawn attention to Levinas' concepts of sensibility and vulnerability as paving the way to an ethics of natality that is sensitive to the demands of the other without equating woman's experience to motherhood (Guenther 2006). According to Guenther, Levinas' theory of responsibility opens the door to a non-patriarchal meaning of motherhood in that it situates ethical vulnerability at the very heart of sensibility. Drawing especially on *Otherwise than Being* and building up a dialogue between feminist and political phenomenology as well as psychoanalysis, Guenther acknowledges Levinas' account of radical responsibility in ethical terms without, however, accepting the implication that women would have a greater share of responsibility and hospitality on account of their reproductive capacity.

Guenther's argument builds on Levinas' concept of anarchic time, which precedes the temporality of consciousness. In Levinas, anarchy refers to a time before the origin, which disrupts the order of historical time through moral proximity, as we illustrated earlier. Guenther interprets this phenomenon in terms of natality, that is, as a time that precedes biological birth and that takes place as a gift from the Other. On this view, to become *like* a maternal body does not require one to give actual birth to a child, nor does it involve an actual feminine body. Donation is rather actualized by acts of forgiveness and promising, whereby I substitute for the Other (that is, take responsibility for them, including the pain they have inflicted on themselves) in motivational rather than causal terms. As Guenther puts it: 'in responding to the Other like a maternal body, I do not insert myself as her cause or origin, but rather give to her a past of forgiveness and a future of promise. To give birth is thus to give time to the Other; it is to make a gift of time that circumvents possession and asks to be passed on' (Guenther 2006, p. 7).[10] Through acts of forgiveness and promising I release the Other from their past, while opening up the possibilities of the future through promising. By interpreting responsibility for the Other in terms of temporality and donation of time, Guenther emphasizes that the obligation of hospitality towards the stranger is a demand that requires no reciprocation, as it is first and foremost an asymmetric relation based on generosity without return or measure.[11] On this reading, intersubjective relations acquire ethical value in that they are inspired by sacrifice, generosity, and hope.

However, how can such a view not turn into martyrdom or even saintliness? And how can the infinite alterity of the Other do justice to the particular cultural, racial, and sexual differences of intersubjective experience? With regard to this, Guenther acknowledges that Levinas was indeed concerned with humanity's aspiration to saintliness, maintaining that holiness represents an ultimate value, even if this is not realized in history (Guenther 2006, p. 131). Nonetheless, Guenther also points out that the relation between carnality and responsibility exemplified by the metaphor of the 'maternal body' is an ethical imperative to listen and be affected by the other, regardless of our bodies and situation. In being exposed to the anarchy of the stranger, whether this is the stranger that gave me the gift of time, or the stranger to whom I donate the gift of time, sensibility is always exposed to the Other and exacerbated by this encounter in the sense of being continuously questioned by the exposure to alterity. As such, sensibility is a call to pay attention to the Other, since, as Levinas argues, sensibility is in itself a condition of vulnerability that can be exploited and persecuted. Given the possibility of abusing the generosity of the Other or of being ourselves abused, Guenther argues that Levinas' theory of responsibility indirectly gestures to a politics of justice that resists reification (including the reification of the female body) and violence.

This excursus into the phenomenology of self and other shows that phenomenological discourse on intersubjectivity is not only concerned with how others present themselves to the self, but also with the problem of understanding others' worldviews, appreciating their moral worth, and participating in their socio-cultural world. As we saw throughout this chapter, a critical-phenomenological approach to intersubjectivity explores how self and other represent not only embodied positions situated in a world laden with values and practical meaning, but also and at the same time – to quote from Lee's 2014 book title – 'living alterities' that require specific forms of attentiveness and critical awareness. In order to explore and understand the identities of others as incarnate alterities, phenomenology shows that it is possible to draw on different practices, including empathy, world-travelling, as well as the cultivation of ethical sensibility. However, if intersubjective experience is in fact the experience of living alterities that are irreducible to a given background or cultural world, it is at the same time necessary to explore what makes such identities 'visible' and how they are positioned with respect to both embodied experience and power relations. To this end, we now turn to the phenomenology of gender and race in order to examine how visible identities are constituted, and the specific challenges that arise from the entanglement between corporeality, social experience, and power relations.

4

Gender and Sexuality

Feminist phenomenology and the politics of gender

Because the body is the instrument of our hold on the world, the world appears different to us depending on how it is grasped, which explains why we have studied these [biological] data so deeply; they are one of the keys that enable us to understand woman. But we refuse the idea that they form a fixed destiny for her.

Simone de Beauvoir, *The Second Sex*

The fear that we cannot grow beyond whatever distortions we may find within ourselves keeps us docile and loyal and obedient, externally defined, and leads us to accept many facets of our oppression as women.

Audre Lorde, *Sister Outsider: Essays and Speeches*

Feminism is historically of the utmost relevance. Since the seventeenth- and eighteenth-century writings of pioneering feminist writers, such as Mary Astell and Mary Wollstonecraft, feminist thinkers have drawn attention to women's condition, especially in relation to the social and political inequalities women experience within a patriarchal society. In recent years, feminism has come to the fore through social movements and activism. A notable example of this is the 'me too' movement started by survivor and activist Tarana Burke in 2006, which went viral in 2017 as the #MeToo hashtag. The 'me too' movement has highlighted the scale and impact of sexual violence and harnessed a collective will to tackle it. Nowadays, feminism is widely discussed in relation to social and political issues, such as femicide, homophobia, and transphobia. The concept of gender is, however, not to be reduced to oppression but to a way of being-in-the-world that calls into question the relation between body, identity, and politics. Such a relation represents a major focus of critical phenomenological explorations of gender. It is also an important part of the politics of gender, a term that we use to refer to the socio-political implications of feminist analysis of gender. On this view, experiences of gender oppression and discrimination are part of a collective or social experience with extended ramifications in individual lives (Hinsch 1970).

Before delving into contemporary accounts of gender, it is essential to situate this concept and its relation to embodied experience, as this emerges in feminist phenomenology. On the one hand, the concept of sexual difference lies at the heart of classical feminist phenomenology, including the works of Edith Stein and Simone de Beauvoir. While not all classical phenomenologists developed an account of gendered experience, their methodological approach provides an invaluable framework for articulating gender as an embodied experience that is also situated in a socio-cultural context, thus connecting woman's experience to the critique of patriarchal settings and culture.

On the other hand, critical phenomenology has developed an intersectional approach to gender, focusing on the relation between gender, sexuality, and political experience, further developing Beauvoir's phenomenological project and tackling situated experiences that are not typically discussed in phenomenology, such as gender identity, heteronormativity,[1] and trans experience. In this respect, critical phenomenology reveals the effects of power relations on both gender and sexuality. In many ways, a critical-phenomenological account of gender does not imply a rejection of the basic concepts and frameworks of classical phenomenology. Rather, critical phenomenology fruitfully employs such frameworks, drawing attention to the differences of gendered experiences and their relation to gender oppression. The result is a rich, multi-textured analysis of women's being-in-the-world, which is both indebted to the philosophical resources of classical phenomenology and strongly critical of the role played by power relations in sex and gender experiences.

Over the last decades, an increasing number of feminist thinkers have relied on the methodologies and insights of classical phenomenology, drawing especially on Merleau-Ponty and Beauvoir (e.g. Bartky 1990; Grosz 1994; Kruks 2001; Young 2005; Al-Saj 2010; Oksala 2016; Fielding 2017; Stoller 2017; Weiss 2021). In this context, in her 'Feminist Phenomenology Manifesto', Fielding emphasizes that feminist phenomenology emerges out of a dialogue with classical phenomenology (Fielding 2017, p. ix). Similarly, Weiss argues that feminist phenomenologists are committed to providing a more comprehensive description of lived experience, one that acknowledges woman's first-person perspective as opposed to a 'gender-blind' phenomenological approach. The core idea is that 'the phenomenological descriptions we provide must express the actual realities of our lives' (Weiss 2021). In this respect, critical phenomenology of gender is simultaneously critical of some aspects of classical phenomenology while keen to utilize its resources for understanding and combatting the oppression of women. As Fischer (2000, p. 33) notes: 'In a fundamental sense the cornerstone of feminist theory and politics is the elaboration and analysis of the particular situation and experience of being a woman.' Thus, one could argue that a critical phenomenology of gender is a core component of feminist theory and politics.

In order to introduce these ideas and issues, the chapter is structured as follows. We proceed with an overview of how sex and gender are thematized in the work of early classical phenomenologists, particularly Husserl, Stein, and Merleau-Ponty, outlining the main criticisms raised by feminist thinkers to classical phenomenology. We then introduce Simone de Beauvoir's pioneering feminist phenomenology, showing how her insights into woman's alienation are developed by two critical feminist thinkers, Iris Marion Young and Sandra Bartky. To clarify the connection between feminist phenomenology and gender politics, we turn to a discussion of how power intersects with the construction of gender by outlining the work of post-structuralist thinkers Michel Foucault and Judith Butler. We consider how a critical feminist phenomenology draws from post-structuralism while also correcting some of its limitations. In the last sections, we consider what a phenomenology of trans embodiment might look like, before concluding with an introduction to the phenomenology of sexuality and sexual orientation.

4.1 Sex and gender in early classical phenomenology

By and large, phenomenological approaches to sex and gender challenge both biological essentialism – the idea that gendered behaviour and gender differences are determined by biology – and the view that gender is exclusively a product of culture and society. The distinction between sex and gender was introduced in the late 1960s and early 1970s in psychology to account for human psychosexual development (Conte 2020). According to this distinction, sex identifies men and women in terms of biological differences (e.g. female and male sex organs, chromosomes, and other anatomical features), whereas gender refers to men and women in terms of the social roles they occupy in conformity to certain societal expectations (e.g. as masculine and feminine). In this standard formulation, the sex/gender distinction relies heavily on the assumption that sex and gender are binary, thereby failing to take into account intersexuality, when people have both male and female characteristics (Stone 2007; Karkazis 2008). The binary distinction has also been widely contested for its inability to account for transsexual, transgender, and queer identities and experiences (e.g. Butler 2004a; Enke 2012; Shrage 2009; Stryker and Whittle 2006), which blur the divide between the two categories, undermining the idea that one can be unequivocally a member of either gender.

However, it is noteworthy that the sex/gender distinction does not necessarily outline either opposition or seamless continuity between sex and gender. Understood in a dialectical fashion, the distinction emerges in an early phenomenologist like Edith Stein to account for sexual difference and to vindicate the intrinsic value and situated character of female experience. In this regard, Stein is the first phenomenologist to provide a feminist perspective on the analysis of the lived body initiated by Husserl (Haney 2000; Luft and Wehrle 2017, p. 337) and further developed by Merleau-Ponty.

While the difference between sex and gender is not thematized as such by Husserl (as it is not captured by the German word *Geschlecht*), his account of embodiment offers a key point of departure for feminist theory.[2] An important aspect of Husserl's approach concerns the relation between drives and habit, which indirectly sheds light on the roles of sexual difference, sexuality, and their respective influence on the psychophysical constitution of self. On Husserl's view, our waking and conscious life is surrounded by a halo of affects, tendencies, and drives, which are not simply 'blind' or irrational, but rather carry an implicit sense insofar as they are based on hidden associations (Husserl 1989, p. 235). In this respect, the constitution of self is simultaneously rooted in the corporeality of sensuous experience, which is pervaded by instincts and drives, but also motivated by certain associations to follow impulses and volitions.

As noted by Lee (1993) and Pugliese (2009, 2015), Husserl's notion of drives is not to be reduced to sheer biological instincts, because they are characterized by a motivational tendency that not only satisfies bodily needs, but also discloses the affective and sensuous orientation of the self. More specifically, the emergence of drives sets in motion a complex entwinement of desires, impulses, and habits. In this context, habit represents the overarching disposition that channels the affective pull of instincts and drives (Husserl 1989, p. 267). In turn, the channelling of drives awakens the self to itself; that is, it leads to the formation of an affective and bodily orientation towards oneself and others. While drives can be inhibited and constrained, they also inform the affective atmosphere of self, as they can be reactivated though passive and active associations in perception, imagination, and thinking.[3]

Husserl distinguishes between drives, as the affective and unconscious background of the self, and the habitual stances that the ego takes up when developing a subjective orientation, which encompasses sexual difference and sexuality (indeed, sexual attraction is a form of affective orientation; see also section 4.6). As we saw in Chapter 2, from a classical-phenomenological point of view, habituality denotes deeply ingrained styles of bodily behaviour that are rooted in corporeal stances, namely bodily ways of acting and being, which range from how we walk to the expression of our emotional reactions, which are produced through constant repetition. Habit informs the acquisition of a style of behaviour, what we may call our 'second nature'. In this regard, gendered behaviour represents a style that is intrinsic to the acquisition and development of a personal stance in the realm of intersubjective experience (Heinämaa 2003). We shall return to this aspect later in the chapter, when we consider the difference between classical phenomenology and the work of Judith Butler, whose concept of gender performativity also revolves on a certain notion of habituality. For now, it is sufficient to note that Husserl does not directly apply his theory of habit to the distinction between the sexes or the development of gender differences, even if he acknowledges that the analysis of the sexes pertains to genetic phenomenology (Husserl 1970, p. 188). Nonetheless, the idea that gender reflects an acquired style of behaviour is central to both Stein's and Merleau-Ponty's accounts of sexual difference, albeit in different respects.

As a Catholic educator who struggled to secure an academic position at a time in which women were not considered for professorships (Sawicki 1997), Edith Stein was quite open to many aspects of the feminist movement. In her writings and lectures on education, Stein quotes from Helen Lange's texts and speeches in favour of a reform of education, aiming to provide young girls with the tools, skills, and abilities to become teachers and access university study. While Stein regards the commitment to Christian life as the fundamental vocation for a woman, she also argues that woman is, alongside man, a type. Unlike pure categories and essences, which are based on formal characteristics that are universally shared (such as, the concept of individual, which serves the purpose of individuating entities), types classify subjects on the basis of contingent features that cannot be predicated of all the members of the species (for example, the type of human with long hair). Types draw attention to differences of bodily constitution and presentation. In this regard, types are often thematized on the basis of one's familiarity with relevant perceived features of objects and subjects, hence types are also influenced by differences of culture and language (Heinämaa 2011). It follows that woman, as a type, includes a number of different characterizations that are not universally shared and that vary across individuals (e.g. the maternal type, the erotic type, the romantic type, the level-headed type, the intellectual type; Stein 1996, p. 155). Stein's view is that men and women embody different types of their common species, that is, humanity. On this view, deviations from standard types are not only possible, but also relevant for a better understanding of female character. Indeed, types evolve 'as sexual evolution advances' (Stein 1996, p. 159).

For Stein, sexual difference is rooted in bodily constitution as a natural phenomenon, but it is also dialectically related to moral and practical orientation. Thus, sex does not correspond to a fixed and static essence but rather develops into a character or spiritual attitude. Rejecting the dualism between mind and body, Stein regards the integration between psychophysical life and spiritual character as the unfolding of an individual's intentional life, having a stable core in the soul, which comes to full realization through acts of communication with other selves. As put by Judd-Beer, 'one is neither born nor becomes a woman: this is a false dichotomy from Stein's perspective. Each woman is longing – longing is an intrinsic part of who she is as a woman and at the same time it is an impetus for her individual existential actualization' (Judd-Beer 2016, p. 44).

As such, the nature of a woman is greatly influenced by environmental and social factors, including the work and activities that woman carries out. In this context, 'individual differences existing within both sexes must be taken into account. Many women have masculine characteristics just as many men share feminine ones' (Stein 1996, p. 78). Stein's remark entails a positive evaluation of androgyny. As Haney puts it, 'the androgyny which Stein recommends is not for the sake of a hypothesized "balance" in sexual being' (Haney 2000). On the contrary, '"masculine" activities and inclinations belong within the make-up of woman if she is to achieve the larger goal, her "true humanity", which includes personal freedom and autonomy for self and others. She seeks to balance her tendencies in order to realize her feminine nature, never to transform it into the likeness of a nature of man' (Haney 2000, p. 234). Stein's view of androgyny is thus connected to her project of moral cultivation, which ultimately coincides with the realization of an ethical vocation that may be in tension with societal norms.

To this end Stein maintains that professions reserved for men should not be prohibited to women, for woman's natural vocation as wife and mother 'is not her only vocation' (Stein 1996, p. 160). On this view, 'individual gifts and tendencies can lead to the most diversified activities. Indeed, no woman is *only* woman. [. . .] Essentially, the individual talent can enable her to embark on any discipline, even those remote from the usual feminine vocation' (Stein 1996, p. 52). Overall, Stein's feminist approach centres on the value of education for women's emancipation, an aspect that she shares with Mary Wollstonecraft's defense of woman's rights (Wollstonecraft 1992; Haney 2000). At the same time, Stein draws attention to the relational and developmental character of woman, which is not defined by feminine standards of behaviour. On the contrary, womanhood involves a relational project of self-discovery and self-appropriation that seeks to affirm woman's vocation in all aspects of social and political life.

Along the lines of Husserl and Stein, Merleau-Ponty argues that the lived body is expressive of a sensuous attitude or style of being towards the world. According to Merleau-Ponty, sexed behaviour manifests itself through gestures, speech, bodily movements, and other aspects of outer behaviour, yet it is irreducible to standardized femininity and masculinity, as it is constantly re-enacted by the self in the context of intersubjective experience. As pointed out by Heinämaa, Merleau-Ponty turns 'from substantial concepts to modal ones. [. . .] In this framework, the differences between human and animal, normal and abnormal, feminine and masculine are not studied as differences of fixed structures or functions. They are understood as differences in the manners of acting and being acted on' (Heinämaa 2003, p. 41). On this view, a sexed being is not causally conditioned by sexual drives and impulses. Sexuality is not located in the body as a sheer biological function or as a conditioning mechanism, but is infused in bodily orientation as a type of erotic motivation.

To illustrate this, Merleau-Ponty discusses in *Phenomenology of Perception* two cases: that of Schneider, the war veteran we encountered earlier in Chapter 2, who reported lack of sexual desire, and that of a young girl who was prevented by her mother from seeing the man she loved. Because of this, the young girl manifested various symptoms, including loss of appetite, sleep and, ultimately, loss of speech. Both cases, according to Merleau-Ponty, can be connected to a fundamental alteration of body's intentionality, and particularly of the body schema. This means that Schneider's lack of sexual arousal did not amount to a weakening of sexual impulse. An explanation of this type presupposes that sexuality is governed by control mechanisms that should have been in fact released by the brain injury (Merleau-Ponty 2012, p. 158). Instead, according to Merleau-Ponty, Schneider's perception had lost its 'erotic structure both spatially and temporally' (Merleau-Ponty 2012, p. 158). In other words, Schneider's symptoms revealed the alteration of an underlying erotic intentionality that informs the body's orientation to situations and events, and which is laden with affective qualities; what Merleau-Ponty calls the 'sexual schema' in analogy with the 'body schema' we discussed in Chapter 2. The disturbance of the sexual schema affects one's sensitivity to the affective and erotic qualities of intersubjective encounters. Events and situations presented themselves to Schneider as having no allure or sensuous depth; hence Schneider found it difficult to connect to women (as Merleau-Ponty assumes he was heterosexual) on an erotic level.

In a similar way, for Merleau-Ponty, the symptoms of the young woman are indicative of a profound disturbance of her own affective and erotic milieu. Her loss of appetite, in particular, symbolizes the young woman's inability to 'swallow' her estrangement from her beloved, hence from their desired togetherness. In both cases, Merleau-Ponty identifies an alteration of the existential projection that underpins the lived body, which impacts the whole attitude of the self towards the world. While Merleau-Ponty's account has not been immune to criticisms (see section 4.2), he is more explicit than Husserl and Stein that sexuality is inseparable from the lived body, and is 'continuously present in human life as an atmosphere' (Merleau-Ponty 2012, p. 171). On this view, sexual difference is integrated in the overall stance of the self, permeating personal life as an existential condition that requires some levels of self-discovery and self-appropriation. We return to Merleau-Ponty's work on sexuality in the final section of this chapter.

4.2 Feminist critiques of classical phenomenology

Classical phenomenology has not been immune to various strands of criticism from feminist thinkers. There are two primary, related charges levelled at thinkers such as Heidegger, Sartre, and Merleau-Ponty. The first critique is methodological and targets the lack of thematization, on the part of classical phenomenologists, of the relation between social norms, gender, and existence. The second critique is about the implicit universalization of the male, white, and straight body in phenomenological accounts of gender and sexuality, including Merleau-Ponty's concept of the sexual schema. Ultimately, both critiques centre on the dismissal of sexed and gendered perspectives from existential concepts like being-in-the-world and motor intentionality. At stake is the worry that phenomenological categories and arguments apply in the same respects and under the same conditions to all empirical subjects *qua* human. In this way, phenomenological descriptions end up universalizing the point of view of a *masculine* subject. As Beauvoir (2009, p. 278) observes, 'the categories in which men think the world are constituted from *their point of view as absolutes*'. On this view, classical-phenomenologists like Heidegger, Sartre, and Merleau-Ponty overlook the ways in which a person's situation is inescapably informed by one's sex and gender.

The first critique can be illustrated by examining Heidegger's phenomenology of being-in-the-world. As illustrated in Chapter 3, Heidegger defines existence through the concept of Dasein, who is thrown into the world and absorbed in everyday concerns. This is a pre-flective, practical orientation in the world, which is structured by a disposition called attunement *(Befindlichkeit)*. Attunement underlies our affective and embodied way of being situated in the world, including moods. In Heidegger, mood means disposition or attunement *(Befindlichkeit)* as well as atmosphere *(Stimmung)*. Both concepts refer to the way in which Dasein is disposed towards the world in terms of affective states. As we saw in Chapter 2, on Heidegger's view, we are always in a mood, whether we are aware of it or not, as moods are part of our 'sense of reality'. Yet a sense of reality is also vulnerable to alterations and affective changes, as happens when the world appears 'uncanny' *(unheimlich)*. The uncanny depicts the mood of 'not feeling at home in a situation', wherein the un-reflected sense of belonging to a practical world is fragmented, and the world becomes 'unfamiliar'. This is best illustrated by anxiety, one of the fundamental moods that Heidegger describes in *Being and Time*.

Unlike fear, which is directed towards a specific object that is the cause of the feeling of being threatened (e.g. fear of wolves or of hurricanes), anxiety – like any mood – lacks directedness to a specific object in the face of which we feel disoriented, oppressed, and ill at ease. As Heidegger puts it: 'that in the fear of which one is anxious is completely indefinite' (Heidegger 2001, p. 231). Anxiety is described by Heidegger as the affective disposition in which we fail to make sense of the world, as existence seems to lack in meaning, coherence, and stability. Yet such disturbance of Dasein's involvement in the world also compels Dasein to interrupt its habitual comportment, as Dasein becomes exposed to the facticity of its condition, and presented with the possibility of taking ownership of its situatedness. Therefore, anxiety is a fundamental mood because it discloses our being thrown into the world as a fact that we can no longer ignore or take for granted. Differently stated, anxiety reveals the web of signification of the things we do and pursue, compelling Dasein to coming to terms with what matters to it and why. The main implication of this view is that anxiety can be a meaningful mood that helps uncover Dasein's comportment in the world, therefore allowing the possibility to seek authenticity over inauthenticity.

From the point of view of Beauvoir's feminist critique, Heidegger's phenomenological reflections overlook, or at least underplay, the extent to which Dasein's fundamental disposition towards the world involves the engagement with a vast array of norms, including gender and sexual norms. For example, for those subjects whose sexuality does not align with heterosexuality (such as homosexuals), the world can appear 'uncanny' because it is already structured by heterosexual expectations and norms. In a similar way, women who are not aligned with patriarchal standards of feminine behaviour experience a continuous conflict between their predispositions and desires and the forms of practical engagement that are available in their context. In such cases, the relation between attunement and being-in-the-world acquires more ambiguous connotations in that the subject's tendency towards anxiety reveals, in fact, a tendency towards guilt.

Related to this, both Heidegger and Merleau-Ponty describe our primordial being-in-the-world as a field of practical possibilities. Both thinkers argue, though in different ways, that our fundamental relation to the world is by way of comporting with objects and other selves within contexts that are already replete with practical meaning. On this view, we are not detached observers looking disinterestedly at a world of 'objects'. As we have seen in previous chapters, from an existential-phenomenological viewpoint, objects and situations are always embedded within a web of practical rules that relate to our bodily capacities and possibilities. However, as Beauvoir observes: 'The world does not appear to the woman as a "set of tools" halfway between her will and her goals, as Heidegger defines it: on the contrary, it is a stubborn, indomitable resistance; it is dominated by fate and run through with mysterious caprices' (Beauvoir 2009, p. 754). Beauvoir's argument is that women have historically dealt with the world of equipment through domestic practices and rituals that were not meant to teach them practical skills and through which they did not acquire any technical knowledge.

Thus, the 'stubborn, indomitable resistance' to which Beauvoir refers is the resistance of the surrounding world, which does not present itself as a potentially continuous field of practical engagement but rather as a discontinuous domain, characterized by ignorance, superstition, and acquiescence. In this sense, for Beauvoir, the notion of fate or destiny is a construct to which women become accustomed and that prevents them from achieving an understanding of their situation. Thus, while

Heidegger's concept of being-in-the-world implicitly presupposes a sub-ject for whom the world can in principle be navigated and even mastered, gender highlights the ambiguity of the taken-for-granted character of the surrounding world, and the constant precariousness of one's involvement in it. This is not to deny that Heidegger's fundamental ontology can be reconciled with the project of a feminist phenomenology,[4] for Heidegger himself acknowledges the disturbances and interruptions of Dasein's comportment. At stake is rather the problem of integrating the role of gender and gender norms in the phenomenological description of human comportment.

The second, related criticism of classical-phenomenological accounts is that they either disregard or woefully misrepresent the phenomenology of sexual difference and gender (e.g. Allen 1982–3). To quote Beauvoir once more: 'There is a whole region of human experience which the male deliberately chooses to ignore because he fails to *think* about it: this experience, the woman *lives* it' (Beauvoir 2011, p. 737). According to Beauvoir, the masculine point of view is established as the standard or norm, against which all other modes of thinking, being and experiencing are evaluated. As a result of this, woman's way of being appears as devi-ant and even inferior in that she does not fit pre-established standards of behaviour (whereas the dominance of the masculine perspective is cemented by the fact that it need not be named – it simply is *the* perspec-tive on the world). As Beauvoir famously states in her Introduction to *The Second Sex*, woman is the 'Other' of man and hence everything that is female/feminine is automatically constituted as an absence, lack, or deviation. This twofold complaint about phenomenology is emphasized by Judith Butler in her critique of Merleau-Ponty, whose account of the subject:

> [. . .] is problematic in virtue of its abstract and anonymous status, as if the subject described were a universal subject or structured existing subjects universally. Devoid of a gender, this subject is presumed to characterize all genders. On the one hand, this presumption devalues gender as a relevant category in the description of the lived bodily expe-rience. On the other hand, inasmuch as the subject described resembles a culturally constructed male subject, it consecrates masculine identity as the model for the human subject, thereby devaluing, not gender, but women. (Butler 1989, p. 89)

As discussed before, Merleau-Ponty acknowledges the relevance of sexu-ality in the *Phenomenology of Perception*. However, for Butler, the entire discussion presupposes tacit assumptions about a male body and a male heterosexual subject, which are presented as *the* body and *the* subject of the phenomenological discourse. Sullivan also contends that Merleau-Ponty's account of the body lacks specificity insofar as it corresponds to an anonymous body that has no particularity, such as those 'provided by gender, sexuality, class, age, culture, nationality, individual experiences and upbringing and more' (Sullivan 1997, p. 1).

Merleau-Ponty's lack of thematization of what it might be like to inhabit a gendered body and to exist as a woman within a social world saturated with gender norms has not gone unnoticed in the scholarship (Heinämaa 2003, p. 22 and p. 73). At the same time, as we mentioned, this lack of thematization of gendered behaviour does not preclude the possibility of a feminist phenomenology that draws on Husserl, Heidegger, and Merleau-Ponty. Indeed, Merleau-Ponty's phenomenology offers the conceptual tools to explore and illuminate gender differences (Heinämaa 2003; Kruks 2006). For example, without an account of how the body is phenomenologically constituted, it would not be possible to thematize responsiveness to other selves and the social context on an affective and perceptual level. In this regard, Merleau-Ponty's account of the 'I-can' as underlying different possibilities for action and movement represents the overarching matrix upon which different possibilities of situated experience can be articulated. Indeed, Merleau-Ponty's view of sexuality as a style can be regarded as the basis of the 'constant indeterminacies' (Kruks 2006, p. 37) that characterize woman's condition. Such indeterminacies include issues of reproduction, pregnancy, and illness that may affect some women but not others depending on their genetic predisposition, race, culture, class, and local environment. For this reason, according to Kruks, the possibility of establishing concrete bonds between women depends on the affective predisposition to relate to the embodied experiences of other women, even and especially when their social identities differ notably from one's own. In this case, as we will see in more detail in Chapter 6, one needs to *choose* to act in solidarity with women (Kruks 2006, p. 43). Accordingly, none of the above criticisms is intended to show that we should dismiss classical phenomenology *tout court*. On the contrary, such critiques indicate that discourse about the facticity of corporeal existence, originally outlined by classical phenomenology, needs to incorporate and reflect a wider spectrum of diverse experiences in order to adequately thematize the lived reality of gender.

4.3 Building a critical phenomenology of gender

4.3.1 Simone de Beauvoir's feminist phenomenology

The work of French thinker Simone de Beauvoir develops many of the core ideas that are at the heart of feminist phenomenology as well as of a critical phenomenology of gender. Beauvoir's work has influenced feminists working within a wide range of different theoretical and political perspectives. While she is well known as an author and existentialist philosopher, Beauvoir's work is central to the phenomenology of sexual difference and gender (Weiss 2002, 2006, 2021; Heinämaa 2003, 2006; Scholz 2006; Webber 2018). This is perhaps most evident in her acclaimed 1949 work, *The Second Sex*, which develops a phenomenological account of gender that applies in an original manner the conceptual repertoire of Heidegger, Sartre, and especially Merleau-Ponty to woman's lived experience. Most notably, Beauvoir explores the relation between socio-cultural norms and woman's experience, highlighting the ways in which the latter has been historically conflated with a standardized notion of femininity. To quote the most famous lines of *The Second Sex*: 'One is not born, but rather becomes a woman. No biological, physical or economic destiny defines the figure that the human female takes on in society; it is civilization as a whole that elaborates this intermediary product between the male and the eunuch that is called feminine' (Beauvoir 2011, p. 330). Taking issue with a whole stratification of cultural and societal assumptions about woman, including – among others – psychoanalysis, history, sociology, and literature, Beauvoir contends that woman's condition is marked by the myth of femininity that is distinctive of patriarchal societies, where women are seen as the 'other' of man rather than as autonomous subjects of feeling, action, and thought.

A major aspect of Beauvoir's work is her exploration of the lived body in relation to woman's situation, following the approach of classical phenomenological analysis: 'one might say, in the position I adopt – that of Heidegger, Sartre and Merleau-Ponty – that if the body is not a *thing*, it is a situation: it is our grasp on the world and the outline for our projects' (Beauvoir 2011, p. 68). However, contrary to these thinkers, Beauvoir does not speak of the lived body *per se*, but rather of women's bodies within particular socio-cultural contexts. She thus insists on the importance of attending to the lived body as a context-dependent reality that is conditioned by cultural values and entrenched social positions, including class and race. From this point of view, the body is both a form of limitation and a field of experience, which woman seeks to appropriate to make it her own within and against socio-cultural standards.

The female body represents a limitation on account of its biological constraints, which are laden with social significance, as we shall now see; but the body is also and at the same time the field through which woman expresses herself. For this reason, Beauvoir speaks of the body as 'one of the essential elements of the situation she occupies in the world. But her body is not enough to define her; it has a lived reality only as taken on by consciousness through actions and within a society' (Beauvoir 2011, p. 71).

In this context, one of the most complex arguments presented by Beauvoir concerns her discussion of female biology. While the first chapter of *The Second Sex* deals extensively with biological descriptions of sex, Beauvoir is very clear that 'physiology cannot ground values', as 'biological data take on those values the existent confers on them' (2011, p. 47). Beauvoir's argument is that biology establishes some fundamental facts about woman's condition, involving various aspects of woman's development across puberty, reproduction, and senility. At the same time, Beauvoir argues that biological data do not define woman's capacity to appropriate and affirm her individual freedom. Like Husserl, Heidegger, and Merleau-Ponty, Beauvoir rejects a naturalistic approach to the lived body, while also outlining a dialectical relation between biology and culture.

On Beauvoir's view, biological data about women (e.g. physical weakness, fragility, less respiratory and muscular capacity than men) significantly shape women's way of being in the world. Indeed, it is on account of woman's biological difference that women have historically occupied a place of subalternity with respect to men (Beauvoir 2011, p. 69). On this view, physical differences between men and women are connected to a historical process of sedimentation of social and cultural norms through which women's sexual and physical difference is made visible and 'othered'. For example, Beauvoir notes that women's muscular inferiority is established by comparison with male muscular strength, but such a physical difference counts as 'weakness only in light of the aims man sets for himself' (ibid.). Woman's muscular capacity appears defective or inferior when it is compared to man's physical attributes, including the practical aims for which muscular capacity is required, like hunting and fighting. This means that women appear fragile and weak where the standards of physical strength are based on male muscular force. This precludes the appreciation of women's distinct physical abilities, including the range of physical and manual tasks they could pursue. At the same time, Beauvoir notes that 'where customs forbid violence, muscular energy cannot be the basis for domination: existential, economic, and moral reference points are necessary to define the notion of *weakness* concretely' (ibid.). Physical weakness is constitutive of woman's condition in comparison to man's where violence defines power authority, but it is not the only reason why women are kept in a place of subalternity. The division of labour and the evolution of customs have historically exacerbated woman's difference in such a way that weakness does not exclusively represent a physical attribute but also a socio-economic position.

With regard to sexual difference, Beauvoir maintains, like Stein, that woman and man represent different types, each having specific sexual characteristics. Unlike Stein, however, Beauvoir insists that sexual characteristics greatly vary across different species, and do not always translate into two distinct sexes. To this end, Beauvoir distinguishes between reproduction (the biological function that enables the maintenance of the species) and sexual difference (the characteristic diversity between male and female bodies). Her view is that, in nature, biological reproduction does not automatically coincide with the hierarchy or asymmetry between the sexes, specifically between an active and a passive pole, which instead characterizes the human species (Beauvoir 2011, p. 44). In this context, Beauvoir pays special attention to the relation between reproduction and woman's existence. Since biological reproduction has historically provided the motive for identifying womanhood with motherhood, Beauvoir notes that the individuality of woman's existence is thereby forgotten: 'female individuality is fought by the interest of the species; she seems possessed by outside forces: alienated' (Beauvoir 2011, p. 60).

Beauvoir describes the condition of woman as being possessed by an external transindividual force, which is the power of the species that perpetuates itself through the female body regardless of woman's individual existence. On this view, women experience their bodies as a source of estrangement and oppression due to the socio-cultural identification of the female body with its reproductive capacity. For example, not all females can give birth for genetic or physical reasons,[5] and not all women regard motherhood as their existential project or vocation. This suggests that, for Beauvoir, sexual difference is a condition that is influenced by both biological and socio-cultural factors. It follows that woman's situation is characterized, for Beauvoir, by a radical ambiguity, as it is both a site of transcendence (in the existential-phenomenological sense of being projected in the outer world through one's body) as well as of immanence (in the sense of being limited by contingency, such as historical and cultural conditions).

As Kruks observes, 'to "become" a woman is to find oneself in a world in which the possibilities close down rather than open up, in which the field of possibilities narrows even, in extreme cases, to the point of disappearing' (Kruks 2001, p. 47). In this regard, Beauvoir draws attention to the tensions that emerge in adolescence, when individual dispositions acquire a more distinct orientation:

> [. . .] for the adolescent boy who is allowed to manifest himself imperiously, the universe has a totally different face than for the adolescent girl whose feelings are deprived of immediate effectiveness; the former ceaselessly calls the world into question, he can at every instance revolt against the given and thus has the impression of actively confirming it when he accepts it; the latter only submits to it; the world is defined without her and its face immutable. This lack of physical power expresses itself as a more general timidity: she does not believe in a force she has not felt in her body, she does not dare to be enterprising, to revolt, to invent; doomed to docility, to resignation, she can only accept a place that society has already made for her. She accepts the order of things as a given. (Beauvoir 2011, p. 398)

Beauvoir argues that young women are less likely to invent, revolt, or be enterprising in comparison to young men, because they are educated to accept their place in society instead of actively pursuing it. This phenomenon is due to consolidated patterns of socialization that influence women's self-perception and self-experience, reinforcing beliefs of weakness, timidity, and fragility. Accordingly, 'many of the faults for which they [women] are reproached – mediocrity, meanness, shyness, pettiness, laziness, frivolity, and servility – simply express the fact that the horizon is blocked for them. Woman, it is said, is sensual, she wallows in immanence; but first she was enclosed in it' (Beauvoir 2011, p. 729). Such a view echoes observations made, some 150 years earlier, by Mary Wollstonecraft, who argued that feminine vices – e.g. obsession with physical appearance, superficiality, and overly emotional behaviour – were the result of an educational and political system that teaches women servility disguised as modesty. Such an educational model contributes to denying women's independence and access to the public realm, while also encouraging the upbringing of women as sexual objects that exist for the sake of men's gratification.[6] For this reason, Wollstonecraft concluded that 'it is vain to expect virtue from women till they are in some degree independent of men' (Wollstonecraft 1992, pp. 252–3).

According to Beauvoir, woman's inhibition is fundamentally connected to physical experiences like menstruation, pregnancy, and menopause, which diminish woman's motor and practical freedom, impacting, since childhood and adolescence, woman's spontaneous and practical orientation in the world. Part of the power of *The Second Sex* lies precisely in Beauvoir's descriptions of 'the primal misery of being a body' (Beauvoir

2011, p. 426), and to the role played by shame in regulating women's relation to their body. For example, Beauvoir notes that women are taught to keep menstruation a secret, and to regard it as something that must be hidden, while simultaneously reminded to fear senility and the crisis of menopause.

On this basis, it is clear why Beauvoir claims that woman is the 'Other'. The 'Other' does not refer to an ethical concept of alterity, as in Levinas, but rather to the historical, cultural, and social representation of women as ancillary and unequal to men. For this reason, Beauvoir describes womanhood as a concrete situation placed in a dialectical tension between nature and culture due to a lack of reciprocity between the sexes. The opposition between the sexes is often framed by Beauvoir along the lines of Hegel's master–servant allegory. In Hegel's 1807 *Phenomenology of Spirit*, self-awareness is the achievement of a subject who experiences self-estrangement and alienation due to a conflictual relation with another subject. In the allegorical version that Hegel presents, the relation between two selves, who are originally equal to one another, develops into an antagonistic relation and, eventually, into a life-and-death struggle for reciprocal recognition, from which eventually the two original subjects emerge as a master and a servant. Despite this unequal situation, the servant is the one who achieves freedom of mind and intellectual independence thanks to his labour.[7]

In applying the master–servant asymmetry to the relation between the sexes, Beauvoir points out that women have historically been prevented from even entering the struggle for recognition, as they are regarded as alien and inequal from the start (Beauvoir 2011, pp. 99ff) due to a combination of biological and social factors. In this context, Beauvoir also maintains that woman needs to work for her liberation, a task that can only be collective (Beauvoir 2011, p. 753). This involves the rejection of the myths of femininity that permeate society and culture as well as the affirmation of woman's economic independence from men. Such independence is necessary for woman to emancipate herself from the place of inferiority and subalternity that women share with workers, Black slaves and colonized natives (though women, as Beauvoir acknowledges, are not a class or minority; Beauvoir 2011, p. 28).[8]

As Beauvoir's thesis that 'one "becomes" a woman' is a fine-grained claim that is attuned to the complexity of woman's condition, it is not surprising that it has sparked a number of debates between feminist thinkers and phenomenologists. Among such discussions, the most relevant for feminist phenomenology involves Butler's reading of Beauvoir's thesis of 'becoming a woman' in terms of gender performativity (Butler 1988, 1993a, 1999, 1990, 2004a). Performativity is a concept that Butler draws from both theatre and speech acts theory. In her view, performativity means that gender is neither an essence nor an attribute of people's behaviour, but rather a 'stylized repetition of acts' that are performed and consolidated through linguistic, social, and cultural practices (Butler 1988, p. 519). On Butler's account, gender is constitutive of corporeal styles of being insofar as it is produced by the repetition of acts and practices that are culturally defined and maintained. Butler has in mind the fact that, from a very early age, we are made to act, look, and feel like a male or a female (e.g. 'this is what boys should wear'; 'this is how girls should play'). Over time, gender attributes and acts are acquired and spontaneously reproduced as natural forms of comportment.

In her work, Butler is clear that gender is neither a 'radical choice' nor an imposition of cultural codes upon the body as a 'lifeless recipient of wholly pre-given cultural relations' (Butler 1988, p. 526). For Butler, gender allows degrees of freedom, as the body inhabits a cultural and social space, which is however structured by limited possibilities for action and expression. Indeed, an individual can only take up one of the two gendered styles that are in place in the social world. In this way, Butler turns the conventional view of gender on its head: it is not that we act, look, feel and talk in some way or another because we are, say, a man or a woman. Rather, we are a man or a woman because we act, look, feel, and talk like women or men do in society (and we only behave in these ways because we were raised to do so).

One implication of this view is that, for Butler, there is no true or right way of being a man or a woman. For Butler, the very concepts of man and woman are socially constructed in that they are informed by social practices and cultural contexts that eventually establish and affirm only two ways of gendered beings, ruling out the plurality of genders. The prescriptive and normative character of gender binary is due, according to Butler, to the fact that gender is maintained through a system of enforcement. This refers to the various ways through which individuals are punished for transgressing gender norms, be it a girl who is told off for playing too roughly, a boy being teased for playing with dolls, or an intersex person being shamed for not being unambiguously male or female. However, given that gender is performative, Butler maintains that there is always the possibility of 'doing gender' differently. While gender is part of a system that regulates sexed and social identity, gendered experience – at an individual level – may consist in the continuous act of subverting certain norms, 'daily and incessantly, with anxiety and pleasure' (Butler 1989, p. 531).

To be sure, Butler's theory shares important aspects with Beauvoir's phenomenology of gender. Both Beauvoir and Butler reject biological essentialism, providing insights into the ambiguity of bodily experience as well as on the complexity of the 'host of "facts and myths" about women' (Stawarska 2018, p. 24; Weiss 2021). However, it is important to note that Butler's view of gender goes beyond Beauvoir's argument (Heinämaa 1997). As Heinämaa argues, for Beauvoir gender is a style or way of being in the world that stands in tension with patriarchal norms. The analysis of woman's condition brings to light the history of norms, beliefs, and practices that inform the visibility and interpretation of the female body as well as the multiple forms of disadvantage caused by gender norms. As Beauvoir's account of woman's alterity is not restricted to female sexual difference, but rather includes the socio-political disadvantage and objectification produced by gender norms, her view is in fact inclusive of the oppression experienced by different gender groups.

Nonetheless, according to Beauvoir, sexual difference and gender behaviour are dialectically related to each other. While they are both laden with social value, they are not determined by the stratification and subsequent acquisition of socio-cultural practices, as they are lived through by the self in relation to a material and biological condition. To this end, Beauvoir offers a dialectical account of sexual difference and gender expression in order to describe how woman stands in a dynamic and often conflictual relation to both nature and culture, and in what ways she is prevented from realizing her existential freedom. This means that the self is not an actor performing a script, but a person striving to realize and appropriate her own style of being. Thus, while Beauvoir's reflections on gender are broadly compatible with Butler's critique of patriarchy and gendered behaviour, Beauvoir and Butler also put forward different methodological and philosophical claims about the meaning of gender and its relation to sex, as testified by the ongoing debate on this topic.[9]

4.3.2 Critical approaches to woman's bodily situatedness and alienation

Beauvoir's feminist phenomenology provides the foundation for much subsequent feminist thought inspired by phenomenological analysis. In particular, Beauvoir's concern with woman's bodily alienation has been further developed by Iris Marion Young and Sandra Bartky, whose works are pivotal for a critical phenomenology of gender. In a series of essays, Young (2005) conducts a phenomenological analysis of women's bodily experiences, drawing on Heidegger, Merleau-Ponty, and Beauvoir. Despite her debt to Beauvoir, Young complains that Beauvoir 'to a large extent, fails to give a place to the status and orientation of the woman's body as relating to its surroundings in living action' (Young 2005, p. 29).

Young argues that although Beauvoir brings to light the existential role of gender, she places too strong an emphasis on the pressure and discomfort produced by female anatomy and physiology. In this way, Beauvoir ends up ignoring 'the situatedness of the woman's actual bodily movement and orientation to its surroundings and its world', creating the impression 'that it is woman's anatomy and physiology *as such* that at least in part determine her unfree status' (Young 2005, p. 29). Young's main concern is that Beauvoir's feminist approach neglects the intentional character of motor behaviour, as social critique overrides phenomenological analysis. Nonetheless, Young herself draws on Beauvoir's methodological approach in order to re-examine phenomenological approaches to motor intentionality, such as Merleau-Ponty's, in light of gender expression. In this respect, Young sets out to describe in what ways woman's motor intentionality is inhibited by contextual factors that are normally taken-for-granted and unthematized.

In doing so, Young is keen to stress that her analysis does not represent a universal account that is true of all women *qua* woman under all circumstances and with the same respects. In fact, her analysis is restricted to the situation of women within the Anglo-American and European culture. Young is also clear that the descriptions she provides of women's bodily experiences are 'probably typical only of women in advanced industrial societies, where the model of the bourgeois woman has been extended to most women. It would not apply, for example, to those societies where most people, including women, do heavy physical labour. Nor does this particular observation, of course, hold true in our own society for women who do heavy physical work' (Young 2005, p. 33, fn. 10).

In this context, in her famous essay 'Throwing like a girl' (originally published in 1980), Young takes issues with the study of German-American phenomenologist and neurologist Erwin Straus, who thematized the difference between girls' and boys' respective posture without giving due consideration to the relation between bodily movements and culturally informed styles of behaviour. Taking issue with Straus' thesis that boys and girls manifest different ways of throwing due to their different use of lateral space, Young draws attention to the relation between motor orientation and self-trust: 'women often approach a physical engagement with things with timidity, uncertainty, and hesitancy. Typically, we lack an entire trust in our bodies to carry us to our aims' (Young 2005, p. 34). To illustrate this, Young offers a personal anecdote based on one of her own hiking experiences. At one point, she needed to cross a stream using stepping-stones. While the men in her group bounded across the stream, confident in their physical ability to do so, Young hesitantly and warily tested the stones, holding onto branches to balance herself, as she slowly made her way across the stream. According to Young, her behaviour revealed two main aspects: (1) lack of confidence in her capacity to act effortlessly and carelessly, despite the fact that her bodily abilities and skills did not cause her any impediments, and (2) a greater fear of getting hurt than men.

From this point of view, it is not just the body as an ensemble of physical skills and abilities that enables woman's motor projection in the world (as in Straus' view) but rather the particular modalities through which woman experiences space, her motility, and her body in general. Young identifies three main modes that distinguish woman's comportment as well as woman's use of motility and spatiality from men's: ambiguous transcendence, inhibited intentionality, and discontinuous unity with her surroundings. Drawing on both Beauvoir and Merleau-Ponty, Young argues that woman's situation is enacted in a constant tension between the motor possibilities that are given through the body and her attunement to the space in which such possibilities are taken up and realized. As most women anticipate the possibility of having to protect themselves, their motor behaviour is more likely to reflect self-conscious direction and motion rather than unrestricted freedom of initiative. Thus, the transcendence of the body (i.e. the body's receptivity and openness to alterity) is 'overlaid' with an awareness of the context. For this reason, when it comes to female experience, motor intentionality appears 'inhibited', revealing a discontinuous relation with the environment rather than a continuous and spontaneous projection in space. Accordingly, women are more likely to experience their bodies as weak, vulnerable, unruly things that hinder the achievement of their aims: 'We feel as though we must have our attention directed upon our bodies to make sure they are doing what we wish them to do, rather than paying attention to what we want to do through our bodies' (Young 2005, p. 34).

On this basis, Young maintains that Merleau-Ponty's account of motor intentionality is not immune to culturally informed constraints, and that differences in motor behaviour across the sexes reveal important variations of posture, motility, as well as of the lived experience of space. At the core of this phenomenon, for Young, is the alteration of woman's self-perception. According to Young, woman's self-perception exhibits a heightened sense of self-consciousness than men's, as woman is more likely to experience herself as an object of the sexist gaze. As she writes: 'An essential part of the situation of being a woman is that of living the ever-present possibility that one will be gazed upon as a mere body, as shape and flesh that presents itself as the potential object of another subject's intentions and manipulations, rather than as a living manifestation of action and intention' (Young 2005, p. 44). Indeed, for the sexist gaze, women are sheer objects that exist to be 'looked at and acted upon' (Young 2005, p. 39). The adoption of the other's point of view onto oneself lies at the core of women's objectifying self-perception. This means, according to Young, that women adopt a negative evaluation of their abilities and capacities by anticipating the look of the other; a phenomenon that occurs even when women's beliefs and values are in sharp contrast with those of the sexist gaze. In this respect, Young's argument shows the extent to which the female body is not only positioned and oriented in space but also habituated to the norms that govern the context, producing a characteristic and dynamic entwinement between motility and self-awareness.

While Young's insights help to articulate the relation between gender and motor intentionality, her argument is not immune to criticisms. For instance, Weiss points out that Young's descriptions of feminine behaviour tend to deflect attention away from the socio-political sources of woman's objectification, focusing instead on women's self-referential pattern of motor intentionality (Weiss 1999, pp. 46ff). Relatedly, when it comes to the analysis of bodily projection in space, Dolezal (2015, p. 115) remarks that Young relies exclusively on stereotypically masculine activities. Young's main examples, such as hiking, running, hitting, throwing, from which the title of her essay, 'Throwing like a girl' derives, are conventional male pursuits, dominated by male standards of bodily skilfulness and dexterity. In contrast, one can note that women often exhibit confidence and skills in other bodily practices and sports, like ballet, yoga or aerobic, where non-stereotypical gendered standards of action and fluency are expected and valued. This reflects the fact that 'the inhibited "female" body that Young describes cannot be put into neat opposition with a completely free and uninhibited "male" body' (Dolezal 2015, p. 115). To put it differently, male and female bodies appear against the background of a socio-cultural context that influences them both. This is indeed how Merleau-Ponty thematizes the flexibility of motor intentionality, which is not meant to be a univocal or fixed disposition of the body, but rather a frame of bodily self-reference that can be varied and shifted across different situations, including cultural and societal ones.

The relation between female embodiment and culture lies at the heart of the work of Sandra Bartky (1990), who explores the political implications of gender by focusing on the relation between sexual objectification and alienation. Specifically, Bartky examines the entwinement between women's lived experience and psychological alienation, blending phenomenological accounts of embodiment with a broadly Marxist framework (Bartky 1990, p. 14). Bartky proceeds by taking into account sexual objectification and its relation to psychological oppression. On this view, sexual objectification is the mechanism whereby a person is identified with her body as a sexual object, a process that suspends or abstracts from a person's defining characteristics in all areas of everyday interactions. To experience sexual objectification is to be regarded as a sexual object, even though one is formally recognized as a person. Bartky refers, by way of example, to catcalling as well as to sexist remarks made by men to women in professional settings (e.g. showing concern for women's appearances or staring at parts of their bodies), which women routinely pretend to ignore, despite being affected by them. All these phenomena are typified by the sexist 'gaze', which apprehends women as objects-to-be-looked at. The sexist gaze operates not only as a form of reification, but it also functions against a backdrop in which such a gaze is endured as something to which men are naturally entitled.

According to Bartky, objectification produces an institutionalized and widespread form of psychological oppression that causes self-estrangement. As she puts it, 'to be psychologically oppressed is to be caught in the double bind of a society which both affirms my human status and at the same time bars me from the exercise of many of those typically human functions that bestow this status' (Bartky 1990, p. 31).[10] On Bartky's view, woman's estrangement is produced not simply by the routinization of the sexist gaze, but also and more importantly by its unquestioned acceptance in public and social settings where woman is supposed to act and behave as a free agent. This form of psychological oppression parallels the process of alienation described by Marx in his early writings. Specifically, Marx describes how capitalist modes of production alienate workers from their labour by estranging them not only from the product of their work (which workers cannot afford to buy), but also and more fundamentally by their productive activity as well as from the human species at large (Marx 1978, pp. 70ff). The worker's labour is mechanical, repetitive, and constrained; hence it impoverishes spontaneity and individual abilities instead of developing them. As Bartky argues, following Marx, to be alienated from productive activity and reduced to a mere means of sustaining life means to suffer fragmentation and 'loss of self' (Bartky 1990, p. 32). In this context, to suffer alienation is not to stumble upon it by accident, but rather 'to have a part of one's being stolen by another' (Bartky 1990, p. 32). In a similar way, women's oppression is a form of psychological domination that deprives women of their freedom of expression and self-awareness, though it does not materially deprive them of their livelihood as in Marx's original argument.

A notable manifestation of this phenomenon is that women may internalize the sexist gaze, developing a heightened preoccupation for their appearances and bodily presentation, as if their worth consisted in being pleasing to men (Bartky 1990, pp. 27–8). This resonates with Beauvoir's concern with woman's education and, indeed, Bartky cites Beauvoir when arguing that woman's situation disposes her 'to apprehend her body not as the instrument of her transcendence, but as "an object destined for another"' (Bartky 1990, p. 38). Psychological oppression manifests itself through various practices of grooming and beautification that are meant to attain an unobtainable bodily ideal. Thus, there arises an unbridgeable gap between the spontaneity of the female body and its cultural domestication: 'The fashion–beauty complex produces in woman an estrangement from her bodily being: on the one hand, she is it and is scarcely allowed to be anything else; on the other hand, she must exist perpetually at a distance from physical self, fixed at this distance in a permanent posture of disapproval' (Bartky 1990: 40). This core alienating process is connected to the saturation of popular culture with various paradigms of 'femininity' that prevent women from taking ownership of their representation across cultural forms of production.[11] From a Marxist perspective, this phenomenon alienates women from their creative activity, and yet, as Bartky notes, women experience such a domination *qua* women and not only as workers in a capitalist society.

From these reflections, however, one should not infer that critical feminist approaches to phenomenology are purely negative and concerned with casting a pessimistic view about society and female bodily experience. On the one hand, Bartky argues that consciousness of victimization is a divided consciousness, as it is both consciousness of weakness and consciousness of strength (Bartky 1990, p. 16). While consciousness of victimization tends to produce confusion, political paralysis, and guilt, it also allows for a productive and fruitful recognition of the practices and mechanisms that produce alienation. Consciousness of strength derives, in this case, from consciousness-raising activities that facilitates critical analysis of the shared concepts and background beliefs that help interpret woman's oppression. Furthermore, understanding the impact of sexual objectification in terms of domination is meant, for Bartky, to reveal the intersectional character of sexual objectification. The disclosure of women's oppression should lead to an understanding of a range of other related forms of oppression of which white women, for example, have until then been oblivious or indifferent to, such as the intersection between gender- and race-based discrimination (Bartky 1990, p. 16).

On the other hand, it is noteworthy that woman's bodily alienation does not always correlate to experiences of oppression and domination. A prime example of this is offered by the phenomenology of pregnancy. As we saw earlier, Beauvoir argues that woman's reproductive role is connected to alienation and loss of freedom.[12] However, when pregnancy and motherhood are actively sought or welcomed, then woman's estrangement from her body can be described as a dialectical expansion into the world (Young 2005, p. 53). Young argues that, while in pregnancy woman's subjectivity appears decentred, split, or doubled, as the movements of the foetus are experienced as the movements of another, those motions are at the same time 'wholly mine, completely within me, conditioning my experience and space' (Young 2005, p. 49). This aspect is especially emphasized by Adrienne Rich: 'In early pregnancy, the stirring of the fetus felt like ghostly tremors of my own body, later like the movements of a being imprisoned within me; but both sensations were my sensations, contributing to my own sense of physical and psychic space' (Rich 1977, p. 47).

According to Young, through pregnancy, women may experience a certain liberation from the sexist gaze, as they witness in themselves a spontaneous process of bodily growth and change that temporarily frees them from sexualization. Furthermore, the boundaries between 'inside' (the awareness of one's body) and 'outside' (the awareness of the external world) are continuously reshuffled. As Young writes: 'in pregnancy, I literally do not have a firm sense of where my body ends and the world begins. My automatic body habits become dislodged; the continuity between my customary body and my body at this moment is broken' (Young 2005, p. 50). Young refers to the radical changes of bodily habits of movement that pregnant women undergo as a result of the alteration of their body shape, which in turn influences their sense of bodily presence and orientation in space.[13]

While Young's phenomenology of pregnancy is mostly concerned with various aspects of bodily change and transformation it is worth noting that such alterations do not disrupt the sense of mineness that characterizes woman's self-relation. In this context, Heinämaa points out that pregnancy indicates a radical transformation of woman's embodied experience in terms of 'temporal processes of bodily transformation and re-formation' that are enacted on a kinaesthetic and sensory level (Heinämaa 2014). Such changes undermine and challenge the dualism between self and other, as they involve the interlocking of two distinct and related sensory-motor beings in the latest stages of pregnancy. From this viewpoint, the phenomenology of pregnancy offers a fruitful ground for rethinking the nature of gestation and the bodily transformations it involves in a more developmental and relational way.

4.4 Power, discourse, and the gendered body

4.4.1 Post-structural critiques: Foucault and Butler

As we have seen in previous sections, feminist phenomenological approaches bring to light the relation between embodiment and domination drawing especially on classical existential-phenomenologists like Beauvoir, Merleau-Ponty, and Sartre. However, feminist phenomenology is also deeply indebted to post-structural thinkers like Michel Foucault and Judith Butler. Indeed, a dominant strand of feminist thinking over the past thirty years or so has been broadly post-structural in orientation, meaning that it has focused on examining the relation between gender, power relation, and social norms. Strongly influenced by the work of Michel Foucault, arguably the most prominent proponent of this tradition of thought is Judith Butler. In this section, we outline the key tenets of this approach to show how post-structural feminist approaches and critical phenomenology are reciprocally connected.

In a series of studies, Foucault examines the various 'techniques of power' that determine how we think, act, interact with others and make sense of ourselves (Foucault 1978, 1980, 1995, 1997). Central to Foucault's work is the rejection of what he calls the 'constituent subject' (Foucault 1980, p. 117). By this, he refers to the notion of a self-transparent subject that provides the basis of objective knowledge about itself and the world. This subject is predominantly associated with Descartes' philosophy, and is, therefore, often referred to as the 'Cartesian subject', but Foucault also sees this account re-emerging in Husserl's transcendental phenomenology and in other classical phenomenologists. Methodologically, Foucault's view is a less an engagement than a rejection of the premises of Husserl's approach that we illustrated in Chapter 1. Far from assuming that the phenomenologist can 'bracket' the world in order to provide an account of the essesntial structures of experience, Foucault argues that philosophical critique should be concerned with the structures of power that inform the understanding of self and world. On Foucault's view, it is not possible to transcend our own cultural and historical specificity, hence any type of knowledge is necessarily localized and partial. In this regard, Foucault maintains that knowledge, subjectivity and experience are constructed in different ways through discourses[14] and practices that determine who we are and how we understand ourselves and the world. On this view, there is no understanding of universal essences to be achieved. This means that, for Foucault, accounts of selfhood must be placed not only within a historical and cultural framework, but also within a particular 'regime of truth' (i.e. within a set of discourses and ideologies that prescribe forms of comportment, including gender, sexuality, mental health) (e.g. Foucault 1988, 1997).

Despite Foucault's rejection of classical-phenomenological approaches to selfhood, it is noteworthy that he does not dismiss the concept of subjectivity altogether. Instead, Foucault insists that subjectivity must be made intelligible within those specific domains of discourse and praxis that constrain it, including especially 'techniques of power' (like the penal system) that disempower individuals (Foucault 1995). Foucault's objective is to provide an analysis of *how* the individual may come to an understanding of oneself *as a subject*, even though such an enterprise is not foundational or conducive to the uncovering of a transcendental truth about human experience. For this reason, while Foucault has been often accused of rendering the self an effect or passive product of discourse and power, it is worth noting that, especially in his later works, he tried to address such concerns by outlining a 'hermeneutics of self'. This project is meant to explore how care for self and other arises through practices of self-interpretation and self-cultivation that are, at the same time, a form of resistance to power (Foucault 1986, 2001).

Perhaps Foucault's most famous work, *A History of Sexuality*, reveals more directly this interrelation of concerns about the constitution of sexual identities and the attempt to liberate the self from a position of disempowerment through the critical reconstruction of discourse about sexuality (Foucault 1978). In the first book, which was followed by two other volumes, Foucault documents the genealogy of sexuality; that is, how particular forms of desire, modes of sexual interaction, ways of experiencing oneself, coalesced into the idea of being 'heterosexual' or 'homosexual'. According to Foucault, in order to understand how the modern individual experiences himself as a subject of sexuality, it is essential first to identify how, for centuries, the western man had been brought to recognize himself as a subject of desire. Foucault refers notably to Christian moral injunctions about sexuality, but he also proceeds to show, in the two subsequent volumes, that the body is not only historically constituted as a sexual, desiring being, but is also capable of re-evaluating pleasure and desire against an overarching ideology. For example, once the relation between power and sexuality is reconstructed, heteronormative codes and expectations are revealed for what they are, namely, as contingent, historical norms that can be shifted, reverted, and resisted. Foucault thus allows the possibility of a critical discourse about sexuality and bodily experience that centres on practices of liberation rather than oppression.

On this front, Foucault's account of sexuality exerted a strong influence on Butler's view of gender (Butler 1990, 2004a). In developing such analysis, Butler draws from a variety of other philosophical traditions, including phenomenological and psychoanalytic thinkers, such as Husserl, Merleau-Ponty, Freud, and Lacan. The result is a complex account of the gendered subject; viz., an examination of what it means to 'have' a gender and how gender is regulated within society. At the heart of this is Butler's concept of gender performativity, which has been central to the development of modern gender theory, especially queer theory. As mentioned in section 4.3, Butler argues that gender must be understood as something we *do*, rather than something we *are*. This is the reason why she defines gender as 'performative': it is something that is brought into being *through* the way we act.

In this context, it is important to point out that Butler inherits Foucault's concepts of discourse and power, but she is also closer to Foucault's later work on practices of liberation. When it comes to gender as discourse, Butler denies that we can freely choose how to 'perform' our gender, and hence she does not suggest that gender is a performance that individuals can choose at will, but a script that prescribes the terms and code of the corporeal space we inhabit. On this view, to be masculine or feminine is to conform to established social discourses and practices that punish and correct individuals who deviate from gender norms. To quote Butler: 'gender is not exactly what one "is" nor is it precisely what one "has". Gender is the apparatus by which the production and normalization of masculine and feminine take place' (Butler 2004a, p. 42). Such 'normalization' occurs in a myriad of ways, from criticizing a girl for being a tomboy, to the medical 'curing' of intersex and trans individuals so they conform to the established model of binary gender. However, Butler argues that no rigid system of gender identity, e.g. being unambiguously 'male' or 'female', can capture the richness and diversity of bodily possibilities. People's desires, feelings, and orientations will always push against the limits of what it is to be recognizably male or female. This is reflected in queer critique of heteronormativity, which refers to the normalization of sexual attraction for people of the opposite sex, which ends up being regarded as a standard for masculinity and femininity (Rich 1980). On this basis, Butler challenges the concept of gender binary, questioning the boundaries of sexual difference, as she argues that this notion is nothing but the stratification of gender discourse upon the body (Butler 2004a).

In their respective ways, both Foucault and Butler highlight the social construction of the gendered subject. On the one hand, both approaches tend to undermine phenomenological analysis of gender, as they downplay the analysis of selfhood and the materiality of bodily experience that are distinctive of classical-phenomenological approaches to gender. On the other hand, however, Foucault and Butler show that contextual knowledge and background beliefs cannot be neatly separated from gender. Indeed, the acquisition of gender is not a movement from a disembodied self to a gendered subject, but a process of acculturation that is not necessarily linear. In this respect, Foucault's and Butler's respective critique of the practices that discipline the social visibility of sexed bodies are meant to challenge unquestioned beliefs and expectations about gender behaviour and gender attributes. While there are a number of related aspects that we cannot here address, it is worth considering whether and how a critical phenomenology of gender draws from this approach, while also offering a corrective to some of the issues that emerge in post-structural feminist thought.

4.4.2 The critical dimensions of feminist phenomenology

A recurrent criticism of Butler's work is that she 'dissolves' the body into a pure effect of discourse. In so doing, she ignores or dismisses what it is like to be an embodied self, privileging the materiality of linguistic acts over the analysis of the materiality of lived bodies (Sullivan 2001, pp. 55ff).[15] In a similar way, Foucault's account can be criticized for describing subjectivity as a socially shaped self, who is positioned in various systems of power relations, thereby lacking an experiential and active viewpoint of his own. Furthermore, the constructivist approach does not sufficiently take into account the differences that characterize and distinguish different types of bodies from one another. As Grosz writes: 'there is no body as such: there are only *bodies* – male or female, black, brown, white, large or small – and the gradations in between' (Grosz 1994, p. 19). The body is not a purely pliable 'putty' from which a specific body is moulded. Rather, it is resistant, unruly, 'volatile' (Grosz 1994), and such modes of resistance, unruliness, and volatility are influenced by material conditions.

From a phenomenological point of view, discourse about gender and sexuality does not *create* the body through practices of discourse, but rather alters the contingent way in which the lived body *expresses* and *orients* itself in the world. A phenomenological approach to gender thus emphasizes the variations of bodily experiences on accounts of both the material and biological constitution of the body as well as of the different socio-cultural systems in which lived bodies are thematized. For example, not all cultures sexualize female breasts. This suggests that the analysis of the socio-cultural framework in which gendered experiences are situated is dependent on the structures of a 'home-world' that does not exclude, but rather depends on the existence of other 'alien-worlds' (Steinbock 1995).

From this point of view, critical approaches to phenomenology seek to account for what is missing in post-structural accounts of gender, retrieving especially the dimension of subjectivity and how it dynamically intersects systems of power relations. As Alcoff argues, 'we need to supplement discursive accounts of the construction of sexual experience with phenomenological accounts of the embodied effects on subjectivity of certain kinds of practices. The meanings and significance of sexual events inhere partly in the embodied experiences themselves, whether or not they can be rendered intelligible within any discursive formation' (Alcoff 2000, p. 55). In this sense, post-structuralism and phenomenology can be brought into a more nuanced and fine-grained dialogue. To this end, Johanna Oksala (2016) argues that phenomenological analysis can offer important insights into how discourses and practices about gender are not co-extensive with one another, and therefore they offer a relevant standpoint for re-interpreting gendered experiences. As Oksala writes:

> Even though women's sexual experiences, for example, are constructed through patriarchal discourses, these experiences are never wholly derivative of or reducible to them. It is possible, for example, that women have, if not a fully articulated feminist critique of their situation, at least a sense of disorientation and dissatisfaction with the dominant cultural and linguistic representations of their experience. It is exactly this dissatisfaction, this gap between their personal experiences and the dominant cultural representations and linguistic descriptions that are available to them that can generate critique as well as create new discourses capable of contesting and contradicting the old ones. (Oksala 2016, p. 45)

As Oksala argues, gender critique does nor aim to reduce women's experiences to existing social norms, but rather seeks to identify the lack of cohesion between cultural and linguistic representation of women and their actual lived experience, which evolves across time in specific socio-cultural contexts. Examples of such a critique, for Oksala, are feminist consciousness-raising practices that utilize women's experience as the basis for social transformation. This occurs by (a) identifying the shared aspects of women's experiences, as a ground for collective awareness; (b) connecting women's oppression to specific socio-cultural factors in order to identify correlated socio-political phenomena; and (c) revealing the implicit beliefs and background norms that influence the thematization of women's experience, showing how such norms produce visible and contingent representations of gender that can be altered (Oksala 2016, p. 48).

Oksala likens this strategy to Foucault's notion of the 'practices of the self' (Foucault 1997), which Foucault developed in his later work as an antidote to the normalizing, disciplining effects of power: 'Viewed as technologies of the self, the aim of the feminist practices of consciousness-raising is not the exposure of deep inner self or an original and authentic womanhood, but rather the problematization of the normalized self. In other words, consciousness-raising practices can be understood as practices of freedom in the sense that their goal is not a naturalization of identity, but its critical transformation' (Oksala 2016, p. 48). On this view, consciousness-raising practices make it possible to 'think oneself differently'; that is, to think about oneself as a centre of feeling, activity, and thinking that is irreducible to a given matrix, which is at the centre of Foucault's political project but also of classical-phenomenological analysis. In this sense, post-structural and phenomenological approaches can form a mutually illuminating, dialectic relationship, with insights from each provoking further insights into the other. It is perhaps at such intersections that a truly critical phenomenology is best realized.

4.5 Trans phenomenology

The discussion we offered so far has outlined the theoretical issues that surround phenomenological approaches to sex, gender, and gender politics. As we mentioned at the outset, the relation between gender and social norms is indicative of the ways in which gender and sexuality can be instrumental in creating systems of oppression. We also saw in what sense gender represents a style of being that is irreducible to standards of feminity and masculinity. An important aspect of Butler's theory of gender performativity is that gender behaviour and gender attributes belong to a spectrum, which reflects the complex and diverse ways in which gender is lived and experienced as a component of one's personal identity. In this context, trans experience represents the experiential domain that most directly reflects the complexity of gender in relation to both gender expression and gender politics. Trans theory and politics had been gaining rapidly increasing attention within feminism and gender theory since the early 1990s, but it is in the last decade that it has become a major topic of public discussion, concerning – among other issues – the accommodation of trans people within existing spaces, and institutions that are historically sex segregated. From a phenomenological point of view, the very concept of 'trans experience' deserves attention, instead of being taken for granted.

One thing to stress at the outset is that there is little consensus on how to understand and thematize trans experiences. The very meaning of 'trans' is debated, although it is often understood to be an umbrella term denoting the variety of ways in which individuals deviate from and confound gender norms based on gender binary. Common to some trans experiences is the phenomenon of 'bodily dissonance' (sometimes called gender dysphoria); that is, the experience of a mismatch between one's physical body and one's sense of gender identity. For a number of years, one way of considering this phenomenon was to assume an internal gendered 'essence' or inner authentic identity, which was supposed to identify one's true gendered self, with which the physical body needed to be aligned. Indeed, autobiographical accounts and self-narratives of transsexuals often invoke the idea of a 'true self' or 'authentic self-hood' for making sense of their embodied experiences and pursue self-transformation (e.g. Gagne et al. 1997; Mason-Schrock 1996). With regard to this, Rubin (2003) has offered a nuanced account of FTM (female-to-male) transsexuals. On Rubin's view, 'authenticity is a leading principle behind an FTM's life. FTM lives are a search for recognition of the innermost self. What FTMs realize is that their innermost selves are authentically male. Once they make this realization, they modify their bodies to express this authentic identity'. Many of the participants in Rubin's study thus 'believe they have always been men, despite their female bodies' (Rubin 2003, p. 143).

However, this theoretical approach is questionable from a number of viewpoints. To begin with, the idea of being 'trapped' in a misaligned body has the implication that the body *must* be altered in order to 'release' the man or woman within. Such a thesis has been viewed with scepticism by a number of feminist and trans theorists in that it reinforces the gender binary by affirming an inner, authentic, gendered self (e.g. Stone 1991; Feinberg 1998; Bornstein 1994). The 'wrong body' narrative is also at odds with the phenomenological and anti-essentialist view of gender. As Beauvoir noted, one *becomes* a woman within an existential situation, therefore one was not born with a pre-formed gendered self. Similarly, Butler's account of gender performativity rejects the 'wrong body' narrative, precisely because Butler denied any inner gendered core or essence. In this respect, the very idea of a gender binary is itself problematic when it is connected to an inner gender identity (e.g. Butler 2004a). Furthermore, as Talia Mae Bettcher points out, it is not always the case that trans people wish to alter their body (Bettcher 2021). Quite to the contrary, trans subjects may feel at home in their own bodily constitution just as it is. Thus, not all trans experiences are alike, nor is dysphoria a necessary precondition of being trans.

Drawing from our discussion of the phenomenology of gender above, we can also note, as Alexis Shotwell (2009) has argued, that being in the 'right body' has more to do with our social world than with any individuated experience of our body. This reflects the fact that our 'embodied being is (trans)formed in and through the discourses and discursive practices that make up systems of power/knowledge' (Sullivan 2003, p. 93). To put it differently, the 'misaligned body' can itself be interrogated when we also challenge the particular regime of truth in which the gendered body is situated, as a system that centres on the gender binary. This indicates that a post-structuralist view of gender can be utilized for a phenomenological investigation of first-person trans experience.

Phenomenology's commitment to first-person descriptions encourages one to attend to the lived experience of trans people, paying attention to their existential situation, including the ways in which the everyday world presents itself to them as hostile and uncanny. In this respect, the fragmentation and alteration of woman's sense of reality, which we explored in Beauvoir and other feminist thinkers, can be explored in the context of trans experience, as reflecting the specific situation and lived horizon of trans subjects. Consider, for example, Andrea Long Chu's description of dysphoria as a 'heartbreak', which Shon Faye aptly comments upon as follows: 'Heartbreak, its incapacitating grief and the sense of absence and loss which activate the same parts of the brain as physical pain, can be so all-consuming it interferes with your everyday life' (Faye 2021, p. 137). Faye is very clear that, while not all trans people experience dysphoria, the distress it causes is as strong as a physical symptom, which impacts one's sense of reality, and it is aggravated by a number of systemic challenges, from healthcare access to stigma, to lack of third spaces, to objectification and stereotypification in popular culture and social discourse. In this context, Faye's comparison of dysphoria with 'incapacitating grief' indicates that dysphoria is experienced not only as a physical symptom but also as an existential orientation. As we saw in Chapter 2, Merleau-Ponty compared the phantom limb to the loss of a friend to emphasize how a physical symptom represents not just a physical alteration of body, but also and more fundamentally an existential alteration of the way of perceiving and relating to oneself (including one's past and present identity) and the world through one's body. Phenomenological accounts of trans experience can help to identify the distinctive shifts and alterations that are involved in the transition from one gender to another, including not only somatic changes but also existential orientations. Indeed, it is possible to think through the phenomenology of trans experience in ways that are still in need of further analysis and discussion.

4.6 Sexuality

The phenomenology of gender is closely related to the phenomenology of sexuality. To this end, Merleau-Ponty's concept of the sexual schema provides an important point of departure for a phenomenological analysis of sexual orientation. According to Merleau-Ponty, the sexual schema 'is strictly individual, emphasizing the erogenous areas, outlining a sexual physiognomy, and eliciting the gestures of the masculine body, which is itself integrated into this emotional totality' (Merleau-Ponty 2012, p. 180). We can think of the sexual schema as an erotic organization of the body, which is subject-dependent and that is simultaneously connected to physiological stimuli, informing – on an affective and pre-reflective level – how the self experiences other sexed bodies. Thus, the sexual schema represents a source of sexual desire that helps to articulate the subject's erotic orientation. Importantly, the sexual schema is, as Merleau-Ponty claims, 'strictly individual'. This aspect is not entirely devoid of ambiguity, but one reading of it is that, despite Merleau-Ponty's exclusive reliance on heterosexual examples, the sexual schema defies reductive categorization in terms of 'male' and 'female' desire, or 'heterosexual' and 'homosexual' sexual orientation. Instead of assuming that individuals do, or should, conform to pre-ordained sexual categories, Merleau-Ponty implicitly suggests that each person's sexuality is unique, and thus can be enacted in different ways. This is compatible with the fact that each individual has unique sexual preferences that evade general categorization. As Salamon writes; 'this insistence on particularity frustrates categorical summary; it means that neither sexual embodiment nor situatedness nor expression can be predicted by membership in any particular category of gender or sex' (Salamon 2010, p. 49).

In this respect, sexuality is a form of erotic intentionality (Salamon 2010, p. 49). By this, Salamon means that sexuality is not just an internal feeling, typically located in the sexual organs. Rather, sexuality is intentional insofar as it is about an object in the world (although not purely about it), while constituting an erotic atmosphere around each individual. As de Preester (2013, p. 180) has suggested, the sexual schema brings about a 'sexual world': it gives shape to our body as a sexual entity and bridges the divide between self and other. Our sexuality moves us and connects us with people or things that we desire. Thus, to enact a sexuality is to inhabit a way of relating to the world. In this context, it is possible to speak, as Salomon does, of 'transposition', a notion that she borrows from Merleau-Ponty's phenomenology to illustrate the climax of desire:

Transposition describes the process by which the desire that houses itself in my body becomes my body itself – not held proximately by thought, but felt and experienced (as opposed to only referred to) through and as the body. [. . .] Simultaneously, my body, in its desire, becomes desire itself. The flesh of it is felt only as an animated leaning, intentional in the sense that the desire animating it has an object – it is desire to the extent that it is desire of – but also intentional in that my sense of it coalesces around a purposeful being towards this desired object. My body becomes a leaning or a yearning, a propulsive force that negates any sense of my body as solid or still, or indeed as mine, in that this sensation owns me more than I own it. (Salamon 2010, p. 52)

According to Salamon, sexual desire underpins a sense of orientation to the desired object that simultaneously turns the body into an affective, erotic force that is less conscious of itself than of the coalescence between one's body and the body of the other. In this sense, the notion of 'transposition' indicates the sense of immersion in an erotic atmosphere that is sustained by the sexual schema in forms and manners that are unique and often unconscious to each of us.[16] However, while the sexual schema is subject-dependent, the way in which we understand and interpret our sexual desires and experiences is also connected to the conceptual framework that operates in a historical-cultural world, through which distinct forms of sexuality are made intelligible and even normalized.

This aspect represents the cornerstone of Foucault's influential work on sexuality, which is concerned with the practices and norms that inform discourse about sexuality. For example, Foucault notably refers to the fact that the category of 'sexual pervert' was created to capture and group together deviant forms of sexual desire and sexual activity, including homosexuality. To this end, Foucault refers to the practices of medicalization that were meant to 'normalize' or 'cure' sexual deviants (an extreme example of this being gay conversion therapy). In a way, this regulation of sexuality is frequent in popular culture, from pop music and Hollywood movies to children's stories and games, all of which explicitly or implicitly assume a heterosexual orientation. In this context, Ahmed thematizes queer sexuality in terms of the dynamic and conflicting relation between sexuality and social norms.

Central to Ahmed's study is a focus on the concept of 'orientation'. Ahmed examines how we find ourselves in the world – how the world appears to us and the directions it points us in –, and how we manage to orient ourselves in it, i.e. how we 'find our way' (or, alternatively, 'lose ourselves') in a place that can be hostile to individual sexual predispositions and desire. In Ahmed, sexual orientation is characterized by the overlap between two directions: the directionality of desire, which is characterized by specific sexual preferences, and the normativity of desire, which concerns how we evaluate sexual desire and make assumptions about the 'right' or 'wrong' forms of attraction. In this sense, on Ahmed's view, heterosexuality is both a sexual preference and an implicit normative standard, where 'straight' refers to the standard form of sexual orientation against which the homosexual orientation appears to be deviant ('bent'). As she writes: 'Sexuality itself can be considered a spatial formation not only in the sense that bodies inhabit sexual spaces, but also in the sense that bodies are sexualized through how they inhabit space [. . .]. Phenomenology helps us to consider how sexuality involves ways of inhabiting and being inhabited by space' (Ahmed 2006, p. 67).

On Ahmed's reading, one's sense of orientation in the world necessarily presupposes confronting and deviating from certain well-trodden paths that are laid out in advance. In this regard, Ahmed offers several examples of ordinary language that reveal the ambiguity of the notion of direction, namely, its being utilized both as an ordinary notion and as the norm against which deviations are evaluated. Life itself has a temporal direction (as an arrow) that one must follow, through a succession of sequential stages that include natural and societal events: birth, childhood, adolescence, early adulthood, job, marriage, family, retirement, death. We speak of people who deviate from pre-established paths as people who 'lose their way', such as the wanderer who quits his job after college or the middle-aged man who returns to his adolescent tastes and fashion. For Ahmed, the notion of a 'direction' in life has a double meaning: it stands for the route through life that one is expected to take as well as for the route that one is told to take (i.e. following directions). The challenge of queerness is that it refuses to align with heterosexual expectations, taking a direction that appears crooked only from the perspective of heteronormativity. On Ahmed's view, 'to act on lesbian desire is a way of reorientating one's relation not just towards sexual others, but also to a world that has already "decided" how bodies should be orientated in the first place' (Ahmed 2006, p. 102).

The main upshot of Ahmed's exploration of the concept of orientation is that it draws attention to the concept of 're-orienting' oneself in the world. This entails coming to terms with how certain directions in one's life are hidden from view, and experiencing the wonder connected with the search of one's sexual identity. As she puts it: 'Becoming a lesbian taught me about how the very point of how life gets directed and how that "point" is often hidden from view. Becoming reorientated [. . .] made me wonder about orientation and how much "feeling at home", or knowing which way we are facing, is about the making of worlds' (Ahmed 2006, p. 20). Following Heidegger, Ahmed argues that being 'thrown' into the world means to find oneself disposed toward objects, other selves, and practical contexts according to different lines of affective relevance. In this context, Ahmed argues that sexual orientation is intrinsic to the comportment or practical stance of self, thereby revealing different affective directions or routes. Even when the direction provided by sexual orientation is not explicit or evident to the self, it remains operative in the way in which one conducts herself towards others as well as towards practical possibilities for action and movement. The fact that such directions are not recognized is an issue that occurs not simply because of the ambiguity of the object of desire, but also and more fundamentally because of the social assumptions that forge one's pre-reflective stance about the direction to take. In this respect, a critical-phenomenology of sexuality aims to conceptualize sexual orientation as a manner of residing in the world, which often exists in a state of tension with the background beliefs and norms of the natural attitude.

5

Race

Phenomenology of race, racialization, and mestiza *consciousness*

If YOU do not reclaim the man who is before you, how can I assume that you reclaim the man that is in you? If YOU do not want the man who is before you, how can I believe the man who is perhaps in you?
                    Frantz Fanon, 'The North African Syndrome'

It's not because the Indo-Chinese discovered a culture of their own that they revolted. Quite simply this was because it became impossible for them to breathe, in more than one sense of the word.
                    Frantz Fanon, *Black Skin, White Masks*

The struggle has always been inner, and is played out in outer terrains. Awareness of our situation must come before inner changes, which in turn come before changes in society. Nothing happens in the 'real' world unless it first happens in the images in our heads.
          Gloria Anzaldúa, *Borderlands/La Frontera: The New Mestiza*

Like the phenomenology of gender, the phenomenology of race has important historical and societal implications. Recently, the explosion of the Black Lives Matter movement, spearheaded by the acquittal of George Zimmerman for the murder of Trayvon Marvin in 2012 and the killing of George Floyd in 2020, has brought debates about institutional racism, racial injustice and everyday experiences of racism to the forefront of Anglo-American scholarship. Such debates, however, have a long history, from the abolitionist movements of the nineteenth century, through the civil rights and Black power struggles of the mid-twentieth century, to the 1999 Stephen Lawrence Inquiry's finding in the UK. Such events and issues reflect W. E. B. Du Bois' claim that the 'problem of the twentieth century is the problem of the color-line' (Du Bois 2007, p. 8). In his seminal *The Souls of Black Folk* (1903), Du Bois draws attention, from both a sociological and philosophical perspective, to the condition of Black people in the United States, confronting the legacy of slavery and the racial segregation of Jim Crow laws. In this sense, the colour-line is a synonym for the racial segregation that existed in the United States long after the abolition of slavery, having a long-lasting impact in the twenty-first century as well.

At the same time, the colour line is also a metaphor for the divisions of humanity and the inequities based on race, as reflected by the development of Critical Race Theory. This approach to legal studies originated in the 1970s in the United States as an academic movement of legal and civil-rights scholars, who brought to light the role of race in American legal culture and, more extensively, in American society (Crenshaw et al. 1995, p. xiii). In this respect, Critical Race Theory seeks to highlight the social and institutional dynamics of racism and racial injustice, challenging the idea that racism is just a problem of individual, subjective attitudes.

As we shall see, a critical-phenomenological approach to race makes important contributions to the analysis of race in relation to both subjective attitudes and cultural and social structures. Specifically, a critical phenomenology of race helps to uncover the phenomenology of racialization (the attribution of socio-cultural and political meaning to race identity) as well as racist attitudes (where racism refers to the deterministic view that regards human behaviour as conditioned by inherited traits that place certain racial groups in a position of superiority towards other groups classified as inferior). To this end, critical phenomenology uncovers the phenomenon of the white gaze and its relation to the constitution of racialized subjectivities. At the same time, phenomenological explorations of race are not to be confined to the analysis of racialization and racism. A critical phenomenology of race also examines race and racial identity in terms of the constitution of multiple identities that foster a renewed and more complex sense of cultural belonging.

This chapter begins by outlining the core features of phenomenological approaches to race, focusing on race as both a 'visible identity' and a background horizon that structures the experience of the socio-cultural world. We illustrate the key tenets of Frantz Fanon's existential-phenomenological approach to race and his analysis of racialization, including Fanon's account of alienation and his critique of the concept of recognition. Fanon's insights are then expanded by considering contemporary critical-phenomenological accounts of the white gaze and racializing styles of perception. We conclude the chapter by discussing racial identity in terms of belonging to multiple cultural worlds and border crossing, drawing on Gloria Anzaldúa's concept of *mestiza* (mixed) consciousness and Mariana Ortega's view of multiplicitous self.

5.1 The phenomenological approach to race

From a methodological point of view, the relation between phenomenology and race is twofold. On the one hand, the most relevant phenomenological exploration of race, combined with a critique of racist ideology, can be found in Frantz Fanon. On the other hand, the phenomenology of race is indebted to contemporary critical phenomenological approaches that tackle race in relation to both racializing attitudes as well as to the concept of racial identity. By and large, the main critical starting point for a phenomenology of race is one that is shared with a phenomenology of gender. This is the claim that phenomenological investigations cannot ignore the role played by race within an existential situation and in relation to empirical subjectivity. Like gender, race represents a contingent and non-deterministic element of the self that is often neglected or non-thematized in the natural attitude. At this level, two important clarifications are necessary.

First, the phenomenology of race cannot be conducted in sharp isolation from the phenomenology of gender, given the significant, complex ways in which both race and gender intersect as axes of social identity, as intersectional theorists like Kimberlé Crenshaw (2012) and Patricia Hill Collins (2000) have pointed out. Second, the 'reality' of race should not be mistaken for a naturalistic or biological category. There is indeed no biological or genetic basis for separating humans into the modern racial categories we employ (Atkin 2012, pp. 33ff). To quote Gutmann: 'There is no genetic evidence that would justify grouping people who commonly identify each other as black and white into two different races' (Gutmann 1996, pp. 116–17). Rather, as Alcoff notes, racial groupings are based on 'biologically insignificant physical attributes such as skin color, the shape of the nose or eyes, of hair type' (Alcoff 2006, p. 164). In this sense, race is a social construct that does not map onto any biologically significant features.[1] A substantial debate thus concerns whether we should avoid using the concept of race altogether, or rather retain it as a social construct, as an important aspect of a person's social identity (e.g. Appiah 1996, 2006; Outlaw 1996; Shelby 2005; Zack 1993, 2002; Mills 2014).

The phenomenology of race is concerned with the critique of a 'colour-blind' account of experience and social identity, which significantly overlooks the reality of race as a historical and socio-cultural phenomenon. In this sense, the notion of race builds on a complex and fine-grained stratification of historical and cultural heritage, lineage, and social experience. To ignore or dismiss race altogether means to also ignore the plurality of cultural heritage that is deposited across generations in the formation of racial identity across different countries. Furthermore, a 'colour-blind' approach runs the risk of ignoring the history of power relations that are connected to racialization and racist ideologies, including the socio-political claims of historically disadvantaged communities under systemic racist structures. For these reasons, the phenomenology of race focuses on the experiential character of race as well as on its socio-political implications. In this sense, from a phenomenological perspective, it can be said, as argued by Alcoff, that race is personally and socially 'real' in a non-deterministic and non-naturalistic manner.

More specifically, Alcoff argues that race does not represent a metaphysical category or a natural difference, but rather a socially acquired framework that 'runs through the domain of the visible (Alcoff 2006, p. 188). In this regard, Alcoff describes race as a background horizon rather than a theme or object of perception. This means that race 'helps constitute the necessary background from which I know myself. It makes up a part of what appears to me as the natural setting of all my thoughts. It is the field, rather than that which stands out' (Alcoff 2006, p. 188). On Alcoff's view, race has a horizontal structure in that it provides individuals with an epistemic access to their position and participation in the social world. As such, race is informed by social and historical beliefs, but it also subjectively developed and carried out. For this reason, however, racializing attributions to self and others are also difficult to discern, since they stem from a background that is normally taken for granted and goes unnoticed in an individual's experience.

To illustrate the habitual nature of racializing attributions, Alcoff draws on Merleau-Ponty's concept of the 'habitual body', which she defines as 'the concept of a default position the body assumes in various commonly experienced circumstances that integrates and unifies our movements through a kind of unconscious physical shorthand' (Alcoff 2006, p. 184). It will be recalled from Chapter 2 that, for Merleau-Ponty, the habitual body is a flexible and adaptable system of orientation based on the body schema, which organizes, on a pre-reflective level of experience, our movements and bodily responses to the environment. In this way, the body schema facilitates the body's effortless and spontaneous interaction with the surrounding world. On this view, the habitual body represents a 'default position', as Alcoff writes, which is both context- and subject-dependent. This entails that the body takes on culturally and socially acquired gestures, postures, body images.

Such a view has a two-fold implication for Alcoff. On the one hand, the body is not a passive receptacle upon which cultural and social meaning (including racializing attributions) can be inscribed in a deterministic way, namely without any awareness or response on the part of subjectivity. The advantage of the phenomenological approach is that it allows for a more complex, fine-grained view of subjectivity. This is a view of self that is not externally conditioned by power relations all the way through, but rather preserves degrees of awareness and flexibility even on a pre-reflective level of experience. On the other hand, the flexibility and adaptability of the habitual body also suggest that racializing attributions are always constituted in a relational framework, namely, in a distinct social and cultural milieu. This indicates that racializing attitudes and behaviour are acquired and enacted habitually through a dynamic and relational process that involves both the subject and the social context.

While one of the sources of racialization has to do with subjective attitudes, racialization is also a significant socio-historical phenomenon. In this sense, racialization occurs when the body's visible identity is used as a category or social marker in a system of social relations that systematically disempower racial groups at the expense of the racial majority, which is – in the socio-political and geographical area we are examining – that of whites. In this context, Charles Mills had argued that racialization is not only a subjective phenomenon, as it is systematically connected to the historical development of modern capitalism. Thus, the reality of race is connected to class inequality, namely to the distribution of wealth as well as of differential access to economic and social opportunities.[2]

In an important way, racialization is also related to the political and economic history of institutionalized racism (such as, in the United States, the history of racial segregation),[3] and its impact is still prevalent today. An important example of this is the frequency with which Black people bear the brunt of police brutality in the United States, as testified by the killing of Black youth. Prominent examples, among many others, include Amadou Diallo, whose wallet was mistaken for a gun in 1999, and Tamir Rice, whose toy gun was taken for a real gun in 2014 (see Yancy 2017, p. 6 for further discussion of this). From a critical-phenomenological point of view, subjective attitudes and systematic practices of discrimination are reciprocally connected. It is precisely because the field of perception is not immune to racializing beliefs that one fails to interpret the behaviour of a person that belongs to a racialized group.

This phenomenon is highlighted by Butler's concept of the 'racial saturation of the field of visibility', which she originally used in relation to the claim made by the defence attorneys for the police in the Rodney King case.[4] The defence claimed that Rodney King, a Black man caught on camera in 1991 as Los Angeles policemen circled him and beat him up with batons, endangered the police. That the video could be used as evidence of violence on the part of the man that suffered violence calls into question, for Butler, the fact of seeing Blackness. More specifically, Butler raises the concern as to whether what is seen is part of a 'racialized *episteme*', namely a set of beliefs and assumptions that influence perception to the point that seeing becomes inseparable from the attribution of intents governed by racial constraints. As Butler points out, 'this is not a simple seeing' but 'the working of racial constraints on what it means to see' (Butler 1993b, p. 16).

Butler's notion of the racial saturation of the field of visibility can be understood in terms of controlling images. Defined by Patricia Hill Collins as hegemonic stereotypes that condition the perception of Black women as fitting distinct types of domesticated, gendered, and highly sexualized behaviour, controlling images inform not simply the social presentation of individuals in interpersonal encounters, but also the background of social contexts (Patricia Hill Collins 2000, 2020). As we shall see, one important effect of a critical-phenomenological approach to race is that it brings to the fore the role played by such background beliefs in perception, and how they affect the experience of the subjects who are at the receiving ends of racializing styles of perception. In this way, it is possible to understand how 'race', as a category of the visible, operates at the level of the background horizon of one's attitude, and how it is connected to the concept of the 'white gaze'.

From this point of view, one of the tasks of a phenomenology of race is to articulate the concept of race across a manifold of experiences: as the background horizon that informs the constitution of racial identity; as the racial constraint that informs the field of perception; and ultimately as the experience of living across borders that are, in fact, different cultural worlds and ways of enacting one's social identity. From this, we can see that race is both highly visible – as the external marker of a social identity – and almost invisible – as part of the background process by which one's being-in-the-world is informed.

5.2 Fanon on the 'fact of Blackness'

5.2.1. Fanon's phenomenology of race

The exploration of race and racial identity is central to the work of Frantz Fanon, one of the most important thinkers of the twentieth century. Fanon was a prolific writer, producing a large oeuvre despite his untimely death at the age of 36. Born on the island of Martinique (a French colony at the time), Fanon worked primarily as a psychoanalyst and psychiatrist, but he was also active as a writer, philosopher, and political activist. In this respect, Fanon is best known as a major figure in anti-colonial struggles, particularly in Algeria, where he was actively involved in the Front de Libération National (FNL), though his influence extends far beyond that. His last work, *The Wretched of the Earth* (1961), which includes a famous preface by Sartre,[5] is based on his experience as a psychiatrist at a hospital outside Algiers as well as on his political involvement for the cause of African decolonization (Fanon 1963). In his writing, Fanon fuses existentialism, phenomenology, and psychoanalysis, producing a powerful account of the lived experience of Black people forced to live in a white cultural world. Indeed, one of Fanon's overarching aims was precisely to understand, describe, and vindicate the reality of Black subjects under colonialism (Gordon 2015). This theme is already developed in his first major work, *Black Skin, White Masks* (*Peau Noire, Masques Blancs*), which he published in 1952 at the age of only 27, when Fanon was studying medicine and psychiatry in France.

As a writer who lived and studied in France, Fanon was immersed in European culture, while also belonging to the West Indian world and fighting for the decolonization of African countries. Deeply informed by existentialist theories, Fanon rejected, like Sartre and Beauvoir, 'all ontology that puts existence to the wayside' (Gordon 1995, p. 35). To put it differently, Fanon rejected metaphysical and philosophical views of being and experience based on abstraction and idealization from human, situated condition. As in line with Sartre's early works, Fanon agrees that 'existence precedes essence', in the sense that there are no pre-given or in-built essential characteristics that define human subjectivity. Instead, human essence is defined by the sedimentation of the projects one chooses and commits to. However, this does not mean that subjectivity is the product of surrounding circumstances. Instead, Fanon argues, like Beauvoir and Sartre, that 'we ought to recognize and respect the structure of human existence' (Webber 2018, p. 152), including the development of one's relation to values and motives for action. At the same time, Fanon puts forward an account of Blackness that challenges the unquestioned premises surrounding race and racial privilege in European discourse. As noted above, in setting up the task of analysing the phenomenon of racial alienation occurring in a colonial regime, Fanon takes into account psychological, psychoanalytic, and philosophical sources, claiming the necessity of adding 'sociogeny' (the analysis of social evolution and development) to 'philogeny' (the study of evolutionary development) and 'ontogeny' (the analysis of biological genesis and development) (Fanon 1986, p. 13).

In outlining such a project, Fanon raises an implicit critique against the psychoanalytic methods of his time, which he found vitiated by evolutionary and biological assumptions, rendering impossible the use of psychology for the thematization and acknowledgement of the humanity of Black subjects. Fanon's worry is that psychoanalysis ended up naturalizing psychic complexes and syndromes instead of contextualizing them within specific institutional practices and discourses. As Fanon shows, an exclusive psychoanalytic analysis of consciousness fails to identify, reconstruct, and assess the internalization of the white gaze, its pervasiveness and sedimentation across all aspects of social life, and its contribution to an enduring structural system of oppression. Fanon's approach to this set of problems is well illustrated by his discussion of 'The "North African Syndrome"' in 1952.

In reporting the clinical encounters between physicians and North African immigrants in France, Fanon documents the systematic indifference and gaslighting to which Black patients were subjected by European doctors. Not only were their symptoms given little attention or concern, the reality of their pain and suffering was also fundamentally denied: 'The North African's pain, for which we can find no lesional basis, is judged to have no consistency, no reality. Now the North African *is* a-man-who-doesn't-like-to-work. So that whatever he does will be interpreted a priori on the basis of this' (Fanon 1994, p. 6). For Fanon, the North African Syndrome epitomizes the widely shared set of biased beliefs about African people held by European physicians. Fanon is very clear that such a lack of care was not due to difficulties of communication, as interpreters were available to translate the reports of African patients. Rather, the problem concerned the attitude of doctors and their 'a priori' assumptions. The Black patient did not set foot in the doctor's office as an ordinary patient awaiting clinical care. Their appearing on the scene is like entering a 'pre-existing framework', where the telling of the patient's experience is met with distrust and diffidence. This signals that the physician has already made up his mind about the Black patient before the patient has even told his story. In this case, racial prejudice reflects, according to Gordon, bad faith, to use Sartre's view of inauthenticity that we explored in Chapter 3 (Gordon 1995). The idea, in this case, is that bad faith results from a commitment to not question the values and projects that consistently inform one's attitude.[6]

Thus, Fanon's critique is that the French medical staff were unable to diagnose North African patients, as if their field of visibility was blocked or racially saturated (as Butler would argue). The patient was treated *as* a socially constructed African, rather than as a human being having a history and medical condition of her own.[7] In this sense, the North African Syndrome reflects both (a) a consolidated and institutionalized pattern of neglect and indifference towards the patient's needs; and (b) the failure of the medical community to practise medicine itself, as medicine requires that one ought to treat the patient first and foremost as a human being. It follows that the syndrome described by Fanon is somewhat ironically turned on its head, as it rests with the European rather than the African mind.

The essay on 'The "North African Syndrome"' reads as a further development of the theory that Fanon illustrates in *Black Skin, White Masks* (1952). In this work, Fanon's diagnosis of the condition of the Black man under the colonial regime in the Antilles is that 'the Black is not a man' (Fanon 1986, p. 10). By this, Fanon refers to the reduction of the notion of humanity to European cultural standards of civilization, which aim to 'educate' different cultures and societies. This means that, insofar as society tells colonized people to be good, it tells them to be white, rather than Black (Yancy 2017).[8] Echoing Beauvoir's account of woman's alienation, Fanon maintains that the alienation of Black people in the colonies is characterized by the foreclosure of the subject's existential projection into the world. At the core of the shrinking of the Black's man existential horizon is, according to Fanon, the fact that Black people in the colonies adopt the racializing styles of seeing and behaviour prevailing in their social environment. Being subjected to the endless repetition and presentation of racialized cultural models, from the movies to newspapers and everyday institutionalized discriminatory practices, Black people in the colonies manifested disturbances of self-perception as well as a conflictual relation towards fellow Black people. Such alterations correlate to the consolidated patterns of identifying whiteness with the standard of behaviour and character.

Fanon proceeds by examining this phenomenon from a psychoanalytic viewpoint, noting the correlations between racialization and psychological complexes, such as the inferiority complex described by Alfred Adler's in *Understanding Human Nature* (1927). On Adler's view, the inferiority complex represents the internalization of feelings of unworthiness due to experiences of neglect and abandonment that make people feel, at a very young age, inferior to others, as if they are less equipped to deal with practical situations than their peers. Adler drew attention to the connection between pedagogical methods, parental behaviour, and the internalization, on the part of children, of feelings of shame, insecurity, and longing to be accepted by adults. As he puts it: 'A child gets the impression that he is a nobody, without rights; that he is to be seen, not heard; that he must be courteous, quiet, and the like' (Adler 2013, p. 71). Adler's thesis is that feelings of inadequacy and insecurity are part of a compensation mechanism, whereby the subject attempts with all her might to master the complex and to be accepted in social life as her ultimate aspiration.[9]

Fanon contends that psychoanalysis fails to take into account the social system in which psychological complexes arise. The application of Adler's inferiority complex to Black people in the colonies would, in fact, infantilize Black subjects instead of making intelligible the structural system of oppression to which they were exposed. Turning upside down Adler's theory, Fanon argues that the 'so-called dependency complex' reflects the relation between self-perception and racialization: 'There is a fact: White men consider themselves superior to Black men. There is another fact: Black men want to prove to white men, at all costs, the richness of their thought, the equal value of their intellect. How do we extricate ourselves?' (Fanon 1986, p. 12). The phenomenon that Fanon describes here is reminiscent of the concept of 'double-consciousness' diagnosed by W. E. B. Du Bois, which occurs when Black people see themselves through the lenses of anti-Blackness. Du Bois articulates this concept in *The Souls of Black Folk* (1903), where he characterizes 'double-consciousness' as a 'sense of always looking at oneself through the eyes of others, of measuring one's soul by the tape of a world that looks on in amused contempt and pity' (Du Bois 2007, p. 3). Du Bois describes double-consciousness as an effect of racial alienation, which produces a split in consciousness, whereby the subject despises and devalues herself. This also contributes to a schism in terms of socio-political identity: 'One ever feels his twoness – an American, a Negro; two souls, two thoughts, two unreconciled strivings; two warring ideals in one dark body, whose dogged strength alone keeps it from being torn asunder' (Du Bois 1903, p. 3). According to Du Bois, being Black is a strife that is based on the dialectical relation between self- and other understanding. The idea of a 'better and truer self' (Du Bois 2007, p. 3) is an achievement that does not aim either to meet the impossible standards of white ideology or to impose a counter-ideology ('to Africanize America', ibid). Instead, Du Bois affirms the need of the socio-political recognition of the Black subject as 'both a Negro and an American, without being cursed . . . without having the doors of Opportunity closed roughly in his face' (Du Bois 2007, p. 3).

Fanon explores the ramifications of double-consciousness in an existential-phenomenological fashion, showing the relation between racialization and the subject's affective and practical orientation. In this context, Fanon notes how feelings, love, and sexual desire are thwarted by the aspiration to be accepted by whites (Fanon 1986, pp. 41ff). In so doing, Fanon shows that the longing for recognition of Black people was not simply the result of a dependency complex, but rather an induced and constructed feeling that was used to manipulate the sense of agency and self-worth of Black subjects. In this way, the dependency complex described by Fanon is synonym for a twofold form of alienation that affects, in different ways, Blacks and whites simultaneously. On the one hand, colonialism and the white ideology that sustains it alienate Black folks from the recognition of their own cultural and social identity, disempowering communities by eroding their sense of agency and reciprocal solidarity. On the other hand, the superiority complex of white people reflects the bad faith of the whites and their fear to confront the system of reality they themselves have created, a system in which white people lose their humanity and authenticity by attempting to deprive Black people of theirs.

From a phenomenological point of view, it is important to stress that Fanon does not present the dependency complex of Black people as a mechanical phenomenon that externally conditions Black bodies, but rather as a fine-grained process that occurs when one's body schema is altered as a result of racialization. To account for this, Fanon employs Jean Lhermitte's concept of the body schema, drawing especially from Merleau-Ponty's phenomenological approach to this concept, which we illustrated in Chapter 2. While Fanon acknowledges that the body schema refers to the flexibility and responsiveness of the body towards the outer world, he also focuses on its relational character. As the body schema is a dynamic and contextual phenomenon, it does not only register contextual cues, but it also interprets and understands them. The movements executed through the body schema are indeed made 'not out of habit but of implicit knowledge' (Fanon 1968, p. 111). Like Merleau-Ponty, Fanon argues that the existential projection in the world made possible by the body schema entails the sedimentation of acquired styles of behaviour, which includes former beliefs and pre-reflective understanding. Thus, the body schema is not a sheer ensemble of motor impulses or reflexes, but a sensorimotor form of attunement to the world.

As Fanon writes: 'In the white world the man of color encounters difficulties in the development of his body schema. Consciousness of the body is solely a negating activity. It is a third-person consciousness. The body is surrounded by an atmosphere of certain uncertainty' (Fanon

1986, p. 110). In describing the experience of racialization, Fanon refers to the moment when the Black person meets the white person' eyes, and how this encounter becomes a source of self-estrangement. The shift from the first-person viewpoint to the impersonal, third-person perspective indicates that the racialized subject does not relate to himself or herself as a subject of feelings, desires, and action, that is, as in a positive or affirmative manner. Rather, one's body is perceived as what it is not (not-white), and hence consciousness of the body is 'solely a negating activity'. Thus, racialization coincides with the phenomenon illustrated by Sartre's notion of the body-known-by-the-other. In one of the most famous passages of the book, Fanon recounts an episode of being pointed at in the street by a white kid, and being called by a racial slur. It is worth quoting at length Fanon's account of his own response:

> I made up my mind to laugh myself to tears, but laughter had become impossible. I could no longer laugh, because I already knew that there were legends, stories, history, and above all historicity, which I had learned about from Jaspers. Then, assailed at various points, the corporeal schema crumbled, its place taken by a racial epidermal schema. [. . .] I was responsible at the same time for my body, for my race, for my ancestors. I subjected myself to an objective examination, I discovered my blackness, my ethnic characteristics; and I was battered down by tom-toms, cannibalism, intellectual deficiency, fetishism, racial defects, slave-ships, and above all else, above all: 'Sho' good eatin'.' On that day, completely dislocated, [. . .] I took myself far off from my own presence, far indeed, and made myself an object. What else could it be for me but an amputation, an excision, a haemorrhage that spattered my whole body with black blood. But I did not want this revision, this thematization. All I wanted was to be a man among other men. I wanted to come lithe and young into a world that was ours and to help to build it together. (Fanon 1986, pp. 112–13)

Fanon refers to the 'crumbling of the corporeal schema', which is ultimately 'replaced by a racial epidermal schema'. The alienating process that Fanon describes in this passage can be understood not only along the lines of the inhibition of motor intentionality, as in Young's feminist account. The epidermal schema does not involve motility but rather visibility and contact.[10] As such, the contraction of the body schema to which Fanon gestures here involves a rupture of the natural 'transaction' (to borrow from Sullivan 2001) between body and world. This rupture simultaneously turns bodily experience into an objectifiable reality. Note, however, that this phenomenon describes the experiential qualities of alienation; it is not a claim about the nature of the body or subjectivity. The racialized self does not lose one's distinctive sense of mineness, as Fanon emphasizes by reclaiming the ownership of his experience as well as his resistance to the objectifying look of the other. Racial alienation, as Fanon describes it, involves loss of practical freedom, annihilation of human dignity, and trauma, but it does not annihilate the sense of being the centre of one's experiences, even when these are traumatic and distressing.

Indeed, Fanon explicitly characterizes racial alienation as a shock and a trauma, as testified by his references to painful and harrowing experiences like 'amputation', 'haemorrhage', and body splitting that accompany the sudden re-presentation of the history of racism and racialization that is sedimented on the Black body. From this point of view, the crumbling of the body schema represents the obstruction of motor agency that is caused by the experience of seeing oneself as an objectified reality for the white man, that is, as a fixed and degrading representation of one's whole race. In this context, Fanon describes racial trauma as a 'dislocation' that occurs in time rather than space. Indeed, Fanon refers to a sense of being displaced across history, as a whole stratification of racist ideology about African culture and civilization is simultaneously re-enacted in the present and thrown back at him, as the representative of that cultural world, in the racial slur. In this way, racial alienation simultaneously identifies individuality with a class or group of subjects, abstracting from the personal qualities of the subject, while also projecting onto that individual a caricature of his lineage, traditions, and historical milieu.

According to Yancy, racialization and racism contradict the Existentialist thesis that existence precedes essence (Yancy 2017). From an existentialist viewpoint, subjectivity cannot be categorized or apprehended through static and categorical essences, as the subject manifests herself through the projects that define her coming to terms with the contingency of a situation. Racial alienation, however, is the reversal of this thesis, as Black consciousness is in fact 'confiscated' from its fields of possibilities and made to coincide with a false representation. Thus, Fanon's analysis points to the fact that racism and racialization cannot be reduced to a subjective attitude but must be situated in a socio-cultural context in which those very false representations flourish and are historically maintained.

5.2.2 Fanon's dialectical view of racial alienation and the struggle for recognition

In the final chapter of *Black Skin, White Masks*, Fanon presents an account of alienation and recognition between Blackness and whiteness that aims to open up the possibility of a transformative praxis in which individuals recognize and acknowledge one another beyond the barriers of racialization. In this regard, Fanon puts forward a dialectical model of recognition that is both a descriptive analysis of racial alienation and a transformative project for Black and white people (Bernasconi 2020). In setting out this dialectical model, Fanon draws on Hegel's master–servant allegory (also known as lordship and bondage) in the fourth chapter of Hegel's *Phenomenology of Spirit* (1807). As we mentioned earlier, Hegel's dialectical philosophy informs the theoretical and methodological background of French Existentialism, infused with Marxist elements popularized in France in the 1930s by the lectures of Alexandre Kojève. By and large, Hegel's *Phenomenology of Spirit* is a description of how consciousness achieves knowledge of the truth by going through a series of dialectical confrontations with different types of alterity, including nature, other selves, culture, and religion. While Hegel's concern in this book is fundamentally metaphysical (as he aims to lay out a theory of truth), the first four chapters of the *Phenomenology of Spirit* take into consideration the point of view of a finite consciousness that confronts reality in an immediate and unreflective way; thus, without having developed any theory about itself yet. Most notably, in the first half of the fourth chapter, Hegel presents the famous antagonistic encounter between two consciousnesses who perceive one another against the backdrop of natural life; that is, as two living beings. Hegel's general argument here is that consciousness does not immediately acknowledge another self as equal to itself, despite sensing on an affective level (what Hegel calls desire) that the other is an independent being, and not a sheer thing.[11] The attempt to achieve recognition from the other as a self-sufficient being engenders a life-and-death struggle in which each consciousness seeks to prove to the other its worth by risking life.

Of these two consciousnesses, the one who is not afraid of risking life until the end establishes itself as the master over the other, who becomes a servant. The servant thus exists as an object for the master in an alienating condition that negates consciousness' original independence. Yet Hegel famously argued that out of such a condition of alienation the servant achieves self-consciousness and freedom of mind by engaging, through his own labour, the surrounding world. Hegel's objective in this section is to show that self-consciousness arises out of a conflicting confrontation with another subject. Such a conflictual and negative situation ultimately motivates consciousness to achieve awareness of oneself as a thinking self. Thus, through labour, consciousness is led to experience its practical capacities and to relate, via the mediation of material reality, to its own being. This provides the basis for more robust forms of knowledge and practical action, a process that is, however, developed throughout the further stages of the *Phenomenology of Spirit*.

A socio-political interpretation of Hegel's allegory informs Sartre's and Beauvoir's respective accounts of alienation in *Anti-Semite and Jew* and *The Second Sex*, as they directly evoke the scenario of the master–servant allegory outlined by Hegel in order to illustrate the 'othering' of Jews and women. In this respect, Fanon's reading of Hegel was certainly mediated by Sartre's philosophy as well as by Alexandre Kojève's lectures on Hegel, though it is not established whether Fanon had directly read Hegel or Beauvoir's *The Second Sex* (as he was familiar with Beauvoir's work).[12] Whether Fanon was directly acquainted with Hegel's *Phenomenology of Spirit* or not does not impact the argument he makes in *Black Skin, White Masks*, as Fanon follows the Marxist reading of the parable of the master and the servant to make a claim about social recognition and emancipation. To this end, Fanon focuses on two key aspects of Hegel's allegory that are also connected to Beauvoir's argument in *The Second Sex*: the conflictual character of recognition and the relevance of reciprocity.

The first aspect is connected to Hegel's seemingly negative appraisal of interpersonal experience. On Hegel's view, basic or elementary recognition between two embodied selves is essential for actualizing individual self-awareness. This is what Hegel means by the famous assertion that 'self-consciousness achieves its satisfaction only in another self-consciousness' (Hegel 1977, p. 110). This longing for recognition, which Hegel calls desire, and that Fanon aptly calls 'the first stage that leads to the *dignity of the* mind' (Fanon 1986, p. 218), is not to be confused with Adler's passive mechanism of being accepted or validated by others. Both Hegel and Fanon argue that subjectivity desires to know itself, and this eventually leads consciousness to experience – through the confrontation with another's embodied perspective – the limit of one's point of view, but also its irreducible uniqueness. As Fanon writes: 'As soon as I desire, I am asking to be considered' (ibid.). In this sense, desire exposes consciousness to the challenges of being a self among other subjects who are equally unique. As a result of this, it appears that desire is the first and most basic motivation that leads individuals to test their subjective certainty through the encounter with others. This stage is the beginning of a journey that will ultimately conduce consciousness to the recognition of the authentic worth and dignity of subjectivity as a 'universally valid objective truth' (Fanon 1986, p. 218). Thus, by resorting to Hegel's dialectic, Fanon argues that the recognition of human worth is a universal principle that connects individuals of all races. The fact that such a recognition must be achieved is not, for Fanon, an issue. Indeed,

Fanon maintains that freedom must be fought for by challenging oneself in the context of reciprocal, interpersonal relations. The fundamental problem, for Fanon, is that – under the systems of colonialism and white supremacy – it is not possible for Black people to engage the confrontation with other selves on an equal footing. As Black folks are already made to be perceived as 'inferior', they are prevented from even entering the fight described by Hegel. A basic or elementary reciprocity is therefore needed prior to the metaphorical fight or dialectical confrontation so that consciousness can actualize itself.

In this way, Fanon draws attention to an important aspect of Hegel's allegory, which is the fact that the two consciousnesses that initially confront each other, prior to the fight, stand in a symmetric relation to one another. In contrast to this, Fanon's point is that in the colonies there cannot be any dialectical confrontation between two different, but nevertheless unequal standpoints. In this context, Fanon also shows the ambiguity of the desire for recognition, as this leads consciousness to experience significant setbacks, oscillating between bad faith (desire to be assimilated) and the need to be acknowledged as a thinking and moral subject (Gordon 1995, p. 111). Bad faith is exemplified by the fact that individuals may deceive themselves about the object of their desire, as they project onto one another a certain picture of who they claim to be. By merging different senses of bondage at once (Adler's inferiority complex, Hegel's allegory, slavery), Fanon argues that emancipation is connected to the struggle against oppression, otherwise people in the colonies are forced to remain in a position of subalternity.

In this respect, Fanon's argument is that the mere granting of emancipation does not correspond to the institution of a just socio-political reality, in which the emancipated slave is regarded and effectively treated as equal to whites. This is one of the claims that writer and abolitionist Frederick Douglass raised in his autobiography, *Narrative of the Life of Frederick Douglass, An American Slave* (1845), where he recounts the struggles he faced when he escaped from the plantations of Baltimore to New York in the hope of finding and being met by a world of free equals (Douglass 1982). Instead, Douglass found out that, after the abolition of slavery, Black people in the United States remained in severely deprived socio-economic circumstances, facing racist attitudes, discriminations, and no access to equal job conditions, which were almost similar to slavery conditions. In a similar way, Fanon argues that the abolition of slavery on French soil 'did not make a difference in the Negro. He went from one way of life to another, but not from one life to another' (Fanon 1986, p. 220). Consequently, Fanon points out that sheer proclamations of political equality do not guarantee social equity. This is why the slave must demand his freedom and hence his subjectivity; he must wrestle it from the white master and define it on his own terms.

Without a true struggle for recognition that reclaims both self-worth and equity, there will remain a fundamental alienation from self that affects not only Black folks but also white settlers. The latter are 'sealed in their whiteness' (Fanon 1986, p. 11), unable to confront the reality of their own society. The white mask that is worn to hide the ideology of colonial regimes and racist society is also the mask that hides bad faith. James Baldwin would make a similar claim in his writings, for example in his 1963 *A Talk to the Teachers,* where he claimed that 'in the doing of all this [racial discrimination] for 100 years or more, it is the American white man who has long since lost his grip on reality' (Baldwin 1998, p. 684). Sartre's notion of bad faith, understood as the attempt to avoid responsibility and flee from the call to authenticity, can then be used to illustrate the self-deception of white people and their failure to take up responsibility for the system of inequity they inhabit (Gordon 1995).

In making these arguments, Fanon departs critically from Sartre's approach in *Black Orpheus* (1948), and more generally from Sartre's overall stance towards race and racism. *Black Orpheus* was written as a preface to a poetry anthology edited by Leopold Senghor, one of the founders of the Negritude movement, which was a literary movement that flourished in the Paris of the 1930s and 1940s, where Black writers joined together to explore, affirm, and keep alive African heritage. A key figure in this movement was Aimé Césaire, who coined the term 'negritude' in his poem *Cahier d'un retour au pays nata* (*Notebook of a return to my native land*).

Black Orpheus manifests, at once, Sartre's commitment to the emancipation of Black consciousness as well as to the Marxist cause of emancipation from the systemic inequity produced by capitalism. To this end, Sartre establishes a parallel between the situation of Black people and that of workers in capitalist society, though he also acknowledges that 'the selfish scorn that white people display for Black men has no equivalent in the attitude of the bourgeois toward the working class' (Sartre 2008, p. 295). Thus, Sartre recognizes that the reality experienced by Black people under racist ideology is not the same as the condition of white working-class people under capitalism. Yet Sartre ultimately envisages a class-less and race-less society as the end goal of the emancipation of Black people. Such a view presented the Negritude movement and the affirmation of Black consciousness as a necessary historical moment that would eventually be overcome by the institution of a just and free society for people of all colours (Sartre 2008, p. 48). Sartre's argument in this

Preface reflects a rough application of the Hegelian notion of 'sublation' (*Aufhebung*). Through this concept, Hegel argued that the different negative moments experienced by consciousness in its quest for knowledge and truth are not left behind but rather preserved in a more mature form. By referring to the notion of sublation, Sartre indirectly suggests that a class-less society that builds on the equality of people of all colours does not cancel or remove the past, but rather preserves it in a more mature and just reality.

Fanon agrees with Sartre that an anti-racist society cannot be built on philosophical and humanistic appeals to equality but, instead, through anti-colonial emancipation for all oppressed racial groups. However, Fanon also contends that the dialectical movement that brings about freedom and emancipation requires the recognition of Black subjectivity as an actual reality that cannot be surpassed, either historically or metaphysically, through the lenses of European civilization. For the Black subjects to be free also means to be free by the notion of a historical development that will eventually set them free. As Fanon writes:

> Sartre, in his work, has destroyed Black zeal. In opposition to historical becoming, there had always been the unforeseeable. The dialectic that brings necessity into the foundation of my freedom drives me out of myself. It shatters my unreflected position. Still in terms of consciousness, Black consciousness is immanent in its own eyes. I am not a potentiality of something, I am wholly what I am. I do not have to look for the universal. No probability has any place inside me. My Negro consciousness does not hold itself out as a lack. It is. It is its own follower. (Fanon 1986, p. 135)

Fanon rejects the Sartrean dialectic that idealizes Black cultural achievements as a moment in the quest for emancipation, in which the future is characterized by 'new values' that would actualize Black consciousness. On the contrary, for Fanon the fact of Blackness teaches that the future of Black consciousness is not to be found in the values set forth by European civilization or in the attachment to Black values as opposed to white values. The opposition between Blacks and whites is indeed still part of the ideology of bad faith that keeps Black consciousness subjugated. As Fanon stresses in the final pages of *Black Skin, White Masks*: 'There is no white world; there is no white ethic – any more than there is white intelligence. There are from one end of the world to the other men who are searching' (Fanon 1986, p. 229). This means that the anti-colonial fight for emancipation needs to be grounded on the value of the humanity of both whites and Blacks as they search for meaning in their common history. Elaborating on this point, Jamila Mascat comments: 'anti-colonial revolution aims to establish a new concept of humanity from which no one is excluded and with this regard it escapes the deadlock of identitarianism and expresses a resolute strive for universality' (Mascat 2014, p. 104). That the fight for emancipation is not to be based on 'identitarianism' means that racial identity cannot be reduced to a sectarian or ideological claim. As Fanon suggests, at the end of *Black Skin, White Masks*, 'my black skin is not the wrapping of specific values' (Fanon 1986, p. 227). For this reason, Fanon appeals to body as the reservoir of meaning that leads individuals to question their identity and position in history without falling back into the trap of either assimilation or white liberation. If the ultimate purpose of history is to open up a future that is entirely in the hands of the subject, it is essential that consciousness *owns* itself, re-appropriating its bodily and affective existence and making choices about its future on its own terms. For this reason, the final line of the book reads: 'O body, make of me always a man who questions!' (Fanon 1986, p. 232).

5.3 Racial objectification and racializing styles of perception

5.3.1 The white gaze

In this section, we develop Fanon's reflections on consciousness and embodiment in light of contemporary critical approaches to the phenomenology of race, focusing on the phenomenon of racial objectification and its relation to the notion of the 'white gaze'. We begin with the insights of philosopher, novelist, and political cartoonist Charles Johnson. In his essay, 'The Phenomenology of the Black Body' (1993), Johnson draws from a number of thinkers, including Hegel, Husserl, and Fanon. Central to his discussion is the concept of 'epidermalization', which illustrates the way in which the visibility of skin colour becomes a social marker that reduces individuals to racial stereotypes. Johnson describes the experience of being placed at the centre of such a horizon in a twofold sense: as the subject of his own field of perception, and as the object of the perceptual field of the white person, who either dismisses or fails to recognize him in social contexts (for example as a professor or as a regular customer).

As we have seen, Fanon speaks of the epidermal schema to illustrate the alteration and reification of motor intentionality. Following Fanon, Johnson argues that epidermalization interrupts the expressive and spontaneous relation between consciousness and the outer world: 'the stain of the black body seems figuratively to darken consciousness itself, to overshadow my existence as subject' (Johnson 1993, p. 604). Johnson describes his experience of walking down Broadway and calling into a bar, until he realizes that he is the only Black person in a room filled with white people staring at him: 'Their look, an intending beam focusing my way, suddenly realizes something larval in me. My world is epidermalized, collapsed like a house of cards into the stained casement of my skin. My subjectivity is turned inside out like a shirtcuff' (Johnson 1993, p. 606). The phenomenon described by Johnson echoes Yancy's reflections on the racialization of the 'Black body', which is denied spontaneity and self-expression, as it is 'thrown outward, assigned a meaning not of my intending' (Yancy 2017, p. 60). According to Yancy, racial objectification is part of a larger, historical process of institutional power. As Yancy writes, quoting from Sartre's *Black Orpheus*:

> Describing the hegemonic structure of the white gaze within the context of a larger white supremacist, asymmetrical social and political world, Jean-Paul Sartre writes: 'For three thousand years, the white man has enjoyed the privilege of seeing without being seen: he was only a look – the light from his eyes drew each thing out of the shadow of its birth; the whiteness of his skin was another look, condensed light.' [. . .] It is this privilege and power of seeing without being seen that bespeaks the structural hegemonic orders that position the white body as the bearer of the white gaze and the black body as the object of the white gaze, the seen, the looked at. [. . .] In short, the performative power of the white gaze is inextricably linked to the sedimentation of white racist phantasmagoric productions that are socially and institutionally shared and 'validated' by white people. (Yancy 2020, p. 70)

Yancy draws attention to the position of Black subjects in a power structure ('structural hegemonic order'), whose normative force depends on a socio-historical framework in which the position of the white man *qua* white is hidden or made anonymous, while the positions of people of colour stand out according to the lines of relevance defined by the point of view of white ideology. Thus, Yancy refers to hegemonic power structures as the system of racializing relations that are socio-historically produced, but also maintained and carried out through social mechanisms of projection. This phenomenon occurs when individuals and groups of colour are identified according to the representations that flow in an unthematized socio-cultural background.

To be sure, from a broad, phenomenological point of view, perception of intentional objects always entails perceiving objects *as x, y,* or *f,* that is, according to certain general types that are connected to a shared social background. This suggests that an interpretative moment is implicit in all perceptual acts, as we identify and recognize objects in the surrounding

horizon through perception. However, at stake for Yancy is the mechanism whereby the perceptual moment of recognition (*seeing* someone in
a context, that is, *as* a man but also as a professor or customer or driver)
provides the basis for a racializing attribution that borrows from the
systems of beliefs of the social background (*believing that* the individual
I am looking at cannot be a professor, driver, customer due to his visible,
racial characteristics).

In this respect, Yancy argues that the white gaze is a 'performative
power', namely a process that brings about the reality of the thing seen
through its performance. This means that the system of beliefs and representations projected by the white gaze acquires social validity and reality
through its being shared in a socio-cultural context. Differently put,
Yancy's idea is that racist ideologies create systems of power when they
are upheld by social practices and common sense.[13] A symptom of this
phenomenon involves the higher expectations or standards of behaviour
to which Black people are held in order to prove that they do not fit the
images or stereotypes of racist ideology. In this regard, for example,
Johnson describes the disciplinary or compulsory effect of the white
gaze, and his own heightened sense of vigilance about how he acts and
behaves in public: 'If I am the sort of "Negro" brought up to be a "credit
to the race", I must forever be on guard against my body betraying me in
public' (Johnson 1993, p. 607).

The relation between racializing styles of seeing and disciplinary
behaviour recalls the system of disciplinary power described by Foucault
with regard to sexuality (Foucault 1978; cf. Butler 1997). Foucault refers
to practices of self-scrutinization through which individuals examine
themselves in fear of departing from heterosexual standards. This power
relation is particularly effective because instead of being exerted on people
from the outside, it is exerted by the subject onto himself. In a similar way,
the white gaze exerts a normalizing power upon subjective behaviour
and manners, which Yancy describes in terms of 'confiscation' of Black
bodies. An illustration of this aspect is provided by Yancy's discussion of
the 'elevator effect', whose name derives from Yancy's experience, which
is familiar to many Black men, of being looked at with suspicion and fear
when entering an elevator already occupied by a white woman:

> I walk onto the elevator and she feels apprehension. Her body shifts
> nervously and her heart beats more quickly as she clutches her purse
> more closely to her. [. . .] The space within the elevator is surrounded
> from all sides with my Black presence. It is as if I have become omnipres-
> ent within that space, ready to attack from all sides. [. . .] The point here
> is that deep-seated racist emotive responses may form part of the white

bodily repertoire, which has become calcified through quotidian modes
of bodily transaction in a racial and racist world. (Yancy 2017, p. 21)

The 'elevator effect' portrays the generalization of the phenomenon of
racialization to ordinary daily situations. Helen Ngo discusses the elevator effect in terms of 'coherence of breadth', 'kind', and 'depth' (Ngo
2017, p. 20) to characterize the sedimentation of racializing practices
and beliefs in the ordinary experience of Black men, specifically in the
United States (though the phenomenon of racialization is not restricted
to Black minorities or the United States). Coherence of breadth and kind
refer to the fact that the 'elevator effect' is experienced by a wide range
of Black men in different socio-cultural contexts. Whether the white gaze
occurs in the elevator, in the lobby of one's building, in the parking lot,
or in college, the objectifying effect is of the same kind. Coherence of
depth refers to the fact that Yancy's situation is aligned with a history of
racist practices and representations of Black people in the United States
and beyond, pointing to a deeper relation between racialization and the
socio-cultural background.

In this context, it is important to note that the fear of the woman
in the elevator should not be dismissed too easily, as at stake is also
woman's vulnerability to male violence, hence an intersection of gender
and race. However, as Ngo argues, the white woman's response cannot
be overlooked by the Black man either due to the compulsory and disciplinary power of the white gaze just noted. Differently stated, for those
who have experienced the brunt of racism (like police abuse), the risks
of underestimating the white woman's reaction are not part of an equal
playing field (Ngo 2017, p. 21). Yancy introduces the concept of 'confiscation' to account for the objectification of the Black body as a form of
essentialization, which denies the existential freedom of Black subjects
(Yancy 2020). Confiscation refers, in a literal sense, to the dispropor-
tionate incarceration of Black youth as well as to everyday episodes of
distrust and discrimination, such as when a Black person is followed by
a security guard as she walks through a department store (Yancy 2017,
p. 18). On this basis, racialization operates not only as a process of social
reification, but also as a phenomenon that displaces racialized subjects
both spatially and temporally. This includes the temporal dislocation
illustrated by Fanon earlier, which Yancy describes as the transformation
of the Black body into a battleground that is historically marked and
scripted (Yancy 2017, p. 17).

In an important way, the 'elevator effect' highlights the role of the
white gaze as an unreflective racializing style of perception. As Yancy
notes, racist attitudes and behaviour need not be reflectively held or

carried out in order to be effective. They can be enacted at the level of bodily gestures or styles of behaviour, even when the subject refrains from holding racializing beliefs. Indeed, bodily responses, like gestures, posture, and facial expressions, are expressive in that they signify, with various degrees of indeterminacy, different types of intentions, emotions, and orientations. In this regard, a key issue for the phenomenology of race concerns precisely the relation between habitual embodied responses and social norms. Both Ngo and Yancy emphasize the impact of bodily responsiveness in racially saturated social spaces, gesturing to the moral relevance of enacting somatic changes, like shifting, readjusting, and altering one's bodily stance. However, somatic changes can as well produce more skilful ways of interacting with others in social contexts that are still characterized by what Sartre would call 'bad faith'. In this case, at stake is not only the relational dynamic opened up by shifts of bodily responses but also the critical task that is required, on the part of the subject, to unlearn ingrained social habits. This entails inquiring into the grounds and causes of those habits, bringing to light the connection between one's style of behaviour and the socio-historical context.

5.3.2 The racialization of Muslim veils

The phenomenology of the white gaze is not restricted to the racialization of Black people, as race operates a socio-historical construct that has important implications for groups and minorities of different backgrounds. In this context, Alia Al-Saji offers a phenomenological account of the racialization of Muslim women that illustrates the intersectional character of racialization. Analysing the French debate that led in 2004 to the banning of conspicuous religious symbols in schools, such as the Muslim headscarf, Al-Saji examines the western representations of Muslim women, connecting it to dynamics of both gender and racial objectification.

Referring in particular to the cultural interpretation of the headscarf as a 'veil', Al-Saji contends that, rather than *representing* Muslim women, these images fulfil a different function: they provide the foil or negative mirror in which western constructions of identity and gender can be positively *reflected*' (Al-Saji 2010b, p. 877). According to Al-Saji, the western representation of the Muslim headscarf as a veil is part of a colonialist and orientalist depiction of Muslim women as an oppressed group. Al-Saji's critique calls into question not just western attitudes towards Islam but also the use of feminist arguments in what she calls the dismissal and 'de-subjectification' of the lived experience of Muslim women. At stake 'is a form of cultural racism that hides itself under the guise of anti-sexist and even feminist liberatory discourse' (Al-Saji 2010b, p. 877), which ultimately works to erase the subjectivity of Muslim women by representing them as passive victims of an oppressive ideology.

To account for this phenomenon, Al-Saji draws on Fanon's essay 'Algeria Unveiled' (Fanon 1965), which describes the French colonial project to unveil Algerian women. Fanon suggests that the veil came to represent Algerian culture as a whole, because it was the most visible aspect for the western eye. However, the aim to 'unveil' Algeria was co-extensive with the colonial aim of eroding and dismissing Algerian culture. Specifically, the colonial attempt to unveil Algerian women was, Al-Saji suggests, a 'mirror' or 'foil' that allowed Europeans to secure a positive self-image by placing themselves in opposition to the negative image of the 'native' culture. Insofar as veiled women are represented as oppressed, unveiled women are instead presented as emancipated, sustaining the west's representation of its cultural superiority over non-western cultures. Al-Saji argues that such a cultural and political phenomenon builds on a mechanism of othering that centres on the naturalization of what is hidden or invisible to the western gaze. The veil serves a means for objectifying Muslim women, producing a static and fixed pattern of recognition whereby 'racialized bodies are not only seen as inferior, they *cannot be seen otherwise*' (Al-Saji 2010b, p. 885).

In this regard, Al-Saji argues that vision unfolds by relying on 'sedimented habits of seeing' (Al-Saji 2010b, p. 884). This means that sedimented and acquired beliefs informs our orientation in the perceptual horizon, bringing into relief certain aspects that are more directly connected to former associations we made between values and intentional objects. It is in virtue of the connection between habit, perception, and beliefs that racializing styles of perception are formed and become operative at a pre-reflective level of experience, in analogy with the white gaze described by Johnson and Yancy.

In this context, Al-Saji points out the connection between racialization and sexism. In particular, she draws attention to the fact that the veil is perceived as an obstacle to the visibility of the woman's body, which supports the desirability of unveiling her. According to Al-Saji, this dynamic is twofold, as it simultaneously regards Muslim women as sexualized objects while also claiming to liberate them from their supposed oppression. As a result of this, the veiled Muslim woman is pictured as subjugated, oppressed, and in need of liberation, discarding the role of the headscarf as part of Muslim women's dressing style. As such, the headscarf is a component of Muslim women's bodily expression, which offers a means for different purposes, including protection from the sexist gaze. Instead, within the colonial gaze, 'the veil becomes a *focal point* in the othering of Islam' (Al-Saji 2010b, p. 887) in the sense that the veil simultaneously enables the objectification of Muslim women and the demonization of Islam.

Al-Saji's account reveals the paradox of Muslim women's position, and particularly the racialization of gender. Her analysis of racializing perception is consistent with the ethics of sensibility that we outlined in Chapter 3, specifically Al-Saji's account of hesitation. Hesitation encourages us to slow down, to resist immediate affective responses and associations, and therefore to attend to what is made to appear invisible in the cultural background. This is not to say that hesitation suffices to counter racism and racializing perception, but that it is a necessary and potentially effective part of antiracist work.

5.3.3 The phenomenology of whiteness

The phenomenon of racialization calls into question the phenomenology of whiteness, which has been widely explored in recent years.[14] According to Ahmed, whiteness can be defined 'as a category of experience that disappears as a category through experience' (Ahmed 2007, p. 150). In other words, for Ahmed, whiteness is a social construct that is, however, experienced as 'a background experience' (ibid.) or as a taken-for-granted contextual horizon of everyday life. Typically, white people are not made aware of their racial identity in a social world that does not racialize them. As a result of this, the different forms and ramifications that whiteness acquires in social contexts remain hidden or unthematized.

Following Heidegger, Ahmed argues that 'the white body' finds itself situated in a practical world filled with instrumental meaning, namely with things that one knows how to use in order to achieve certain goals. From this point of view, whiteness is 'an orientation that puts certain things within reach', which includes 'not just physical objects, but also styles, capacities, aspirations, techniques, habits' (ibid.). On Ahmed's account, whiteness is a socially constructed orientation that informs the sense of one's practical possibilities, or lack thereof, as happens when certain things are perceived as out of reach. Ahmed develops this idea by revisiting Merleau-Ponty's idea of the habitual body, as a body that smoothly facilitates action; a body that does not get in the way of action but, rather, is '*behind the action*' (Ahmed 2007, p. 156). Ahmed's argument is that whiteness is like a second nature that informs how individuals experience the world around them as in principle accessible and capable of being navigated. This is not to say that white bodies do not experience differential access to objects in the world due to differences in class, age, disability, nationality, and gender.[15] Ahmed's point is rather that, as long as whiteness informs a subjective orientation, white people are not called upon to confront the *fact* of their whiteness, as people of colour must do. In other words, whiteness remains invisible to white people as a phenomenon, despite offering them such a privileged position, namely that of not being identified with their race in everyday life.

This is what Mills has called 'white ignorance', that is an epistemic disposition that, while not being insuperable or uniformly common among the white population, involves 'not merely ignorance of facts with moral implications but moral non-knowings, incorrect judgments about the rights and wrongs of moral situations themselves' (Mills 2007, p. 22). Moral ignorance, for Mills, implies not simply that one does not know what is ethically required of them in a given situation, but also that one fails to realize that such non-knowing has in itself moral implications. Mills points out that white ignorance is rooted in perception, which relies on individual and social beliefs, as well as on individual and social memory, thereby constituting an epistemic environment (or a belief system) in which particular varieties of racial ignorance flourish.

From a critical-phenomenological viewpoint, white ignorance is connected to the fluidity of action and movement that is familiar to white people. As Ahmed notes, 'whiteness is not a property that white bodies possess but rather a structuring process that makes the world appear white, and therefore "ready" for certain kinds of bodies, as a world that puts certain objects within their reach' (Ahmed 2007, pp. 153–4).[16] Ahmed highlights the way in which white subjects in a predominantly white culture and social space do not have to confront themselves as objects of racializing styles of perception; they are not called into question as 'others' on account of their skin colour, precisely because the racialized world accommodates them. As Sullivan (2006, p. 143) argues in relation to unconscious habits of white privilege: 'far from being a neutral, empty arena in which people of various races are located, space both constitutes and is constituted by white privilege' (Sullivan 2006, p. 143). In contrast to Johnson's description of how Black people need to monitor their outer behaviour and bodily movements, the white body dwells in social spaces, it is at home in them. There is a certain unconsciousness about such movements, as 'all cultural and social spaces are *potentially* available for one to inhabit. The habit of ontological expansiveness enables white people to maximize the extent of the world in which they transact' (Sullivan 2006, p. 25, our emphasis). As Ahmed puts it, the white person's 'reach' is greatly extended in a world that is receptive to them, indeed, is built around them. Naturally, the white person is rarely conscious of this. The feeling of belonging, of being-at-home, is not a feeling that is typically or easily present-to-mind. It is rather like a noise that one does not notice until it is interrupted by unexpected circumstances that challenge ingrained assumptions and expectations.[17]

5.4 *Mestiza* consciousness and the multiplicitous self

As we have shown, racialization is connected to experiences of dislocation and displacement; that is to say, to a fundamental sense of non-belonging to the common, social world that is normally taken for granted. However, as noted at the outset of this chapter, race and racial identity should not be identified with racialization and non-belonging. Quite to the contrary, racial identity can be explored as a rich, complex, and multiple stratification of cultural heritage, social traditions, values, and linguistic repertoire despite and against racialization and racism. In fact, social identities express different affective and cultural forms of belonging, which are not limited to citizenship or to the fact of inhabiting a specific geographic territory. As we pointed out in Chapter 3 in relation to Lugones' account of world-travelling, multiple cultural and social worlds can be travelled in virtue of the cultural identities that co-exist in an individual standpoint. Thus, while the notion of 'racial identity' may implicitly suggest the association with one race, it may in fact be connected to a plurality of ethnic backgrounds. While in Chapter 3 we explored world-travelling as a practice of interpersonal understanding that enriches and potentially transforms intersubjective experience, here we illustrate how Latinx philosophy, specifically Anzaldúa's and Ortega's approaches to racial identity, can be fruitfully employed to explore issues of multiplicity and belonging in the phenomenology of race.

Anzaldúa was born in the Rio Grande Valley of south Texas, which borders Mexico. Her family was of Spanish American and Native American descent and, while her father's family was once (poor) aristocracy, they ended up living in poverty and her father died during her adolescence. Anzaldúa was a cultural theorist, poet, and feminist, whose work explores themes such as borders, belonging, liminality and marginality, sexuality and colonialism. Her work has been taken up by critical phenomenologists to examine gender and racial oppression, sexual identity, and being-with others. An abiding aim of her work is to challenge the construction of barriers, both literal and conceptual, and to encourage the thematization of plural social identities. Her work draws heavily from her own experiences as a form of self-critique, which deconstructs fixed categorizations and explores ways of re-interpreting one's social identity. Indeed, Anzaldúa regards the practice of self-examination and self-transformation as an important part of social transformation. As Keating and González-López (2011, p. 2) note: 'For Anzaldúa, "inner work" and "public acts" are so intimately interrelated as to be inseparable.'

This aspect is reflected in her most famous text, *Borderlands/La Frontera: The New Mestiza* (Anzaldúa 1987), which is a semi-biographical work examining the condition of women in Chicano and Latinx culture. Anzaldúa draws on her life experiences in a border community as a queer intellectual, confronting sexism, racism, and homophobia. Thus, Anzaldúa's work is concerned with different types of borders: between nations, cultures, classes, genders, and languages,[18] with a focus on how bridges can be built across them. This exploration of plural identities is reflected in how *Borderlands/La Frontera* is written, which comprises both poetry and essay-writing in a mixture of languages (including standard Spanish, Chicano Spanish, Mexican Spanish, standard English, slang English, and Mexican Spanish dialect) that intermingle through the text. Thus, the text itself performs this fusing of worlds and bridging of boundaries, reflecting her desire to break down dualisms and categorizations.

As noted above, Anzaldúa's writing reflects a process of self-exploration, which she describes through the image of Shiva, one of the principal deities of Hinduism:

> Think of me as Shiva, a many-armed and legged body with one foot on brown soil, one on white, one in straight society, one in the gay world, the man's world, the women's, one limb in the literary world, another in the working class, the socialist, and the occult worlds. A sort of spider woman hanging by one thin strand of web. Who, me confused? Ambivalent? Not so. Only your labels split. (Anzaldúa 1983, p. 205)

This quote points out Anzaldúa's intention to cross boundaries, and to inhabit multiple, apparently incompatible worlds (e.g. the straight world and the gay world; the working-class world and the literary world). It also captures the possibility of multiple schisms within a person, and possibly between groups of people, as these are generated by the process of labelling and constructing mutually exclusive social categories. In *Borderlands/La Frontera*, Anzaldúa develops this theme through the concept of '*mestiza*' (mixed) consciousness, which refers to her mixed ethnical and racial heritage, as a woman who is both Spanish Caucasian and Central or South American Indian. '*Mestiza* consciousness' is a self who is culturally inclusive, containing a multiplicity of social and cultural identities that merge and clash within one person.

To live as a *mestiza* consciousness means to be open to difference, but also to confusion, ambiguity, and liminality. It also involves engaging with the competing sets of meaning, social values, and practices that are distinctive of the different social identities one travels. As Anzaldúa writes: 'Cradled in one culture, sandwiched between two cultures, straddling all three cultures and their value systems, *la mestiza* undergoes ... a struggle of flesh, a struggle of borders' (Anzaldúa 1987, p. 78). While to live as a *mestiza* is a challenge, it also evokes the possibility of a more complex coexistence between people of different races, ethnicities, sexualities, genders, religions, among other aspects.

Anzaldúa has inspired important phenomenological explorations of racial identity, including Mariana Ortega's work, which is closely connected to both Latinx phenomenology and Heidegger's ontological phenomenology.[19] In this context, Ortega introduces the concepts of 'being-between-worlds' and 'being-in-worlds' to illustrate the situation of individuals of mixed racial and ethnical backgrounds, who find themselves inhabiting multiple, sometimes irreconcilable cultural worlds. According to Ortega, being-between-worlds brings to light the continuous ruptures in everyday life that are experienced by 'the self in the borderlands, or the self that world-travels' (Ortega 2016, p. 50). Ortega's idea is that the self in the borderlands travels between social worlds, negotiating the demands that each context makes of them, and ensuring that they follow the appropriate norms and rules embedded in those contexts. As such, according to Ortega, Dasein's relation to the surrounding world is mediated by an implicit or practical knowledge of social and cultural norms, which are constantly negotiated in crossing the borders of different social frameworks. For example, a Nigerian queer woman attending an English secondary school will have to cope with the social rules that are appropriate within the context of her Nigerian family, but that may not be appropriate in her English secondary school. Ortega's idea is that one does not simply move across different practical contexts but also enacts different social and cultural identities that co-exist in each context that the self navigates. Coping with such demands compels individuals to be more reflective about the social norms they relate to as well as of the activities they carry out, and for this reason there cannot be a homogeneous and continuous form of attunement to the world.

With regard to this, it is essential to clarify the difference between Heidegger's and Ortega's respective approaches. As we illustrated in previous chapters, Heidegger stresses that Dasein's practical concern with the surrounding world is not an uninterrupted practical orientation to the world. The things ready-at-hand that Dasein encounters are part of a holistic network of meaning, as they are the things that Dasein has learned to deal with different practical contexts (Heidegger 2001, p. 191). However, such things can also break, fall apart, and become conspicuous for Dasein. Ortega's worry is that, in Heidegger's account, the interruptions of Dasein's practical orientation are always discrete, that is, they occur as gaps within a fundamental, basic interpretation of the surrounding world. In contrast to this, the traveling-self experiences continuous ruptures in her natural orientation, as she is constantly exposed to the clashes and differences that emerge in the totality of her involvements with the world.

This aspect leads Ortega to concentrate on Heidegger's concept of anxiety, i.e. the experience of not being at home in the world. As we pointed out before, anxiety in Heidegger is a fundamental mood, where moods refer to 'the sense of reality', as Ratcliffe aptly calls it, of subjective experience. The sense of reality underpins the sense of belonging to a world that is normally taken for granted in the natural attitude. In this context, anxiety signals, for Heidegger, the fragmentation of one's natural relatedness to the surrounding context. Ortega points out that 'despite the fact that anxiety is the mood that presents the uncanny in the world, that makes Dasein not feel at home, it is also the mood that allows for the possibility of self-awareness and a life in which the self understands and accepts the responsibility for making choices' (Ortega 2016, p. 53).

The connection between anxiety and the responsibility of choice is central for *mestiza* consciousness. Ortega describes this aspect as the anxiety of not knowing to *which* world one belongs, including the anxiety that accompanies the experience of crossing different worlds. How does a queer writer, born in a disadvantaged and homophobic environment adopt the habits, techniques, and worldviews of her native childhood environment, while also coping with the demands of the Anglophone, academic, and middle-class world that she navigates in her everyday life? Clearly, the choice is not whether one form of comportment is more authentic than the other, as those modes of behaviour intermingle in the stream of one's experience. Yet the co-presence of different and even opposite standards of comportment to which one holds oneself accountable makes the pursuit of authenticity inseparable from inauthenticity in a more radical sense than Heidegger may have suggested. Indeed, *mestiza* consciousness is often, or even always, in a state of unease and of detachment from the world, rather than immersion in it (Ortega 2016, p. 59). As Ortega writes:

> The ruptures in her everyday existence, given her multiple, social, cultural, and spatial locations, prompt her to become more reflective of her activities and her existence, what we may describe as a life of

not being-at-ease. While all selves may experience not being-at-ease occasionally, multiplicitous selves at the margins experience it continuously. (Ortega 2016, p. 60)

According to Ortega, Heidegger's account of anxiety could be enhanced by the 'recognition of and engagement with the experiences of a life of constant ruptures prompted by marginalization and a life at the borders and borderlands' (ibid., p. 61). She refers specifically to the notion of 'multiplicitous selfhood', which she contrasts with the view of self as simply plural (as in Lugones' account). While plurality suggests multiple, distinct, and in principle distinguishable selves, multiplicity 'suggests a complexity associated with one self'. To put it differently, multiplicity highlights the ontological continuity of the self as living across different worlds and dwelling in liminal spaces, insofar as one occupies a number of positionalities in terms of social identities, whether it is through one's race, gender, sexuality, ability, age, nationality, or ethnicity. In this respect, Ortega emphasizes that temporal displacement and unease are constitutive of selfhood.

At the same time, Ortega is keen to stress that experiences of not being-at-ease and being-between-worlds are not wholly, or even predominantly, negative phenomena. In other words, being-between-worlds is not a problem to be solved or escaped, but an ontological condition, which provides the means to bridge differences and construct new, intersectional identities. In this respect, being-between-worlds helps to transcend the antagonisms that imbue many racist or homophobic relations today. Indeed, as Lugones has argued, being immersed in the world, being too at-ease, 'tends to produce people who have no inclination to travel across "worlds" or no experience of "world" traveling' (Lugones 2003, p. 90). In a similar vein, Ortega redefines authentic intersubjectivity as 'critical world-traveling', which consists in an ongoing process of interpretation and evaluation not only of what is learned through traveling but also of the very practices of 'traveling across worlds' (Ortega 2016, p. 131).

6

Social Experience and Political Action

Communal life, political space, and solidarity

Since the man without a state was an anomaly by definition, he was completely at the mercy of the police, which itself did not worry too much about committing a few illegal acts in order to diminish the burden of the undesirable.

Hannah Arendt, *The Origins of Totalitarianism*

If it is the person, or the people, who are deemed dangerous, and no dangerous act need to be proven to establish this as true, then the state constitutes the detained population unilaterally, taking them out of the jurisdiction of the law, depriving them of the legal protection to which subjects under national and international law are entitled.

Judith Butler, *Precarious Life. The Power of Mourning and Violence*

We stated at the outset of this book that critical phenomenology explores phenomenological and existential questions concerned with the relation between self, social experience, and social norms, including the critique of the social presuppositions at stake in such a relation. The themes and arguments thereby provided shed light on how individuals are differently situated in a world that is also extremely conflictual, as it involves unequal power relations and discrimination. In particular, Chapters 4 and 5 illustrated several issues connected to sexism, racialization, and racism. At the same time, we have also shown that critical-phenomenological analyses seek to identify and articulate the dialectical relations between self and world through which social identities become visible without reducing gender or race to experiences of oppression.

In this final chapter, we explore how phenomenology is directly concerned with social and political phenomena. Guiding questions include: What is the nature of a social community, and what are the mechanisms through which individuals and groups may be excluded from it? What contributions can critical phenomenology make to the concept of political action as well as to the thematization of struggles for social justice? As we shall see, this chapter weaves together the themes of embodiment, intersubjectivity, and social identity that we have discussed in the previous chapters, bringing them to bear on political issues and social concerns, such as precariousness and solidarity.

In this context, it is worth stressing that investigations of socio-political experience are not foreign to classical and existential phenomenological discourse. Indeed, phenomenologists of different schools and traditions have long concerned themselves with the description and analysis of 'the political'.[1] This notion encompasses, among other aspects, the nature of the community and the state, the role of political agency and political space, as well as issues surrounding political and social participation. In particular, two main strands of research in classical phenomenology appear relevant from a critical point of view: (1) the analysis of social experience, including the thematization of the 'we'-subject (in early classical phenomenology) and collective praxis (in existential phenomenology), and (2) the investigation of the political space as the foundation for political freedom, which is prominent in the thought of Hannah Arendt.[2]

With regard to the concept of social experience, it is noteworthy that Husserl was not only familiar with the works of German sociologists like Ferdinand Tönnies and Georg Simmel, but his work also includes an analysis of communal life and social life, which was further elaborated and developed by early phenomenologists like Edith Stein, Gerda Walther, Adolf Reinach, and Max Scheler, among others (Szanto 2020). Classical phenomenologists are very clear that political investigations require an account of how individuals participate in social life and contribute to the constitution of social structures.

In this respect, phenomenologists like Stein maintain that social reality is constituted by social relations (e.g. associations, community, the state) that develop historically and whose ethical content (e.g. questions of duty, authority, solidarity and justice) requires an analysis of values. For early phenomenologists, the goal of political community is not simply to ensure freedom through the State, as advocated by German Idealists, such as Hegel and Fichte. On Stein's view, modern philosophical approaches to the State and political freedom fail to appreciate the *motives* that inspire and guide social relations as inwardly felt orientations, including, for example, empathy, sympathy, friendship, and solidarity. For this reason, for early classical phenomenologists, political communities are not only based on political and juridical structures, but also permeated by lived experiences that are ignited by value-oriented affects and communal action. To the extent that affect, social practices, and group association inform social structures, social reality is largely based on webs of social relations that make possible the thematization of collective agency. This aspect makes classical phenomenology particularly relevant for sociological investigations on the nature of social reality. A good example of this type of research can be found in Alfred Schütz, one of the most prominent social theorists inspired by phenomenological research in the twentieth century.[3]

The discussion of social experience in existential phenomenology is closely related to the relation between phenomenology and Marxism, which primarily involves French existentialism.[4] Historically, existential phenomenology has been more directly related to issues of social justice, praxis, and Marxist politics that rely on dialectical philosophy (Crowell 2000). Sartre, Beauvoir, and Fanon, in particular, were preoccupied with issues concerning political association, group membership, and anti-colonial struggle in order to challenge existing sources of oppression through class struggle. As a result of this, existential phenomenologists appear less concerned than early classical phenomenologists with the analysis of the genesis of community and communal life. Instead, they focus on how discrimination and oppression are perpetuated and maintained in society as well as on concrete forms of liberation and emancipation.

In this regard, for example, Fanon diagnoses the relation between institutions, culture, and racism as the invisible, yet 'crudest' structure of racist society. He makes clear that 'racism is never a super-added element discovered by chance in the course of the investigation of the cultural data of a group', but rather a 'cultural whole' entrenched in the fabric of everyday life, from the culture industry to ideology and social commentaries (Fanon 1994, p. 36). On this view, racism cannot be dealt with as a prejudice, bias, or subjective 'quirk', but rather as a 'disposition fitting into a well-defined system' (Fanon 1994, p. 41); that is, a system that uses advanced technological power to exploit and disempower colonies and minorities.

It is in such a context that concepts like solidarity acquire both ethical and social relevance. In his unfinished ethical theory contained in his posthumous *Notebook for an Ethics*, Sartre argues that solidarity represents the end goal of acts of recognition as a way to realize freedom against alienation. Solidarity emerges as one recognizes the freedom of the other as a value that needs to be realized 'not because it is mine, not because it is a value, but because it is a value for someone on earth' (Sartre 1992, p. 281). Sartre's view of solidarity informs his conception of collective praxis, which aims to transform the static and oppressive power of existing material conditions through the conscious and organized activity of a plurality of subjects. Central to Sartre's project of collective praxis is the mobilization of the members of an oppressed class in order to resist systemic structures of oppression through the solidarity and collective action of the group.

In the thought of Hannah Arendt, political freedom has a special relevance from both a phenomenological and ontological perspective. Not only did Arendt witness the origins of totalitarian regimes in Europe, she also diagnosed social maladies like political exclusion, marginalization, and political disempowerment. For Arendt, solidarity involves acknowledging other subjects as co-builders of a common space through which individuals manifest themselves in the public realm. As we will see, Arendt's analysis seeks to provide a critical counterweight to the logic of concentration camps, whose objective was not simply to exert power over individuals, but also to modify the very dimension of human nature, starting with the annihilation of feelings of solidarity.

From this brief overview, it can be argued that the relation between solidarity, social experience, and political action is central to classical phenomenologists of different traditions, hence of political phenomenology. As we will see, such concepts and the issues they posit are also at the heart of contemporary critical phenomenology. Borrowing from Bedorf and Herrmann (2020), it can be argued that three main areas of investigation are at stake in political phenomenology, and by extension, to critical-phenomenological approaches to politics: (1) an analysis of *socio-political* experience; (2) an inquiry into the *ontological* foundations of political action; and (3) a phenomenology of political *episteme* that tackles the relation between knowledge, understanding, and power.

In line with the method of previous chapters, we proceed by introducing the critical aspects of classical-phenomenological discourse, and how they intersect contemporary critical-phenomenological analysis across the three domains of research identified by Bedorf and Herrmann. To account for the collective character of socio-political experience, we draw attention to the relevance of communal experience in classical phenomenological analyses (section 6.1). We then present the ontological foundations of political experience through Arendt's reflections on political space, which pave the way to contemporary critical accounts of social death and social invisibility (sections 6.2 and 6.3). We continue by presenting phenomenological approaches to epistemic injustice (section 6.4), which illustrate the relation between knowledge, understanding, and power from a phenomenological point of view. We conclude by considering how critical phenomenology weaves together the themes of solidarity, vulnerability, and precariousness (section 6.5).

6.1 Communal life and affect

From a phenomenological point of view, to be a 'person' is to exist within a community. This is made clear by Husserl and Stein in *Ideas II*, where they argue that human beings are regarded as persons only insofar as they are members of 'a moral association of persons in which the world of morals is constituted' (Husserl 1989, p. 200). A community is both the social organization that sustains people's flourishing and the social space that is constituted through the value-oriented acts of its members. From this point of view, classical phenomenological accounts of social experience build on the phenomenology of intersubjectivity, including empathy, which we explored in Chapter 2. Indeed, since empathy (in the Husserlian sense described in Chapter 2) forms the basis of interpersonal experience, it is involved in social acts of communication and reciprocal understanding.

However, while social acts of communication have their basis in empathy, they should not be equated to empathic experience. From a Husserlian viewpoint, empathy is a form of perception that is at stake in the direct experience of other selves, such as face-to-face encounters. Empathic acts make possible the recognition of another self as a distinct centre of intentional life. Social relations, however, are not necessarily forms of direct experience, as they consist of normative acts of mutual recognition between persons or moral agents (Szanto 2020). In a social relation, moral agents bring into existence a social content that has normative value, namely, it is valid for the members of the group. As such, social relations build on acts of commitment on the part of practical agents as well as on their mutual acknowledgment as fellow group members.

Stein was particularly interested in exploring the motives of social experience, and how this leads to the formation of communities understood as 'moral associations of persons'. Unlike a contractual association, in which a subject deals with another out of some interest (so that the other subject is in fact the 'object' of a negotiation), a community is based on a shared relation between two or more subjects. A community involves shared experiences, but also shared values and norms. On this view, being part of a community entails being a member of a 'we-relation' that has the capacity to enrich and empower individual life. For example, an individual with a predisposition to artistic endeavours would gain inspiration and energy by joining a community of artists. The reason for this is that, within the artists' community, individual capacities are awakened and given the opportunity to develop further. As Stein puts it: 'a whole range of original predispositions can atrophy because there is no opportunity for their activation' (Stein 2000, p. 199). While the individual core of the artist's personality is irreducibly unique, it may remain hidden or undeveloped until one's psychic and affective dispositions are given the opportunity to flourish and develop. Sensitivity to values also diminishes when one's abilities lack training and support through social experience.

At the same time, the life of the community also depends on the contribution of the individual *as* a member of the community. This means that, within a community, individuals do not act as isolated and atomistic bodies, but rather as subjects who contribute to the 'life and soul' of the group. In this regard, Stein speaks of the 'life-power' of the community in analogy with the 'life-power' of the individual. The notion of 'life-power' refers to the development of psychophysical abilities that stem from the body, particularly from sentience (Stein 2000, p. 22). While the life-power is a real property of the subject, it does not coincide with the essence of the person, which in Stein corresponds to the inner core of the self. By arguing that the life-power of the community is based on the life-power of its members, Stein highlights the reciprocal relation that obtains between the self and the group. On the one hand, individuals contribute to the life of the community in their various capacities and physical abilities. On the other hand, owing to the dynamic we pointed out earlier between the flourishing of individual predispositions and social life, the community also invigorates and sustains the life-power of individuals. It follows that the circulation of life-power in the community is always twofold, and it can be weakened or diminished depending on how individuals contribute to it (Stein 2000, pp. 205).

Moreover, since the life-power is a psychophysical quality of self that requires cultivation and practice, the analogy between the self and the community indicates that concrete acts of communication between subjects are necessary to create a community. However, the core essence of the community depends on the relations of motivation that take place between individuals, specifically by the free attitude or stances that subjects take toward one another and the community itself. In analogy with the structure of the person, the core part or soul of the community consists in the bonds that group members form, and that motivate them to come together. As Stein puts it: 'Where persons are living in common without being inwardly given over to each other and to the community, you cannot talk about any soul of community. You might think of fellow-travellers, residents of a house, or students in a class, who have found themselves together by accident and live with one another, but do not get close to one another inwardly' (Stein 2000, p. 274). The essence of the community depends on the interest or investment that individuals have in the community itself and the positions they adopt to carry on communal life.

From this point of view, communities are instituted out of shared social experiences, but they are not limited to the sameness of culture, ethnicity, language, or territory (Drummond 2000). A social community institutes a sense of belonging that is transformative, dynamic, and rooted in the way individuals are inwardly motivated to live together by acknowledging each other as free and responsible members. Indeed, it is only when subjects come together in virtue of their freely abiding by communal norms that genuine communities are generated. In this context, an important aspect of communal life in classical phenomenology concerns precisely the distinction between a community and the mass, and relatedly, the role of individual agency.

The concept of the mass dates back to Gustave Le Bon's mass psychology (1895), according to which isolated individuals that gather together in a crowd under the influence of violent emotions display a type of behaviour that is comparable to a "collective mind". In this case, individuals feel, think, and act in a manner that is quite different from the way in which they would normally feel, think, and act as isolated individuals. In fact, as a member of the collective mind, the subject appears infected by a propagation of emotion or affective contagion that unconsciously conditions her. Le Bon's study anticipated in many ways the emergence of the mass in the twentieth century, and particularly during fascist regimes. Stein argues that the affective flow that permeates communal life is not to be ascribed to an affective contagion, as if the individual stances of group members were taken over by a flow of collective energy. To this end, Stein distinguishes between the affective current of the community and the contagion that occurs in the masses. In the former, collective energy depends on the character of individual members, each having their own stance and attitude towards a common object. In so doing, different subjects motivate one another to acts of communication that preserve the difference of the individual positions involved. In the case of the mass, instead, Stein notices a propagation of convictions and feelings that have no logical and axiological basis; that is, they lack sensitivity to reason and values. On the basis of certain moods or suggestibility, people endorse the convictions of others without identifying the sources of those beliefs, thereby forsaking the use of their own mind as well as their individual agency.

An upshot of Stein's argument is that group members are responsible as individuals for the role they play in a community. In so doing, Stein departs from Scheler's approach, according to which every societal unity, whether religious, social, or political, is founded on an a priori spiritual core, namely on the adherence to the hierarchy of values that informs personal life. For Scheler, members of the community are held responsible as 'persons', meaning as carriers of spiritual values, and not as free-standing and independent individuals. On this view, individual agency is grounded and made possible by value-responsiveness. Therefore, for Scheler, it is the '*identical personhood* of every individual in the community, not the *individuality* of the person, that founds responsibility along with autonomy' (Scheler 1973a, p. 497, emphasis is ours).

This means that every individual in the community is simultaneously co-responsible for others and not only for their own individual actions. This principle, which Scheler identifies with solidarity, links together individual and collective responsibility, establishing the basis for various degrees of merit and guilt in addition to and independent of individual guilt and merit. On this view, I am co-responsible for my neighbour as a member of the 'collective person' that the community represents, and not only as an autonomous and independent individual. Against Scheler, Stein reclaims the positionality that individuals retain while joining the community, and that holds them responsible for the actions they abide by as *free*, autonomous subjects. This is not to deny the role of collective responsibility, but rather to preserve the individual core of agency in communal experience, especially the quality of 'free mentality'. Thus, while Scheler's view of solidarity makes individuals co-responsible *as* group members insofar as they are carriers of values, Stein argues that responsibility in a community is based on individual free choice and understanding.

While classical phenomenological views on communal life are irreducible to a single, unitary account, they ultimately highlight a fundamental relation between communal life and affect, particularly solidarity. The peculiarity of social acts consists in the fact that, within the community, individuals are confronted with an affective environment that is part and parcel of individual experience. In this context, solidarity represents the affective drive of genuine communities, which entails, in both Scheler and Stein, sensitivity to the experiences of others as well as ethical responsiveness to communal bonds. In a way, solidarity shares important similarities with the Kantian concept of respect for humanity as a universal source of ethical obligation. Yet solidarity is not an impersonal and rational obligation but the motive that prevails in the stream of social experience and that binds individuals together as group members.

Moreover, by placing affect and social experience at the core of communal life classical phenomenologists indirectly address the vulnerability of communities. Drawing on such an approach, Calcagno (2018) draws attention to the tensions that characterize immigrant communities when new generations move away from the traditions and social customs established and handed down by their ancestors. In such cases, the older generations feel nostalgia and solidarity for a former past of the community that is no longer shared. Instead, new generations do not identify with or feel deep ties for the habituated form of communal life shared by their parents and grandparents. Thus, the shared experiences that form communal life allow degrees of strength, depth, and duration of the value-oriented stances that inform them. This indicates not only that changes of beliefs and customs are intrinsic to the flourishing of a community, but also that, as different habituated styles arise and inform communal life, there may be conflicting tendencies within the same community. Furthermore, deceptions and mistaken value-judgements constellate the historical evolution of communal life, as it happens when people lose trust in their respective groups and political associations.

Loss of social trust and radical alterations of the sense of belonging to a given community are especially relevant if one considers that a number of classical phenomenologists experienced first-hand exile, deportation, and migration. The most prominent examples, among others, include Edith Stein (who was deported to Auschwitz), Alfred Schütz and Hannah Arendt (who both experienced political exile from Nazi Germany). In a 1944 essay dedicated to 'The Stranger', Alfred Schütz describes the 'shock' experienced by the immigrant who moves to a new country and finds his habitual patterns of interpretation altered and shattered. The immigrant, like any social agent, is a member of a social group based on cultural patterns of interpretation that have been handed down to them by ancestors, teachers, and authorities as 'an unquestioned and unquestionable guide in all the situations which normally occur within the social world' (Schütz 1944, p. 501). This is the knowledge of 'trustworthy *recipes* for interpreting the social world and for handling things and men in order to obtain the best results in every situation with a minimum effort by avoiding undesirable consequences' (ibid.). Schütz's argument is that social understanding relies on a whole repertoire of previously acquired knowledge (what he calls 'stock knowledge'), which provides 'recipes' for communicating one's intent in an appropriate way. Such recipes are also necessary for interpreting cultural patterns and understanding the intents of other subjects. The use of recipes is not a matter of linguistic proficiency, as a migrant may master a foreign language while still experiencing clashes in the course of everyday situations.

On Schütz's view, the stranger finds himself at a loss as to how he can make himself understood in the new social environment, while also struggling to decipher and interpret the symbols and social codes of the host country. This is due to the fact that the stranger approaching the local group in the host country can no longer trust his taken-for-granted knowledge to get by in the new environment. Thus, his former certainty about how to conduct himself in life falls to pieces. Schütz maintains that such experiences of readjustment and adaptation are not limited to migration, as they are intrinsic to our general interpretation of social contexts. On Schütz's view, in our everyday life, we constantly rework our general schemes of interpretation in order to make them compatible with newly acquired information. 'If we succeed in this endeavour, then that fact which formerly was a strange fact and a puzzling problem to our mind is transformed into an additional element of our warranted knowledge. We have enlarged and adjusted our stock of experiences' (Schütz 1944, p. 507). Thus, Schütz suggests that the process of navigating the social world, including its customs, rules, and norms is, at least on a subjective level of experience, a continuous process of adaption, learning, and unlearning of previously acquired information.

As Evandro Camara argues, however, the progressive adjustment of one's stock of knowledge through conflicting social experience is the aspect that is most ambiguously at work in political and social forms of discrimination caused by power-based group manipulations (Camara 2021, p. 145). As we will see in the next sections, for those who are systematically excluded from the social space, the structures of the social world are not only perpetually thrown into question, but also experienced as precarious and lacking ontological stability.

6.2 Phenomenology of political space

A phenomenological exploration of the ontological foundations of the political world can be found in the work of Hannah Arendt. Arendt's interest in the significance of the political world, and the experience of being excluded from it, has a strongly personal dimension. Indeed, Arendt was forced to flee Germany for France in 1933, due to Hitler's rise to power, and in 1941 she had to flee France for the United Sates. During her time in France, Arendt worked with several Jewish refugee organizations, thus deepening her analysis of statelessness, which features prominently in *The Origins of Totalitarianism* (1951).

A former student of Jaspers and Heidegger, Arendt did not consider herself a phenomenologist, but rather a political theorist. Yet in *The Human Condition* (1958), she goes to the roots of the constitution of the political space, developing a phenomenological account of 'publicity', i.e. the 'public realm' (*res publica*). Arendt conceives the public realm as a 'space of appearances,' which is brought to life through the activities by means of which human beings appear to one another, specifically through their speech and acting. To account for this, Arendt carries out a phenomenological exploration of the activities that distinguish the existence of human subjects 'in the midst of the world' (Moran 2002). To be in the midst of the world is not simply to navigate a world of equipment or things ready-at-hand, as in Heidegger's account of being-with, but rather to bring into existence shared spaces that serve different purposes. To this end, Arendt argues that the public realm does not always exist, as it is brought about by individuals who act in public as free subjects in concert with each other, and not as private individuals.

The difference between the private and the public sphere is central to Arendt's analysis in *The Human Condition*. The private sphere is the realm of subjective and material interest and needs, which are connected, especially in the modern era, to the private pursuit of wealth. The foundation of the private sphere is, for Arendt, the household, whose constitution is relatively independent from state interference. In contrast, the public sphere is, for Arendt, a *political* realm, as it represents a space for action within a community of peers.[5] As such, the public realm is an actual shared world (*Mitwelt* in German) that precedes and grounds political institutions and that is not to be confused with material or economic interests. The peculiarity of the political space, as Arendt describes it, is that it provides the ontological ground for the manifestation of individual agency. As such, individuals like the slave, the foreigner, or the 'barbarian' in antiquity can be deprived of the political space, and confined to only inhabiting a private, hidden space.[6]

Moreover, the public space is not a reality that is inhabited at all times, as it depends on the presence of other people. Recalling Aristotle's idea that man is not only a *zoon politikon* ('political animal'), but also a *zoon logon ekhon* ('a living being capable of speech'), Arendt argues that to be human means to be among other people: 'No human life, not even the life of the hermit in nature's wilderness, is possible without a world which directly or indirectly testifies to the presence of other human beings' (Arendt 2018, p. 22). Arendt's view is that man is not simply a herd animal, but also and more fundamentally a subject of action; that is to say, an agent, who has the power to disclose 'who' she/he is through speech and acting. As Loidolt has pointed out, to relate to a person as a 'who' (as opposed to a 'what') means that individuals manifest their uniqueness in the context of intersubjective experience, hence they cannot be regarded from an impersonal standpoint (Loidolt 2016). The public realm is therefore, on Arendt's view, the ontological domain in which the pursuit of action corresponds to the actualization of the self. As such, action is not governed by utilitarian goals or private interests, but rather it is concerned with the manifestation of who one is and what one can do (Arendt 1970, p. xiii).

As to be human is to be alongside others in the common world, Arendt's view of subjectivity entails that the constitution of one's identity is based on thinking and acting in relation to others. The realm of action discloses who we are, but such actions acquire meaning through how others interpret and respond to them. The relation between selfhood, appearance, and intersubjective experience reveals that individuals are reciprocally connected in the public realm. This, however, does not mean that an individual's identity is entirely dependent on how one's actions are interpreted by others. Indeed, for Arendt, action is a process of actualization of the self that cannot be reduced to the perspective that others cast on self. In this sense, Arendt stresses that the appearances through which an individual manifests herself have a fundamental relation to who one is, as an ontological, unique being. As Arendt writes: 'By acting and speaking, men show who they are, reveal actively their unique human personalities and thus make their appearance in the human world' (Arendt 2018, p. 179). Since acting and thinking involve the presence of an addressee, and are both dynamic activities that express or reveal the self in a world, one's identity is a dynamic and unpredictable phenomenon. To quote Arendt (2018, p. 192): '[. . .] one discloses one's self without ever either knowing himself or being able to calculate beforehand whom he reveals.'

On Arendt's view, the concept of identity resists reification, namely, the reduction of selfhood to an objectifiable, tangible reality. Even the stories or narratives that we can give about ourselves reveal a fundamental difference between agency and authorship. The agent is the *initiator* of a speech or an action, whose outcome are stories, whereas the author is the *producer* of those stories. While each individual life can be told as a story, 'nobody is the author or producer of his own life story' (Arendt 2018, p. 184). Arendt's distinction has to do with the ontological character of stories and narratives, which represent finished products, having a beginning and an end, as opposed to the open-ended and unpredictable character of human existence. Action and speech unfold over time in ways that we cannot fully foresee or determine: 'strength of the action process is never exhausted in a single deed but, on the contrary, can grow while its consequences multiply. [. . .] The reason why we are never able to foretell with certainty the outcome and end of any action is simply that action has no end' (Arendt 2018, p. 233). Consequently, there is an element of risk and vulnerability in acting, for we cannot know beforehand what the results of our actions will be. As Arendt puts it, 'although nobody knows whom he reveals when he discloses himself in deed or word, he must be willing to risk the disclosure' (Arendt 2018, p. 180).

In this context, Arendt maintains that action is constitutive of freedom. For Arendt, freedom does not equate either to 'non-interference' (freedom not to be prevented from doing what one wants) or the ability to act upon one's free will, which roughly corresponds to Isaiah Berlin's distinction between 'negative' and 'positive' freedom respectively (Berlin 1969). Arendt's view of freedom overcomes such a distinction in that she connects freedom to natality, which is the capacity to initiate something new or to bring forth a novel and unexpected change in the world. As action actualizes an individual's power to act, and it is bound by the presence of others within a shared world, individuals are free as long as each of them enacts a new beginning.[7] For Arendt, action should not be mistaken for activities that either reproduce biological life or that are concerned with the production of an external output. I do not 'act' – in the sense of Arendt's view of action – if I merely raise my arm to scratch an itch in my face or if I cook dinner. Rather, 'action' in Arendt is close to Aristotle's view of happiness as *eudaimonia* or flourishing, which is an activity whose end is internal to the development of the activity itself, bringing forth what is most distinctive about humans, namely the use of reason. Importantly, action is realized *with* others. Examples of action, in an Arendtian sense, include speaking and listening, civil disobedience or non-violent resistance, promising, and forgiving.

Arendt's examples indicate that action is inseparable from plurality. Plurality denotes 'the fact that men, not Man, live on the earth and inhabit the world' (Arendt 2018, p. 7). Arendt's view is that to be in the world means to share a common space with other subjects who are irreducibly unique. No two human lives are the same and hence each life brings about new changes in the world. As Arendt puts it in the *The Human Condition*:

> The fact that man is capable of action means that the unexpected can be expected from him, that he is able to perform what is infinitely improbable. And this again is possible only because each man is

unique, so that with each birth something uniquely new comes into the world. (Arendt 2018, pp. 177–8)

Arendt weaves together the concepts of action, natality, and plurality as the unexpected performance of a subject that unsettles the world, while opening up new possibilities for thinking and acting. This reveals that action is laden with possibilities that are in principle capable of connecting and bringing together different subjects. However, while action is inherently unpredictable, it is also fundamentally irreversible, as it unfolds over time, hence it cannot be taken back. Both features – unpredictability and irreversibility – are best illustrated by looking at Arendt's two main examples of action in *The Human Condition*, namely promising and forgiving.

Promising binds us to a commitment to others, even if the circumstances under which our action will take place are uncertain. For example, when I promise to my children that I will spend time with them, I do not simply commit myself to a course of action (such as, playing or taking a walk together) that will take place in a given time frame (e.g. tomorrow or on the weekend). My promise voluntarily binds my future to the future of another despite the unpredictability of life. In this sense, promising serves as a 'remedy' to the unpredictability of human existence, including the contingency of the circumstances.

Forgiving addresses the irreversibility of action in light of how it affects others. When I ask for forgiveness, I am asking to be absolved from my mistakes, including the unintended consequences of my deeds. Forgiving resists the identification of a subject with the outcome of his or her actions. Therefore, forgiveness restores freedom by recognizing the uniqueness of each person, including the possibility of their changing. Thus, when I forgive my friend for the harm she caused me, I liberate her from the identification with her mistakes, allowing her to let go of her past. In so doing, forgiveness restores human agency: 'Without being forgiven, released from the consequences of what we have done, our capacity to act would, as it were, be confined to one single deed from which we could never recover; we would remain the victims of its consequences forever' (Arendt 2018, p. 237). Both promising and forgiving free us by allowing us to be who we are: the former by binding us to a future with others, and the latter by absolving us from the harm we have done in the past to others. Hence, promising and forgiving reveal the essential temporality of action as well as its relation to plurality, for both actions require the presence of others and their involvement in our lives (d'Entrèves 1994, pp. 82–3).

On this view, the political realm, as the space of freedom, is intersubjective in that it is constituted by a plurality of subjects that think and act together. This indicates that action 'not only has the most intimate relationship to the public part of the world common to us all, but it is the one activity which constitutes it' (Arendt 2018, p. 198). In this respect, acting together provides the basis for solidarity, which does not only acknowledge the right of every person to manifest themselves, but also their right to a space that allows the coming-to-be of the diverse appearances of each individual. As Arendt writes, it is out of solidarity that individuals 'establish deliberately and, as it were, dispassionately a community of interest with the oppressed and exploited' (Arendt 1990, p. 88). Solidarity is the affective bond that reveals the necessary inter-dependence between a plurality of subjects, whose actions make the political space possible. In this respect, solidarity is informed by a deliberative stance, which is the capacity to think in concert with others, that is, to discern the good without yielding to self-serving interest. This coming together of individuals is necessarily fragile, owing to the finitude of action; yet it is also essential, for this is how we collectively 'establish relations and create new realities' (Arendt 2018, p. 200).

In this context, it is important to note that Arendt conceives the political realm as the space that sustains human rights. Specifically, human rights represent the universal norms through which one's ability to participate in the public world is acknowledged and protected. At the same time, Arendt argues that it is only when the political realm is established as such that human rights can be upheld. As she writes: the 'only given condition for the establishment of rights is the plurality of men; human rights exist because we inhabit the earth together with other men' (Arendt 1951, p. 437). Arendt does not thematize human rights as universal principles grounded in either natural law, human reason, or God's will. On the contrary, Arendt argues that rights are a fragile, contingent accomplishment that must be sustained by the reality of the common world (Parekh 2008, p. 5). On this view, human rights are defined by the condition of belonging 'to some human community' (Arendt 1951, p. 439). As Parekh has pointed out, this does not entail that human rights are arbitrary or simply relative to culture. Arendt does not reject the universality of rights but their abstract formulations. For example, Arendt criticizes the modern conception of human rights as a natural and inalienable possession of humankind, since this view presupposes that rights would exist outside a civil framework. In fact, this is not the case of stateless people, such as exiles and refugees, the group that most radically experienced social alienation in the twentieth century (as Arendt argues in the *Origins of Totalitarianism*).

As Parekh remarks, at the heart of Arendt's account is an apparent paradox. On the one hand, stateless subjects are those who most need the recognition of their human rights in order to receive protection from a political body. On the other hand, without the action of political institutions that recognize the political status of migrants, exiles and refugees cannot be granted their human rights. The paradox, then, is that 'being *nothing but human* means that one can no longer rely on your human rights' (Parekh 2008, p. 11). This is an aspect that the European migrant crisis has made painfully clear in our century, as millions of refugees across the Middle East, the Mediterranean Sea, and Eastern Europe are left to suffer in make-shift camps along borders, forced to make extremely dangerous, frequently fatal crossings across the sea, or are remanded in migrant centres waiting indefinitely for their case to be processed. Such denial of the political space amounts, for Arendt, to a retreat, on the part of modern society, in the realm of private concerns and interests. Consequently, Arendt argues that the most important right is *the right to have rights*, which means, politically, the right to appear in the common world; to be recognized as a fellow member of the community; to be able to speak and to act meaningfully with others (Parekh 2008, p. 12).

6.3 Phenomenology of social alienation

From a critical-phenomenological point of view, a useful exploration of the Arendtian concept of the 'right to have rights' involves the concept of 'social death', which dates back to Orlando Patterson's study of slavery (Patterson 1982). According to Patterson, common to various forms of slavery practised across different civilizations and cultures is the fact that the slave is a 'socially dead' person.[8] While not literally dead, the slave 'had no socially recognized existence outside of his master, he [or she] became a social nonperson' (Patterson 1982, p. 5). A central element of the concept of social death is the fact that the slave is cut off from meaningful kinship ties. Slaves are severed from family, becoming an anonymous being without a past (i.e. without forebears) or, as Patterson puts it, a 'genealogical isolate' (Patterson 1982, p. 5). This concept has been further explored by Guenther from a critical-phenomenological viewpoint:

> To be socially dead is to be deprived of the network of social relations, particularly kinship relations, that would otherwise support, protect, and give meaning to one's precarious life as an individual. It is to be violently and permanently separated from one's kin, blocked from forming a meaningful relationship, not only to others in the present

but also to the heritage of the past and the legacy of the future beyond one's own finite, individuated being (Guenther 2013, p. xxi).

While slaves did form relationships, such groups were born out of opposition and resistance to the system that rendered them socially dead. As such, the social groups formed by slaves were extremely precarious, as they could be torn apart at any moment. For example, slave children were frequently separated from their parents and sold to other slave holders, hence such a threat was always hanging over families. The only sustained relationship that the slave had was to their master, which was a non-reciprocal relationship in which the master wielded absolute power over the slave. The slave was, in a sense, a part of the master's person, rather than being a person in their own right. As a result of this, the slave was confined to a liminal, ghost-like existence, as slaves were denied the formal and concrete recognition of their personhood and made socially invisible by their masters and the community. This echoes the reflections of the narrator of Ralph Ellison's novel *Invisible Man*, which describes the racial abuses and discrimination experienced by a Black man living in the United States in the 1930s:

> I am an invisible man . . . I am a man of substance, of flesh and bone, fiber and liquids – and I might even be said to possess a mind. I am invisible, understand, simply because people refuse to see me. Like the bodiless heads you see sometimes in a circus sideshow, it is as though I have been surrounded by mirrors of hard, distorting glass. When they approach me, they see only my surroundings, themselves, or figments of their imagination – indeed, everything and anything except me. (Ellison 1995, p. 1)

While Ellison's novel is not about slavery, it is worth noting that scholars such as Caleb Smith (2009), Joshua Price (2015), and Lisa Cacho (2012) have consistently developed the concept of social death to illustrate the status of Black people post-emancipation. In particular, these studies address the targeted imprisonment of the racialized poor, their subjection to systematic violence, their denial of fundamental rights and their exclusion from political decision-making (Zurn 2020, p. 310).

In this context, a fruitful discussion of the concept of social death in phenomenology has been developed by Lisa Guenther, who has documented the experiences of prisoners placed in solitary confinement. Guenther's argument is that social death aims at removing inmates from their natural contact with other living beings, excluding them from any shared or common space, including the possibility of touching or being touched. Guenther shows how exclusion from such a shared affective realm impacts the inmates' ability to perceive adequately, to trust their feelings, and to organise their thoughts, to the point that they lose trust in the existence of the surrounding world. Sensory deprivation affects both humans and nonhumans alike, confirming the phenomenological insight that the need of contact and everyday interpersonal experience lies at the core of carnal existence. On this view, any institution seeking to establish social death as a norm produces ontological violence. As Guenther puts it:

> Solitary confinement does not simply dehumanize prisoners, cutting them off from the social relations that sustain them as social animals, and it does not only alter their very existence as living beings, pushing them beyond the boundary between humans and animals toward the nonliving status of a stone; solitary confinement is a violence so radical that it could even alter the ontology of a stone. (Guenther 2013, p. 143).

Guenther's description shows that solitary confinement pushes the boundaries between living and nonliving existence, and not simply between human and non-human life. In this context, she reports that 'many prisoners describe their experience in solitary confinement as a form of living death', with one inmate calling it a 'living tomb' (Guenther 2013, p. xii). Another inmate reports that, 'when they talk of ghosts of the dead who wander in the night with things still undone, they approximate my subjective experience of this life' (Guenther 2013, p. xxv), echoing Ellison's imagery of a shadow-like existence. Guenther connects social death to the exploitation of prison labour, which treats inmates not simply as labourers but rather as natural resources to be exhausted. For this reason, she argues that social death goes beyond dehumanization in that it reveals an intrinsic form of de-animalization. This phenomenon consists in the violation and exploitation not only of prisoners' human dignity but also of their dignity as living beings in general (Guenther 2013, p. 140).

On her account, the testimonies of prisoners subjected to prolonged solitary confinement reveal the erosion, and even the collapse, of their sense of reality. For example, Guenther reports that some prisoners were unable to ascertain the real from the unreal, experiencing hallucinations, such as seeing other people in their cell or noting the surface of the prison's walls bulging (Guenther 2013, pp. 34–5). In this regard, Guenther argues that '"becoming unhinged" is not just a colloquial expression; rather, it is a precise phenomenological description of what happens when the articulated joints of our embodied, interrelational subjectivity are broken apart. Solitary confinement deprives prisoners of the bodily presence of others, forcing them to rely on the isolated resources of their own subjectivity, with the (perhaps surprising) effect of eroding or undermining that subjectivity' (Guenther 2013, p. xii).

This leads Guenther to inquire into the relation between social death and the concept of personhood in Husserlian phenomenology: 'What are the conditions for the possibility of such a radical physical, emotional, cognitive, and social deterioration of the prisoner in isolation? How must concrete personhood be structured in order to be diminished so radically by the prolonged deprivation of the bodily presence of other people?' (Guenther 2013, p. 23). We have seen that for Husserl and other classical phenomenologists, the subject is not a solitary, atomistic being. We do not exist as persons without belonging to a world shared with other subjects, and a shared sense of reality with other fellow human beings is in turn essential to establish the objective reality of the world. It is this fact, that we are deeply interconnected beings on both an embodied and a practical level, that makes solitary confinement a 'living death'. Drawing on Husserl's account of the body as a centre of orientation that is transcendentally related to an *alter ego* or other self, Guenther questions whether the transcendental sense of being a 'person' can be eroded by experiences of solitary confinement that systematically deny contact with other people.

As we pointed out in Chapter 1, from a Husserlian viewpoint, the transcendental self is a condition of possibility for thematizing subjective experience and identifying the essential structures that make the experience of the world a meaningful and coherent experience *for* a subject. Connected to this, we saw in Chapter 3 that the most basic and fundamental experience of the self is the experience of another subject. Thus, to be a self is to be exposed to the alterity of others through one's corporeal existence. To objectify transcendental subjectivity by regarding it as an external and independent power with respect to the world risks losing sight of the fundamental concept that Husserl theorized and put at the centre of his phenomenology, which is intentionality. It is this fundamental directedness (or aboutness) that makes possible philosophical discourse about experience, meaning, and objectivity. In this respect, Husserl was concerned with a method that would allow the thematization of those general structures of experience within which it becomes possible to also thematize structural variations and deviations, including the erosion of psychological identity, temporal continuity, and affective connection to other selves.

From this point of view, it is essential to distinguish between transcendental selfhood and the attribution of personhood. While the latter requires normative recognition, the former is the sense of mineness that is given even in the absence of mutual recognition from others in a practical context (as we pointed out when discussing Fanon's account of racial objectification). It follows that social death highlights the diminishment and infringement of the affective, moral, and social bonds that makes possible the actualization and recognition of personhood. In this context, selfhood refers to the transcendental ground of personhood; it does not exist as a separate or independent entity apart from embodied subjects, but as the source of the meaning-bestowing activities of consciousness across all the spectrum of human experiences (including hallucinations and trauma).

At the same time, it is worth noting that Guenther's description of social death entails the erosion of the affective attunement to a shared world. This means that social death underpins not only a lack of affective and social interaction, but also and more fundamentally the erosion of the experience of *being with* others. Indeed, Guenther highlights the necessity of affective and embodied intersubjectivity as a primordial and basic experience for the thematization of the world as a necessary correlate of human experience. As Guenther claims: 'To the extent that we regard the prisoner as an individual who is separable from the world and from others, even if we acknowledge that this individual is a "social animal" whose "environment" has some sort of effect on physical and mental health, we fail to grasp the depths of the harm inflicted by solitary confinement' (Guenther 2013, p. 35). Guenther's thesis that the subject–world relation cannot be modelled upon the ordinary concept of 'social animal' is aligned with the classical-phenomenological insight according to which the subject is not a sheer physical or biological entity that exists independently of the surrounding world. This means that it is possible to approach the erosion of self-experience in the context of social death by recognizing its relation to the denial of the *possibility* of being with others. Indeed, as Ratcliffe (2015) has pointed out, appreciating someone as a person involves not only interacting with them, but having the possibility of doing so.

From this point of view, social death represents a nihilation or collapse of the basic and fundamental relatedness between self and other in the world. This makes social death more radical than other forms of alienation occurring within the social world, including the phenomena we discussed in previous chapters connected to gender and racial alienation. Nonetheless, gender and racial oppression can produce estrangement from the very fabric of the common world. At first sight, it may seem as if classical phenomenologists did not concern themselves with such a possibility. For example, while Arendt was all too aware of the issues connected to political exclusion and exile, she was less clear about forms of social and racial discrimination.[9]

This reflects a more general concern with accounts of social experience within classical phenomenology, which is often criticized by critical phenomenologists for not providing an adequate account of power relations and how they structure social experience and the political realm more generally. One way in which critical phenomenology seeks to develop classical phenomenology is by imbuing it with an account of power relations that draws on the work of Foucault.[10] As we discussed before, in Foucault power operates as a form of normalization that disciplines subjects to make them conform to established discourses about the self. An important aspect of Foucault's work is that power operates across all domains of experience, hence society itself can be understood as a system of micro-networks of power relations that function to perpetuate social norms. On this view, each individual is a potential conduit for power, including social practices that indirectly sustain normalizing behaviour (from raising children to behave like 'boys' or 'girls', to labelling someone 'weird' because of their disability, or blaming and mocking men if they do not demonstrate sexual interest in women). Thus, everyday social interactions indirectly facilitate and sustain power relations, even in those cases where individuals would disagree with or reject the norms underlying those practices.

Despite Foucault's disillusionment with classical-phenomenological accounts of the political, his view of power may shed light on the socially constructed character of the stranger and the paradoxical 'visibility' of social invisibility. As Ahmed argues, 'strange' bodies are symbolically marked in ways that determine who does and does not belong in a social space (Ahmed 2000).[11] This means that the historical and political failure to enact the political space in the Arendtian sense depends on the paradoxical *visibility* of the stranger. Indeed, 'strangers' are those who are identified *as* such. They are familiar as the 'unfamiliar' or as the 'out-of-place''. As Ahmed writes: 'strangers are not simply those who are not already known in this dwelling, but those who are, in their very proximity, *already recognized as not belonging*, as being out of place' (Ahmed 2000, p. 21). The construction of the category of the outsider enforces the boundaries of social space, demarcating who is allowed or not allowed to enter it.[12]

The politicization of the figure of the 'stranger' has important implications for institutional and social practices. For example, it connects to Robert Bernasconi's account of the institutional invisibility of racial minorities in the public realm in the United States. Bernasconi points out the relation between racial prejudice and lack of access to equal opportunities, ranging from access to loan approvals to educational, health, and employment opportunities (Bernasconi 2000, p. 185; but see also Barber 2001). Reflecting on these issues, Bernasconi argues that Arendt 'provided an account of political community that lacked the resources necessary to address the divisions sustained by racism' (Bernasconi 1996, p. 4). A similar critique is raised by McGowan, who notes that Arendt 'devotes too little attention to the possibility of unequal and nonreciprocal relations among humans in public spaces' (McGowan 1993, p. 67). Similarly, Herrmann argues that Arendt's reflections on the public realm 'soon reach their limit as they lack a concept of power through which the epistemic conditions of visibility and voice can be grasped' (Herrmann 2019, p. 278). According to such views, Arendt's conception of the public realm would be inattentive to issues concerning equity and social justice, which are connected to the deprivation of political agency. This calls into question Arendt's account of the 'right to have rights', which refers to citizenship but should be equally connected to access to social opportunities.

As we pointed out earlier, Arendt is very clear that the political space does not always exist, in that it is brought forth through acting and thinking with others. From this point of view, practices like racial discrimination are consistent with Arendt's thesis that the political space cannot exist where deeds and discourses reverse the shared sense of reality that is constitutive of the common world. Furthermore, Arendt's view of the political space cannot be equated to or identified with an institutional space. Instead, the political space represents the ontological foundation that helps to think through the conditions that should be enacted by an actual political community. Ultimately, Arendt's account of the political space can actually offer a way to rethink issues of inclusion and marginalization. On this view, the thematization of social alienation is less a critique of the Arendtian concept of political space, than a problem that refers, as we shall now illustrate, to the epistemic conditions that guide the interpretation of social injustice.

6.4 Phenomenology of epistemic injustice

The concept of epistemic injustice has been spearheaded by the work of Miranda Fricker (2007). We encountered this concept before in the context of the phenomenology of illness and the epistemic injustice of the healthcare system in Chapter 2. Epistemic injustice is worth explaining in more detail here, as this notion addresses social invisibility from a specific angle that connects the notion of power to discursive and epistemic relations. Epistemic injustice concerns our interactions with other subjects as *knowers*, namely, as agents who possess epistemic abilities to acquire, share, and produce information. In Fricker, 'knowledge' refers to practical understanding, and it includes discursive and propositional beliefs such as information about the world that can be true or false (e.g. knowing who the prime minister of England is), but also skills and technical know-how.[13] Ultimately, for Fricker, knowledge refers to a broad set of abilities and skills through which socially valuable information is exchanged in social interaction.

According to this view, the attribution of epistemic status depends on being recognized as a reliable and trustworthy informant by others. In such a case, the knowledge one shares and communicates is also trusted, whereas it is disregarded if one is judged unreliable or even outright untrustworthy. It follows that deficit and excesses of credibility affect epistemic relations among knowers. According to Fricker, credibility judgments can be influenced by prejudice, which is often consciously upheld by the subject, but it also operates on a pre-reflective level. As Fricker puts it, 'human societies have prejudice in the air, and these prejudices will tend to shape hearers' credibility judgements regardless of whether they have succeeded in eliminating prejudice from their beliefs or not' (Fricker 2007, p. 96). Therefore, the crucial factor in epistemic relations is whether or not credibility judgments are warranted; specifically, whether there is something in the context that causes the hearer's judgment to deviate from the assessment of the speaker's competence and sincerity.

In this regard, Fricker speaks of 'testimonial injustice' to refer to the kind of injustice that occurs when a person's statements receive less credibility from the hearer because of a credibility deficit in the speaker's competence and sincerity due to the hearer's prejudice. When this happens, one is not treated as an epistemic equal, hence one is denied the status of knower to the point of being epistemically objectified (Fricker 2007, p. 133). This means to be treated as a mere source of information, that is, as an exclusive and passive medium from which it is in principle possible to extract some information, disregarding the general status of the speaker as a subject of knowledge. In this sense, epistemic objectification excludes the speaker from 'the community of trusted informants' (Fricker 2007, p. 132), with the result that one is unable to actively participate in the sharing of knowledge (except in so far as one can be used as a source of information). Testimonial injustice often occurs when the hearer holds prejudicial views about the social group to which the speaker belongs. Fricker's examples include situations in which men ignore or dismiss a woman's contribution, especially in one-off exchanges, namely, when there is no actual communication in place. This happens, for instance, when a man ignores a woman's comment about football, assuming that women would know very little about sport. By extension, this applies to both those women and men who hold men more reliable for manual jobs. Testimonial injustice can operate through many forms of prejudice that involve various aspects of social identity, such as race, ethnicity, age, and language.[14]

An example of how accent affects the reliability of speech is provided by Beata Stawarska (2017), who refers, in this case, to 'unhappy speech', borrowing from J. L. Austin's account of 'felicity conditions' of speech acts. Felicity conditions broadly refer to whether and how the hearer takes up the solicitation or request of the speaker's speech. Stawarska provides the example of an academic classroom in which the instructor speaks with an accent that, despite being understandable, breaks the expectations of what is commonly regarded as a familiar accent. In this case, speech is vulnerable to the infelicity of misunderstanding in that the instructor is not heard and her request is not executed due to a lack of credibility based on one's accent. While, on Austin's view, the speaker is not always in control of the effects of her speech on others, Stawarska draws attention to the connection between the performance of a speech act and the hearer's contribution to its success. On this account, an unhappy speech is a speech that fails in its effects (what Austin calls its 'illocutionary force') due to the lack of involvement of the hearer. Thus, unhappy speech is unsuccessful speech; it does not achieve what it aims to do because the listeners do not respond to it – not because of the intelligibility of the *content* of the speech, but rather because of the *form* of the speech, including the presentation of *who* speaks, such as, how they sound.[15]

Testimonial injustice reflects a similar set of issues. Specifically, testimonial injustice wrongs someone 'in their capacity as a subject of knowledge, and thus in a capacity essential to human value; and the particular way in which testimonial injustice does this is that a hearer wrongs a speaker in his capacity as a giver of knowledge, as an informant' (Fricker 2007, p. 5). According to Fricker, epistemic injustice erodes the status of individuals as rational knowers, which is symbolically related to the degradation of someone *qua* human, due to the close relation between being a subject and being an epistemic knower (Fricker 2007, p. 44). Epistemic injustice can be a source of social disadvantage, especially when it occurs in socio-political settings, for instance during job interviews or trials. Recalling Arendt's account of the political space, it can be argued that testimonial injustice undermines the ability of the subject to contribute to the public sphere, which is based on speaking and listening.

Testimonial injustice also highlights the fact that, in many of our daily epistemic interactions, we do not reflectively decide how much credit to assign to a person's statement. This points to the relation between perception and belief as well as to the unquestioned set of background assumptions that inform perceptual reliance on different 'social types'. On Fricker's view, perception entails the exercise of rational sensitivity, which is not based on inferential reasoning or reflective judgments but rather on one's upbringing and moral training. This means that, when one is confronted with a certain action or situation, it is not necessary to work out its implications in order to grasp its moral connotation. One just sees actions that way, namely, as kind, selfish, charitable etc. (Fricker 2007, p. 72). On this basis, Fricker argues that the hearer can train her testimonial sensibility in order to attend critically to the interlocutor's words. This coincides with the exercise of a 'virtuous perception' which brings together epistemic and moral elements inspired by Aristotelian ethics. The main aspect of this account is that one does not need to apply any theory while attending to what the speaker says. The virtuous listener does not arrive at the formation of perceptual judgments by codifying some complex norm that would be implicit in her judgment. Instead, one needs 'to adapt and rework her thinking to the indefinitely diverse contexts liable to confront her' (Fricker 2007, p. 73).

In this context, Herrmann (2019) argues that Fricker's account of how judgments of credibility work can be elaborated further by drawing on Merleau-Ponty's phenomenology of perception. As illustrated in Chapter 2, Merleau-Ponty argues that perception is organized by relational patterns (for example, the background-figure relation), in that we do not perceive entities as discrete and isolated things but, rather as grouped together by patterns that make up for structured wholes, also known as holistic configurations. This view was originally introduced by Gestalt psychology, a school of thought that emerged in the twentieth century in Austria and Germany, and that Merleau-Ponty extensively discusses in both *The Structure of Behaviour* as well as in *Phenomenology of Perception*. According to Gestalt theorists, through perceptual acts, we intuitively grasp the inner structure (in German, *Gestalt*) or organization of an object. Thus, perception spontaneously recognizes simple geometric forms, like circles and triangles, in place of missing spaces and juxtaposed lines. Similarly, perception naturally seeks coherence and completeness over discontinuity and incompleteness, which is the reason why patterns like figure-ground, proximity, similarity, continuity, closure, and connection constantly emerge in the description of perceptual content.

In *Phenomenology of Perception,* Merleau-Ponty draws on the findings of Gestalt psychology to account for the flexibility and spontaneity of perception. In so doing, Merleau-Ponty departs from Gestalt theorists in that he does not regard organizational patterns like figure and ground as fixed or essential structures of perception based on mathematical and geometric regularity. Instead, Merleau-Ponty argues that those meaningful patterns are generated through the body's orientation and directedness to the felt 'physiognomy' of objects. This means that shapes and figures acquire meaning in virtue of the subject's habitual movements, perspective, and affective situatedness. On this view, the *Gestalt* of a circle is not grasped as a geometric shape formed by a number of points that are equidistant from a centre, but is rather recognized by the subject due to the her affective and sensorimotor familiarity with circular shapes or modulations (as happens, for example, when a child is used to playing with hula hoops).

On Herrmann's view, social classifications can be understood as gestalt-building principles. This means that perceptual cognitive competencies depend on overarching patterns that are acquired through culture and education, while also varying across subjects on the basis of their upbringing and situation. According to Herrmann, social classifications 'do not simply form the background in front of which our perception operates but rather guide its formation' (Herrmann 2019, pp. 288–9). Like Fricker, Hermann argues that stereotypes and prejudices are not subsequent evaluations of perceptual acts but are integrated in the structure of background knowledge that is passed down through social habits, customs, and traditions. It follows that negative prejudices not only affect how subjects are reciprocally positioned towards one another as epistemic agents, but they also posit issues in terms of how background cultural information is structured.

To be sure, this would make epistemic injustice all the more difficult to rectify, because of the way in which stereotypes and prejudices may enter the pre-reflective perceptual thematization of the social context. In fact, styles of perception can be corrected, but that such a work involves restructuring both subjective styles of seeing as well as the cultural background knowledge that is passed down through generations. The implications of this approach have both moral and social relevance. On the one hand, as we pointed out in previous chapters, the process of habit formation is not entirely passive. On the contrary, it involves some level of responsibility on the part of the perceiver. In light of Fricker's analysis as well as of Herrmann's phenomenological re-appraisal, it is possible to qualify this type of responsibility in terms of epistemic responsibility,[16] which is connected to practices of 'attentive listening' (Stawarska 2017).

On the other hand, however, it is equally necessary to consider the means that serve the goal of countering epistemic injustice on a social level. To this end, Herrmann refers to practices of non-violent resistance, like civil protests, as a fundamental tool to challenge epistemic injustice. Historically, civil protests have not only affirmed plurality through the action of agents in concert with one another. They also testify to the power of direct action to challenge epistemic silencing and correct unquestioned common-sense views that circulate in social backgrounds. As Herrmann aptly puts it in relation to the protests of Black Lives Matter: 'instead of looking at black bodies and perceiving them as a source of danger, the white gaze should be enabled to perceive the endangerment of black bodies and the violence that is inflicted upon them' (Herrmann 2019, p. 296). A main upshot of this perceptual shift is that it makes available the perspectives that belong to the political space, enlarging the ground for political speech as well as for political disputes that are integral to democratic and deliberative life.

The revision and correction of contextual knowledge is particularly relevant in light of the relation between knowledge, context, and power. In this regard, Fricker identifies a second type of epistemic injustice, which she calls 'hermeneutic injustice'. While testimonial injustice addresses the recognition of epistemic competence and sincerity, hermeneutic injustice occurs when one lacks the semantic or conceptual resources that are necessary to interpret and communicate experiences of exclusion and discrimination. Fricker provides the example of Carmita Wood, who had difficulty understanding or adequately describing the mistreatment she experienced at work because she was unfamiliar with the concept of 'sexual harassment'. Thus, while Carmita Wood was subjected to treatment that is recognizably sexual harassment, she could not thematize it as such. A person like Wood may be confused, frustrated, and/or angry at the way she is being treated, but she does not have the hermeneutic tools to identify it as an injustice, and therefore as something against which she has a right to be protected. This is the reason why, for example, one of the goals of the 'me too' movement is to raise awareness about the magnitude of the problem of sexual violence as a way to empower women by recognizing the phenomenon itself.

Both forms of epistemic injustices (testimonial and hermeneutic) wrong someone as a subject of knowledge, and therefore 'in a capacity essential to human value' (Fricker 2007, p. 5). As such, epistemic injustice can affect both individuals and groups, underpinning phenomena of social invisibility. In this respect, it is worth noting that both forms of epistemic injustice are at stake in Fanon's account of racial alienation (Guenther 2017). As we noted earlier, for Fanon, racism is not just a matter of subjective attitudes but also a cultural problem that is entrenched in contextual knowledge and power structures. For Fanon, the rectification of racist attitudes requires not just changes in embodied orientation and style of seeing, but also consistent cultural and political practices of resistance to racism as well as of affirmation of humanity. In this context, Fanon's experience as a psychiatrist is consistent with a decolonial praxis that actively fights both testimonial and hermeneutic injustice. Recall, for example, Fanon's diagnosis of the North African Syndrome that we discussed in Chapter 5. Related to that, in *The Wretched of the Earth*, Fanon details how the reports of African patients were systematically dismissed, treated as irrelevant, or else classified as symptoms of laziness and whining by white doctors. Using Fricker's theory of epistemic injustice, we can see to what an extent Fanon sought to dismantle the axes of epistemic oppression in two main ways: first, by 'listening' to the reports of Algerian patients and by acknowledging their histories of abuse and suffering, Fanon vindicates their testimonies, granting them equal dignity and validity.[17] Second, by diagnosing the contextual roots of pathology (for example, by highlighting the connection between colonialism, mental disorders, and racial trauma), Fanon sought to offer the semantic and hermeneutic resources for conceptualizing the relation between racial alienation and institutionalized racism. From this point of view, Fanon's practice aims not just to awaken the consciousness of oppressed people, but also to question the professional medical practice in order to sustain projects of social reform.

6.5 Solidarity, vulnerability, and precariousness

6.5.1 Solidarity and women's coalition

Building on the set of issues discussed so far, we consider, in this final section, how critical approaches to phenomenology thematize solidarity as a shared awareness of common interests, sustained by affective sharing and acting in concert with others.

An important point of departure in this regard is Sonia Kruks' *Retrieving Experience* (2001), which highlights the importance of phenomenological analysis for feminist philosophy. As a political philosopher, Kruks draws from classical and existential phenomenologists to thematize solidarity as a form of coalition among women. Methodologically, Kruks builds on Husserl's concept of 'bracketing' our presuppositions in the analysis of experience. As we saw in Chapter 1, the suspension of the natural attitude is thematized by Husserl as a critical tool that allows the phenomenologist to pursue rigor and clarity in the investigation

of phenomena. As a complete suspension of our cultural presuppositions is never realizable, Kruks follows Merleau-Ponty in arguing that
the bracketing can be used as a heuristic method (Kruks 2001, p. 8).
Specifically, according to Kruks, bracketing can be used for bringing into
relief established or naturalized assumptions about women.

In a way, Kruks' strategy is closely related to Foucault's tactic of
'de-familiarization'. For Foucault, tactics of de-familiarization are a type
of deconstructive work that can be used to revisit and question social
practices and beliefs that have historically 'sedimented' to the point of
being accepted as unquestioned truths about ourselves (Foucault 1997).
By rendering such beliefs 'de-familiar' through genealogical analysis,
that is, by reconstructing the ways in which systems of beliefs operate,
Foucault argues that it is possible to appreciate the ultimate contingency and hence alterability of different styles of being. While Kruks'
approach is partly inspired by Foucault's, she is very clear that, among
the assumptions that should be bracketed, there are also post-modern
theories of gender. Against such approaches, Kruks seeks to retrieve the
focus on 'lived experience' that is distinctive of classical and existential
phenomenology, and that is absent in postmodern theory of gender. On
Kruks' view, 'a focus on what we might call a *sentient* subject allows
us to rethink a range of questions: about volitions, knowing, acting,
about relations with others, and about how differently sexed and raced
(and aged and abled) bodies imbue subjectivity differently' (Kruks 2001,
p. 13).

In her project, Kruks emphasizes the relation between affective sharing and collective agency to build an account of solidarity. According
to Kruks, solidarity consists in acts of generosity and respect guided by
the recognition of the injury suffered by women, even and especially
when that injury is not familiar to the subject. This is what Kruks calls
'respectful recognition', namely 'a relationship in which one is deeply
and actively concerned about others, but neither appropriates them as
an object of one's experience or interests nor dissolves oneself in a vicari-
ous experience of identification with them. Such a relationship allows
other space of their own and recognizes a distance between us that is
not the distance of unconcern' (Kruks 2001, pp. 154–5). Kruks avoids
identifying respectful recognition with empathy, as her account is strictly
concerned with a stance of concern and care for women's bodily and
lived experiences, including women's vulnerability to sexual violence.
Nonetheless, her view of respectful recognition shares at least an important aspect with the Husserlian and Steinian account of empathy that we
introduced in Chapter 2.

From a classical-phenomenological viewpoint, to empathize with another does not require that one has to undergo the same experiences of the person we empathize with. Similarly, Kruks argues that respectful recognition does not require identity of experiences. For example, it is possible for a man to recognize the pain of a woman who experienced sexual abuse without that man having endured that hurt himself, and despite the diversity of sexual characteristics. Drawing on Lugones' account of world-traveling, Kruks argues that respectful recognition entails: (1) feeling-with, which is an affective response to women's suffering that is enacted not just through perception, but also by imaginatively connecting to women's experiences; and (2) a commitment to make the pain and suffering of women an object of ethical concern.

Kruks' account of respectful recognition presents several challenges. On the one hand, the focus on pain runs the risk of objectifying the experiences of women as victims, thereby turning respectful recognition into acts of condescension and pity. On the other hand, as feeling-with does not rule out the use of imagination, there is a risk of intellectualizing women's experience, especially when it comes to the pain of women of different socio-cultural backgrounds. Such limits can be partly accommodated by considering that respectful recognition is an ethical stance of solidarity, and not a universal manner of apprehending or perceiving women regardless of their context. Indeed, respectful recognition is at stake in the comprehension of women's situated experience. In this sense, respectful recognition contextualizes the position of both the women one feels-with and the stance of the subject that attends to those experiences. In so doing, respectful recognition creates affective bonds that are based on the acknowledgment of differences among women, instead of building on either identification or projection. To this end, Kruks stresses that respectful recognition is 'a double awareness, involving immediate affective response to another's pain and a simultaneous awareness that my response is not the same as the other's suffering' (Kruks 2001, p. 175).

By and large, Kruks' account of solidarity aims to inspire and sustain a collective feminist politics. Solidarity motivates women to act together, despite their social and cultural differences. Accordingly, feminism, as a political movement, can be centred on the recognition of difference as well as on the reciprocity of social and political interest, overcoming the risks of reducing the project of women's coalition to some female essence that all women would share *qua* woman. Starting with Beauvoir, the notion of feminine essence has been widely criticized in feminist theory (e.g. Lorde 1984; Fuss 1989; Spelman 1990; Heyes 2000). The feminine essence epitomizes approaches to gender based on the universalization of a particular way of being a woman, thus erasing substantive differences between women, especially when it comes to race, class, and sexual orientation.

In this context, Betty Friedan's *The Feminine Mystique* (1963), is often regarded as an example of the difficulties feminists have faced historically in addressing issues related to diversity. Friedan's argument revolved around the description of experiences of middle-class white women, and their struggles to pursue higher education, careers, or a political voice (Friedan 1992). To be sure, Friedan's work played a key role in feminist discourse and feminist movements, as it challenged the attribution of the role of housewife to women. However, her book also deflected attention from the reality of women for whom a career, a house, or a family are economically unattainable, as well as from those women who do not consider a career a value, as they find fulfilment in non-conventional roles. This is the main critique that emerged in the United States, especially across Black feminists (see also Combahee River Collective 2014). Drawing especially on the works of bell hooks, Black feminist thinkers have argued that the cultural and radical feminist movements of the 1960s and 1970s erased racial and class differences between women, ignoring in particular the experiences of poor women of colour. As hooks states, 'when women are talked about the focus tends to be on white women. Nowhere is this more evident than in the vast body of feminist literature' (hooks 2015, p. 7). In a similar vein, Audre Lorde famously warned white women against the risks of universalizing their experiences to the point that the experiences of women of colour are reduced to the experiences of the 'outsiders'. As Lorde explains, failure to acknowledge the concept of difference in feminism leads to political fragmentation, precipitating collective action: 'Refusing to recognize difference makes it impossible to see the different problems and pitfalls facing us as women' (Lorde 1984, p. 218).

Kruks aims to counter these issues by paying attention to the differences between women without forsaking the goal of promoting collective solidarity. Her view is that solidarity builds on what she calls 'an *affective predisposition* to act on behalf of women other than and different from oneself: a predisposition towards forms of feminist solidarity (Kruks 2001, p. 150). This affective predisposition is rooted in the commonality of sentience as well as in the use of imaginative understanding, sustaining Lugones' view that a 'coalition' between women is ultimately possible as long as white women learn to 'travel' the world of women of colour, developing 'insights into each other's resistant understandings' (Lugones 2003). Differently stated, as white women are exposed to the sexist gaze as well as to gender discrimination, they can draw on such a repertoire of knowledge and experience to travel the race-based oppression of women of colour, from which they are protected by their whiteness. The goal, in this case, is not to identify oneself with another woman by projecting onto her one's personal experiences, but rather to resist the logic of oppression that pits women against each other. This is possible by enacting one's knowledge in an empathetic and politically oriented way. In this sense, a shared coalition of women is capable of resisting social fragmentation through mutual understanding and collective action.

An important example of political action that builds on this insight is the 'Take back the night' movement, which campaigns to end sexual violence. The movement originated in 1970s protests against assaults on women, and the term was used in 1977 as the title of a memorial read by Anne Pride at an anti-violence rally in Pittsburgh. While this movement has predominantly focused on ending sexual violence against women, more recently it has signalled its support for ending sexual violence against different gender identities from all backgrounds around the world.[18] The primary mode of activism of 'Take back the night' consists in marches on the street, typically at night, to highlight the dangers women face when being out at night, and to reclaim streets as places of safety for women, thereby promoting a wider concern for the safety of vulnerable subjects. Participation in these marches highlights the importance of creating and maintaining affective bonds in the sense indicated by Kruks, that is, by connecting people through the respectful recognition of women's experiences and the ethical demands they pose.

6.5.2 Between vulnerability and precariousness

An important upshot of Kruks' phenomenological discussion of solidarity is that it brings to light the dimension of shared vulnerability that underlies and unites women's experience. From a phenomenological perspective, vulnerability is a relational concept rooted in affective experience. Classical, existential and critical phenomenological arguments converge that the lived body is a reality that is simultaneously available to the gaze of the other as an objectifiable reality, while retaining its own characteristic spontaneity and unpredictability. For this reason, vulnerability cannot be equated to fragility and weakness *tout court*. While fragility centres on precarity, weakness, and mortality, the characteristic relationality of vulnerability is rooted in the sphere of sensibility as a place of self-displacement and intercorporeal understanding. At the same time, however, violence constitutes the most radical subversion and denial of the sensitivity upon which vulnerability builds. This calls for a further analysis of the relation between vulnerability, power, and political action, as indicated by the significant attention that the concept of vulnerability has received in recent years across phenomenology, feminist philosophy, and critical theory (see especially Murphy 2012; Petherbridge 2016; Gilson 2018).

From a classical-phenomenological point of view, ontological vulnerability is connected to Merleau-Ponty's account of the flesh in *The Visible and the Invisible* as well as to Levinas' view of sensibility (see Chapter 3). On this view, ontological vulnerability depends on the receptivity of sensibility, understood as the capacity to affect and to be affected by others. These insights have exerted a strong influence on Judith Butler's development of the concepts of vulnerability and precariousness (e.g. Buter 2004b, 2005, 2009), which form part of her project to develop what she calls a 'new bodily ontology' grounded in relationality (Butler 2009, p. 2). Drawing from the work of Levinas, Butler aims to show that the other self that is encountered in intersubjective experience is the very heart of embodied human existence. Specifically, Butler follows Levinas in maintaining that selfhood is constitutively defined by ethical obligations towards others, thus rendering us dependent on – and hence vulnerable to – other people as well as the environment we inhabit. In so doing, Butler also seeks to challenge the view of a sovereign and self-sufficient self that has dominated western political thinking.

Butler uses the term 'precariousness' to denote this universal human condition of interdependence. Precariousness is a fundamentally egalitarian concept, given that each person's existence is equally 'precarious' (Butler 2009, p. 22). It is this shared condition that, Butler thinks, can form the basis of a universal ethics and social solidary: 'From where might a principle emerge by which we vow to protect others from the kinds of violence we have suffered, if not from the apprehension of a common human vulnerability?' (Butler 2004b, p. 30). However, Butler also acknowledges that vulnerability is 'allocated differentially' around the world (Butler 2004b, p. 31), as some groups and individuals are more vulnerable than others due to their different involvements in relations of power, oppression, socio-economic or political inequality, and systematic injustice (e.g. institutional racism). These different conditions, which Butler identifies with 'precarity', build upon the general sense of precariousness that is shared by all human beings within a natural environment that involves non-humans as well. On this view, although we each share a basic ontological condition of *precariousness*, the lives of certain groups, such as women, homeless people, and people of colour, are – in different ways – rendered more precarious than others, and thus experience varying degrees of *precarity*.

Butler connects the process by which differential states of precarity are created with the concept of 'grievability', which denotes the extent to which we are able to mourn the suffering or death of other people. Butler explores how some people's lives do not count as mournable because of how they are represented across the media and within social discourses. Writing in the aftermath of the 9/11 terrorist attacks to the Twin Towers, Butler notices that one effect of America's national response was to cast the lives of those killed by the United States' military as ungrievable. This generated a moral and affective indifference towards the experiences of, for example, those detained and tortured in Abu Ghraib prison as well as towards the death of Afghan citizens following the US occupation of Afghanistan. The asymmetry of mourning is part of Butler's long-standing concern with the way in which only certain lives appear to be recognizable as distinctively human and hence liveable (Butler 1990; 2004a). For example, within the heteronormative, binary model of gender, trans individuals are constitutively unrecognizable, which renders their lives both *symbolically* unliveable (namely, ostracized and othered) and, in tragic cases, *literally* unliveable (in the sense, for example, that trans people are exposed to violence and risks of suicide).

Underpinning this analysis are perhaps the two most fundamental questions to Butler's work: who is recognized as human, and what happens to people who are not considered to be fully human? To return to Arendt's paradox of rights, it seems clear that the lives of migrants trying to enter the United Kingdom are not grievable in the same way or to the same extent as British citizens, especially white British citizens. The Black Lives Matter movement can also be interpreted as an ethical demand that (white) Americans mourn the death of a person of colour with the same intensity as they grieve the death of a white person. In this sense, the lives of the people who are particularly precarious, and whose suffering and death are made ungrievable, are often more vulnerable to violence, either because there is little public response to the violence they experience or because they are considered suitable targets for violence precisely because they are not considered fully human.

Such a distinction between different types of precarity and grievability has been taken up by Erin Gilson to reframe the ethical demands posited by vulnerability. Gilson distinguishes between a primary, 'ontological vulnerability', which is a universal condition that all share regardless of sex, gender, race, abilities, and age, and a 'situational vulnerability', which denotes specific forms of socially induced vulnerability. This latter includes, but is not limited to, psychological/emotional, corporeal, economic, political, and legal vulnerabilities (Gilson 2014, p. 37). On this view, it can be argued that, while all of us are vulnerable to sexual assault, young women are more vulnerable because of a patriarchal culture that depicts women as sexually available to men, fostering the idea that men are *entitled* to women's bodies for their sexual pleasure (hence the resentment when such access is denied). This is coupled with a legal system that woefully fails to protect young women from sexual assault, reflected in the shockingly low conviction rates for rape cases. In turn, these systemic relations sustain and promote the belief that one can get away with sexually assaulting women.

One important reason for distinguishing between ontological and situational vulnerability is that we have good reasons to try to eradicate many forms of situational vulnerability, whereas ontological vulnerability provides the basis for the cultivation of solidarity, including an appreciation of our mutual interdependence as precarious beings. By and large, Gilson's argument aims to correct and expand feminist approaches to vulnerability and violence, showing that vulnerability provides the basis for: (1) comprehending our connectedness to others; (2) responding to the claims and needs of vulnerable groups; and (3) understanding the propensity for violence and its ramifications. Such conditions enable the transformation of those theoretical and mundane practices on the basis of which we tend to regard one another as independent and unrelated subjects of experience. From a normative viewpoint, however, the concept of vulnerability posits significant challenges. For example, Ann Murphy has questioned the ethical and political potential of the concept of vulnerability. While acknowledging that the recognition of our vulnerability can elicit empathy and care, Murphy points out that an appeal to vulnerability as a state of dispossession and availability to others may fail to indicate prescriptive, normative indications that would translate into effective moral norms or political action (Murphy 2012, p. 68).

6.5.3 The power of public assembly

The project of linking together the concept of bodily vulnerability with coalitional politics has been explored more closely in recent years by Butler. In *Notes Toward a Performative Theory of Assembly* (2015), Butler addresses the issues posited by precariousness and their relation to social justice. Butler proceeds by examining recent upsurge in popular protests, from the Arab Spring in the early 2010s (especially as it played out in Tunisia and Egypt), to Occupy Wallstreet, to the 'me too' and Black Lives Matter movements. Butler considers these movements as driven by, and aimed at ending, experiences of precarity. In so doing, she also draws attention to the challenges posited by vulnerability and their relation to precarity.

According to Butler, the political movements above mentioned have in common the fact that they involve physical spaces of mass assembly.

These are the spaces where people mobilize collectively, bringing their own bodies, as it were, to assemble in a public square and across the streets. To be sure, to speak of 'bodies' in general terms is an ambiguous expression, and indeed Butler is well aware that the phrase 'bodies on the street' can refer equally well 'to right-wing demonstrations, to military soldiers assembled to quell demonstrations or seize power, to lynch mobs or anti-immigrant populist movements taking over public space' (Butler 2015, p. 124). Thus, the crux of the matter is to identify under what conditions public assemblies 'are in the service of realizing greater ideals of justice and equality' (ibid.).

Engaging with Arendt's account of the political, Butler describes the act of protesting as the right to appear in public. Butler's argument centres on the concept of political movement, which aims at inspiring social change by placing a plural, embodied 'we' at its centre. In this respect, Butler agrees with Arendt that freedom is a relational concept. As Butler writes, 'freedom does not come from me or from you. [. . .] It is not a matter of finding the human dignity within each person, but rather of understanding the human as a relational and social being, one whose action depends upon equality and articulates the principle of equality' (Butler 2015, p. 88). However, Butler also emphasizes that public protests are enacted by a plurality of bodies, 'as the precondition of all further political claims' (Butler 2015, p. 182). Butler's view is that, prior to the formulation of political demands, the visible and bodily exposure of the group brings forth the demand to recognize human needs of liveability. The difference between the upsurge of the violent mass and the public assembly that asks for democratic changes lies precisely in the fact that the latter surges forth 'in ways that claim and alter the attention of the world for some more enduring possibility of livable life for all' (Butler 2015, p. 183).

Accordingly, Butler refigures the relation between political assembly and bodily experience as interconnected forms of political action. On her view, the very assembling of people constitutes a 'body' (the 'body politic'), which itself is composed of subjects coming together in a space through their interconnected movements, gestures, and speech. Thus, the 'public realm' is an actual, physical space that is inhabited by multiple subjects who manifest themselves through embodied forms of non-violent communication. Butler is keen to stress that the right to appear in public is much more secure for some people than others. Specifically, those bodies that are deemed acceptable can mobilize or move together with more freedom, flexibility, and security than those deemed unacceptable or targeted as outsiders.

From this point of view, the very act of appearing in public can be an important political event. For example, part of the power of Gay Pride street parades is that they demand and celebrate the right of a gay body to appear in public. As Butler writes: 'When the bodies of those deemed "disposable" or "ungrievable" assemble in public view [...] they are saying, "we have not slipped quietly into the shadows of public life: we have not become the glaring absence that structures your public life"' (Butler 2015, p. 152). Echoing Arendt's claim that the most important right is the right to have rights, Butler's theory of assembly implies that the most important social struggle is the demand to be able to appear in public in order to make political demands (that is, to enact specific social claims for justice).[19] On this view, those unable to assemble are fundamentally disempowered. Think, for instance, of the dispersion of homeless people, aided by laws that make it illegal to sleep in public, which works to isolate them as homeless individuals, thus rendering their situation a *personal* one – perhaps to be explained by or blamed on drug abuse or domestic abuse – rather than a *political* one, which governments bear a responsibility for tackling appropriately.[20] As homeless people lack the organizational and social power to form a political body – to mobilize collectively to demand reforms – they are prevented from appearing in public as agents, and therefore they are thoroughly de-politicized. This reflects the fact that a whole network of power and privilege supports people's ability to demand social reforms, from having the time and money to travel to public spaces (which presupposes public transport infrastructure in the first place), to possessing the technology required to coordinate the assembling (which is why mobile phones and social networks were so pivotal in organizing the public protests in places like Egypt). To quote Butler, 'we cannot even fight for infrastructural goods without being able to assume them to one degree or another, so infrastructural conditions for politics are themselves decimated, so too are assemblies that depend on them' (Butler 2015, pp. 126–7).

Ultimately, Butler understands the struggle for social change to be focused on making more lives liveable (and, relatedly, to make lives more liveable). In this sense, Butler considers our shared bodily vulnerability, our inescapably precarious existence, as the basis for a coalitional politics, aimed at securing the conditions in which bodies can exist and, ideally, flourish. Thus, in a way that is not dissimilar to Kruks' argument, Butler thinks and hopes that solidarity can be cultivated when people struggle together to secure the conditions required for bodies to survive, whether that be campaigning to make streets safer for women by ending rape and sexual harassment, or by tackling the problem of homelessness. However, Butler goes further than Kruks by suggesting that the very act of assembling can promote feelings of solidary; simply coming together can foster a sense of togetherness. Thus, it is not always necessary to establish a strong sense of solidarity *prior* to political mobilization. Instead, solidarity can emerge through the collective struggle itself, for example, when people come from very different backgrounds). We need not prove there is a unique or dominant social identity before we can act in concert to secure change about liveability.

Butler's proposal is not without challenges, as it overlooks the analysis of the epistemic and normative conditions that would allow for the *recognition* of the demands for a more liveable life. In the absence of deliberations that sustain normative claims, demands for change can be easily overthrown, restoring the original *status quo*. This is one of the worries that Arendt raises in her account of civil disobedience (Arendt 1972), where she nonetheless defends the power of civil disobedience as a form of voluntary association. In fact, Arendt notes that it was the movement of civil rights, and not the law, that brough into the open 'the American dilemma', forcing the recognition of the crime of chattel slavery, and the 'unique responsibility' that people have inherited (Arendt 1972, p. 81). However, Arendt also stresses that the performances that take place in the political space are the performances of people who *think* and *act* together, thereby constituting a deliberative space.

At the same time, Butler's view can be read as a development and an ameliorative critique of Arendt's account of the political space, with which we opened this chapter. Like Arendt, Butler regards non-violence as the fundamental requirement of public assemblies. Similarly, Arendt contends that, while – from a historical viewpoint – the occurrence of violence seems inevitable, the use of violence should be starkly distinguished from power, which underlies political action and is inherent in the formation of political communities. On Arendt's view, all political institutions are 'manifestations and materialisations of power' (Arendt 1972, p. 140) in the sense that they embody political authority and rely on the force of their governing bodies. For Arendt, the notion of power goes back the Ancient Greek concept of *dynamis*, meaning potency. On her view, power expresses the human ability to act in concert with others for a common purpose. Violence, by contrast, is in itself anarchic, as it is designed for the purpose of 'multiplying natural strength' until it can substitute it (Arendt 1972, p. 145). This means that violence disrupts not only the space of appearances, hence the domain of human and social interaction that power seeks to preserve, but it also affects and destroys the very ability of acting and instituting a shared world. Indeed, violence does not bring forth anything new, for it consists in the nihilation of plurality. Ultimately, from Arendt's point of view, violence lends itself to a breakdown of the horizon of sense that could in principle be pursued by an agent (Dodd 2009).

Moreover, as Amy Allen points out, Arendt understands solidarity 'as a kind of *power* that arises when we make commitments to each other and act in concern. Thus solidarity is achieved, not assumed in advance' (Allen 1999 p. 114). In a similar way, Butler argues that solidarity is enacted by the coming together of an embodied 'we' for the cause of making lives more liveable. At the same time, Butler may provide an ameliorative critique of Butler's account, as she takes into account the intersectional axes that impinge on the positions of the subjects in the political space. Relatedly, according to Butler, if we are to preserve the open-ended and plural character of our living together, we need institutions and policies that acknowledge the demand of hunger, shelter, and social trust. On Butler's view, Arendt did not make space in her account for a geopolitical view that centres on overcoming inequality in food distribution, affirming the rights of housing, and targeting the inequalities of labour.

The discussion of such similarities and differences between Butler's and Arendt's respective approaches to the political may help shed light on the ways in which critical phenomenology can be fruitfully engaged today in dialogue with classical and existential phenomenology. Indeed, the fact that critical approaches to phenomenology consistently use and revolve on classical-phenomenological concepts and arguments should compel us to engage their respective differences, clarifying theoretical divergences but also common philosophical concerns. Such a dialogue helps to thematize in more robust ways the intersectional character of lived experience, and its relevance for the project of an effective feminist coalition. Furthermore, the interrelations between classical and critical phenomenology may contribute to uncovering the connection between epistemic and ethical responsibility in the context of discrimination and injustice. Finally, the investigation of critical topics in classical and contemporary phenomenology sustains the recognition that a shared, liveable world is the condition of possibility for political action and the ethical demands it posits.

Notes

Introduction

1 This book was originally conceived as a continuation of Käufer and Chemero's 2015 introduction to phenomenology, to which we direct the reader for further analysis and discussion of the key ideas and arguments of classical phenomenology. In this connection, see also Zahavi 2019.

2 Critical theory is the denomination of an intellectual tradition and socio-political theory developed in the 1930s by Max Horkheimer, including – among other thinkers – Theodor Adorno, Erich Fromm, Herbert Marcuse, Jürgen Habermas, and Axel Honneth. As we indicate in Chapter 1, critical phenomenology shares the concerns and questions of critical theory, though their respective methods of analysis do not coincide.

3 For an overview of the use of critical phenomenology in other fields, such as cultural geography, see Simonsen and Koefoed 2020.

4 In this book, we have decided to capitalize the term 'Black' to signal that this word refers to a social identity and not to a natural category. As we argue in this volume, racial identities are historically created, and Black identity is shared (in a non-univocal way) by descendants of the African diaspora and beyond due to the history of colonialism. For this reason, 'white' is not capitalized when using the word to refer to white people, as the term does not signify a historically constituted social identity. While there is no consensus on how to capitalize 'black' and 'white', the choice to capitalize the word 'Black' is aligned with the philosophical arguments presented in this book.

228 Notes to pages 14–22

1 What is *Critical* Phenomenology?

1 Both terms derive from the Ancient Greek *nous* (mind or intellect in the sense of the faculty capable of apprehending its object in the understanding rather than in sense-perception).

2 For further analysis, see McIntyre and Smith 1989.

3 This is the idea that history is driven by reason and that the course of history is motivated by an inner, rational purpose which coincides with the fulfillment of humanity's highest end; that is, the actualization of reason. Historically, this view is connected to Hegel's philosophy of history, and his account of the so-called progress of history, of which Husserl was, nonetheless, quite critical, being in this regard closer to Fichte's idealism.

4 See especially Husserl's *Kaizo* articles in Husserl 1988 (partial English translation included in Husserl 1981). These articles refer to a series of essays that Husserl wrote from 1923 to 1924 for the Japanese journal *Kaizo*, where Husserl outlines the task of developing a rational, a priori science of morality for the improvement of society.

5 See in this context Fink's account of the 'operative shadows' that are at stake in Husserl's phenomenology in Fink 1981 (originally published in 1957). As Fink puts it, 'the presence of a shadow is an essential feature of finite philosophizing' (Fink 1981, p. 69).

6 It is also worth noting that the critical-phenomenological critique of Husserl does not apply to all critical-phenomenological works. For an appreciation of Husserlian phenomenology, see, for example, Davis 2020; Rodemeyer 2020; Morris 2020; and Weiss 2018. It is also important to consider that Guenther's critique of transcendental phenomenology is not a rejection of Husserl's insights; see, for instance, Guenther 2017. During the final copy-editing process for the book, we came across Guenther's newly published paper (Guenther 2021), which sets out her understanding of the concept of 'critique' within critical phenomenology. While it was not possible to incorporate a detailed discussion of this contribution, it confirms that the relation between transcendental and critical phenomenology is pivotal for a reconsideration of what makes phenomenology 'critical' in a sociopolitical sense.

7 See also, in this context, Zahavi and Loidolt's critical concerns in Zahavi and Loidolt 2022.

8 For a systematic and thorough introduction to the main themes, problems, and thinkers of critical theory, see Allen and Mendieta 2019.

9 Honneth has developed an influential theory of recognition, at the centre of which is the idea that a just society can be understood in terms of appropriate and normative relations of recognition. While Honneth does not draw on classical phenomenology, his work explores the effects

of misrecognition on embodied experience and the role of affects in the struggle for recognition. For a critical-phenomenological appraisal of Honneth's work, see Oliver 2001. With regard to the theoretical continuity between Honneth's theory of recognition and classical phenomenology, see Jardine (2015, 2017) and Petherbridge 2022. See also Petherbridge's study of Honneth in Petherbridge 2013.

10 For further analysis and discussion, see Moran 2012.

11 For further analysis and discussion, see Gallagher and Zahavi 2007; Käufer and Chemero 2015; Zahavi 2019.

12 For an analysis and discussion of the development of the concept of the life-word in Husserl's phenomenology, see Carr 2014.

13 As Dermot Moran points out, 'it is undoubtedly true that Husserl's careless remarks about Gypsies "vagabonding" around Europe and not contributing to the ideal of universal humanity, and his condescending remarks about the humanity of Papuan natives, sound remarkable for someone who as a Jew was himself subjected to abuse in similar terms. The itinerant position of the Roma Gypsies surely occupies the role here of the "wandering Jew"' (Moran 2012, p. 61).

14 On this basis, Husserl's continuous concern with the universal and transcendental principles that underlie the life-world can be understood as an inquiry into the conditions of 'homeworlds'. This concept refers to the sense of inhabiting a life-world from within, by appropriating a social and cultural tradition and sharing it with fellow companions or 'home-comrades' (Steinbock 1995). As homeworlds are not defined by birth, nationality, or territory, they represent liminal fields that are necessarily co-generated with 'alienworlds', namely worlds that, despite being unfamiliar, are necessarily implicit in the formation of a familiar world-horizon. According to Steinbock, such a critique of historical tradition is best understood in terms of the project of "generative phenomenology" (Steinbock 1995), which inquires into the structure and development of socio-cultural temporalization, rather than simply into the structure of egoic temporalization.

15 Hegel's reception in France was mediated in particular by Alexander Kojève's lectures on Hegel in the 1930s (see Stone 2017a). The master–servant allegory was at the time isolated from the rest of Hegel's *Phenomenology of Spirit* and identified with the core theory of Hegel's dialectic, exerting a significant influence among French Existentialists.

16 For a helpful contrast, compare Sartre's account of the Jewish condition with Hannah Arendt's biography of Rahel Varnhagen, a German writer of the nineteenth century in *Rahel Varnhagen. The Life of a Jewish Woman* (Arendt 1974).

2 Corporeality

1 This is what Drew Leder (1990) calls the dys-appearance of the body, using the Greek prefix "dys", meaning 'bad, hard, ill'.

2 Interestingly, Sartre does not mention either sex or gender. See Chapter 4 for a discussion of gender that draws on Simone de Beauvoir.

3 See also Petherbridge 2017.

4 Nevertheless, according to Ngo, Merleau-Ponty's phenomenology provides a framework to investigate 'how racist practices can become inscribed in bodies', but it 'fails to account for how one's body is experienced in the case of those who are at the receiving end of such practices' (Ngo 2017, p. 64). Like Sullivan, Ngo raises the concern that Merleau-Ponty's critique of corporeal existence admits an 'epistemological level playing field' (Ngo 2017, p. 21) that does not adequately account for the relation between bodily experience and power relations.

5 This is an aspect that will come up again in Merleau-Ponty in the context of intersubjective experience, as we will see in Chapter 3 in relation to Merleau-Ponty's view of intercorporeality as well as to Al-Saji's theory of hesitation.

6 Classical behaviourism of the twentieth century maintained that the organism's behaviour could be understood in terms of how the body reacts to physical external conditions (i.e. stimuli) set by the outer environment to condition biological responses. Merleau-Ponty had already departed from a behaviouristic understanding of human psychology in *The Structure of Behaviour*.

7 Elizabeth Grosz draws attention to the fact that Schilder's use of psychoanalysis centres on a male/heterosexual model of sexuality, which does not simply overlook female sexuality, but also risks reducing the latter to experiences of 'lack' based on the comparison with male sexuality. (Grosz 1994, p. 83). For a discussion of Schilder, Lacan, and narcissism see also Weiss 1999.

8 As Legrand argues in her discussion of anorexia, 'the subject suffering from anorexia is demanding nothing, literally no thing: she does not demand any thing, any matter, any food that would answer her hunger, fulfilling her need; rather she desires the "bare responsiveness" of others, the manifestation of their sensitivity to her intransitive demand, their sensitivity to her presence as a subject who needs *no thing, no food, no answer,* but who desires others, their response to the calls she addresses them' (Legrand 2015).

9 See especially Zaner 1981; Ratcliffe 2008; Carel 2016; Stanghellini et al. 2019.

10 For an accurate and thorough analysis of this concept, including an account of how Heideggerian moods play out in phenomenological psychopathology, see especially Ratcliffe 2010.

3 Intersubjectivity

1 For an overview and critical discussion of empathy in the phenomenological tradition, see especially Zahavi 2001, 2014, and Szanto and Jardine 2017.

2 As Zahavi points out, the concept of empathy runs through all the works of Husserl, spanning over a period of thirty years, testifying to Husserl's continuous engagement with and revision of his own theory of intersubjectivity (Zahavi 2014).

3 To illustrate this, Husserl borrows from Leibniz the notion of monadic life. The monad is a living centre of activity, including passions and volitions. For Husserl, each transcendental ego is, at the same time, incarnated in a concrete monad, which is open to alterity while retaining a characteristic sense of mineness; that is, an intrinsic first-person perspective. Thus, the sphere of ownness refers to the domain in which the concrete, incarnated ego stands in relation to other selves as sources of intentional activity.

4 Edith Stein nonetheless criticizes Scheler's theory for this lack of specification. For a discussion, see Dahlstrom 2021.

5 According to Moran (2005), Heidegger did in fact develop Husserl's theory rather than simply departing from it.

6 For a discussion of the role of Estelle in the play, see Webber's analysis in Webber 2018, pp. 95–112.

7 According to Weiss, a major difficulty with Lugones' theory is that her description of the process is too one-sided, as it does not make clear whether Lugones' mother, for example, would engage the world-travelling attitude (Weiss 2008, p. 112).

8 This is, however, one of the trajectories of critical phenomenology that is more directly connected to intersubjectivity in terms of social perception. This is not exhaustive of all the research directions in critical phenomenology that contextualize or address intersubjective experience. A significantly different approach concerns, for example, the relation between intersubjectivity and dialogue, which draws on Martin Buber's existentialism. See especially Stawarska (2009).

9 It is worth noting that Levinas' concept of otherhood refers to both human subjectivity and God, hence it admits both an ethical and theological interpretation (Bloechl 2011, p. 233).

10 Guenther's appraisal of maternity is informed by Arendt's concept of natality, which we discuss in Chapter 6.

11 For a critical view of Levinas' account of generosity, see Stawarska (2009).

4 Gender and Sexuality

1 The notion. of heteronormativity refers to the assumption that heterosexuality is the standard or normal mode of sexual orientation. This concept is used by gender theorists to challenge norms and cultural practices that stigmatize homosexuality. An important early discussion of this concept is Adrienne Rich's paper, 'Compulsory Heterosexuality and Lesbian Existence' (1980).

2 For a critical-phenomenological account of gender that integrates Husserlian phenomenology, see especially Weiss 1999, 2008; Heinämaa 2003; Al-Saji 2010a.

3 In this respect, Husserl's genetic phenomenology can be brought into dialogue with psychoanalytic approaches to the unconscious (Bernet 2002; Pugliese 2009).

4 See for example Holland 2001; Freeman 2011 .

5 In this sense, female sexual difference includes a set of possibilities of the body towards biological reproduction (e.g. the ability to give birth or lactate), whether or not such biological possibilities are realized (in the sense that not all females can give birth or lactate) (see also Alcoff 2006, p. 172).

6 Wollstonecraft points out the relation between education, social conditions, and moral development, noting that women who are raised to please men and to depend on them are also more likely to be 'cunning, mean, and selfish' (Wollstonecraft 1992, p. 253).

7 In this connection, see Chapter 5, where we discuss Fanon's use of the master–servant allegory.

8 Beauvoir's comparisons between gender, race, and class oppression are not devoid of difficulty. A major concern is that Beauvoir draws such analogies without examining in more detail the overlaps between gender, race, and class oppression, centering her analysis on the experiences of white women. For a discussion, see Spelman 2008 and Gines 2014b. Compare also with Bauer's account of Beauvoir's humility (Bauer 2001).

9 See, in particular, for further discussion on Beauvoir and Butler, Heinämaa and Rodemeyer 2010; Oksala 2016; Groenhout 2017; Stawarska 2018; Weiss 2021.

10 Bartky's account of psychological oppression is highly indebted to Frantz Fanon's account of racial alienation, which we illustrate in the next chapter.

11 See Dolezal (2015) for a phenomenological exploration of women's experiences of shame and how this is used to regulate women's bodies and behaviour, such as the pressures to diet and undergo cosmetic surgery.

12 For a critical overview and discussion of Beauvoir's account of pregnancy and the debates surrounding it, see especially Stone 2017b.

13 Naturally, such bodily changes, and pregnancy more generally, need not be experienced as a positive expansion in the world, as Young herself notes. Pregnancy posits significant physical challenges, be it nausea, aches and pains, difficultly of sleeping, or anxiety (Staehler 2016). See especially Young 2005, pp. 55ff and Rich 1977. Both Rich and Young also highlight the issues posited by the medicalization of pregnancy, when the pregnant woman is treated as a passive vessel. See also Bornemark and Smith 2016.

14 Discourse or discourses, in Foucault's sense, are specific bodies of knowledge through which we make sense of the world, including ourselves. Such bodies of knowledge are historically and socially produced, as they are conditioned by what *can* be said, written, or thought in a historical period. Part of Foucault's work aims to reconstruct the genealogy of discourses, that is, how specific bodies of knowledge (for example, about sexuality or mental health) are produced, established as specific disciplines, and hence accepted as true. See also McHoul and Grace 1993.

15 See especially *Bodies That Matter* (Butler 1993a) for an attempt to think through the materiality of the body within a broadly post-structural framework.

16 For a discussion of the relation between Merleau-Ponty's concept of sexual schema and the Freudian unconscious, see Mooney 2017.

5 Race

1 The average genetic difference between two randomly chosen individuals from anywhere in the world is 0.2% of the total genetic material, which means that humans share 99.8% of the genetic material. Of the 0.2% genetic variation between humans, it appears that there is more genetic variation within the same population or ethnicity (e.g. among Italians or British), than between groups that are considered racially different (such as Caucasians and Asians). Those genetic differences that can be accounted for also have little if no scientific relevance. See Lewontin 1972, and also Gutmann 1966 and Atkin 2012 for further discussion.

2 According to Mills, white supremacy is an ideology system of advantage that is interlocked with capitalism, 'where white people are both the

victims of capitalist exploitation and the beneficiaries of racial exploitation'. For a discussion, see Mills 2014.

3 For a philosophical-historical overview, see also Kendi 2016.

4 Rodney King was an African-American man who, in 1991, was severely
beaten during his arrest by police officers for driving while intoxicated,
following a high-speed chase. Footage of the event was filmed by an
onlooker, the global publication of which caused a public outcry against
police brutality towards African-Americans. The four police officers
involved were put on trial on the charge of excessive use of force. Three
officers were acquitted and the jury could not reach a verdict on a charge
for the fourth officer. The news of the acquittal caused riots in Los
Angeles, which lasted six days and resulted in the death of 63 people
and injuries to 2,383 people. A later trial resulted in two of the officers
being sent to prison, while the two others were acquitted. For a philosophical and socio-political analysis of this event, see the contributions
in Gooding-Williams 1993.

5 Sartre's Preface to *The Wretched of the Earth* placed special emphasis on
the role of violence in anti-colonial revolution, contributing to a misun-
derstanding of Fanon's view of emancipation and anti-colonial struggle.
Hannah Arendt was notably critical of Fanon's justification of violence
(Arendt 1972). For a discussion of Sartre's Preface which contextualizes
Sartre's role in the legacy of Fanon's theory of anti-colonial revolt, see
especially Butler 2006. For further discussion about Arendt's critique of
Fanon and Sartre, see Bernstein 2011.

6 In this regard, Gordon stresses that racist beliefs are voluntarily adopted
and are not simply part of the social background without any corresponding responsibility on the part of the subject who upholds them.
On this front, Gordon departs from Appiah's account of racism, which
instead makes more room for ignorance and lack of reason. For further
discussion see Appiah 1996 and Gordon 1995, pp. 67–77.

7 'Every Arab is a man who suffers from an imaginary ailment. The young
doctor or the young student who has never seen a sick Arab *knows* (the
old medical tradition testifies to it) that "those fellows are humbugs"'
(Fanon 1994, p. 9).

8 To quote Fanon: 'The torturer is the black man, Satan is the black, one
talks of shadows, when one is dirty one is black – whether one is thinking
of physical dirtiness or moral dirtiness . . . In Europe, whether concretely
of symbolically, the black man stands for the bad side of the character . . .
Blackness, darkness, shadow, shades, night, the labyrinths of the earth,
abysmal depths, blacken someone's reputation; and, on the other side,
the brightly look of innocence, the white dove of peace, magical, heavenly
light. A magnificent blond child – how much peace there is in that phrase,
how much joy, and above all how much hope!' (Fanon 1986, p. 189).

9 Fanon also refers to Jacques Lacan's theory of the mirror period, which is the stage when children learn to recognize their reflection in the mirror as their own image. Fanon notes that this theory does not take into account the fact that racialized children project whiteness in the course of the recognition of their own body image. See Fanon 1986, pp. 161ff. For a discussion of Fanon and Lacan, see also Weiss 1999, pp. 26–34.

10 A similar experience to Fanon's is recounted by Audre Lorde (1984). She describes an occasion from her childhood, in which she was sitting next to a white woman on the New York subway. The white woman pulled her coat away from Lorde's snowsuit. Lorde wondered whether there was an insect on her coat that the woman was trying to avoid. However, she realized that *she* was what the woman was trying to avoid contact with: 'When I look up the woman is still staring at me, her nose holes and eyes huge. And suddenly I realize that there is nothing crawling up the seat between us; it is me she doesn't want her coat to touch' (Lorde 1984, pp. 147–8). In both Fanon's and Lorde's narrative, racist categorization produces shame: 'Shame. Shame and self-contempt. Nausea. When people like me, they tell me it is in spite of my color. When they dislike me, they point out it is not because of my color. Either way, I am locked into the infernal circle' (Fanon 1986, p. 116).

11 Hegel's account of desire as mediating the encounter between self and other lends itself to phenomenological explorations, as it provides a remarkable contrast to classical-phenomenological accounts of empathy. For a discussion, see Bergo 2018.

12 For further discussion, see especially Stone 2017a.

13 Compare with Mills' account of white ignorance, in Mills 2007.

14 See also Yancy 2004, 2010, 2015, and Sullivan 2006.

15 Ahmed is aware of such differences, observing that 'some bodies, even those that pass as white, might still be "out of line" with the institutions they inhabit' (Ahmed 2007, p. 160). Although Ahmed does not go into further detail here, it is important to stress that 'whiteness' can only operate effectively with other aspects of privilege. To give an example, even white disabled subjects will experience objects as out of reach, if social spaces are not structured to accommodate them. Thus, 'whiteness' is contextually dependent on the *type* of opportunities white people have access to.

16 As Ahmed also writes: 'It is important to remember that whiteness is not reducible to white skin, or even to "something" we can have or be' (Ahmed 2007, p. 159).

17 This conception of whiteness is also connected to issues related to institutional spaces, to which Ahmed refers, including universities (Ahmed 2007, p. 157).

18 See on this especially Casey 2014.
19 See also Jacqueline Martinez (2000).

6 Political Experience and Political Action

1 See especially Thompson and Embree 2000; Jung and Embree 2016; Gurley and Pfeifer 2016; Bedorf and Herrmann 2020.
2 This is a necessarily limited characterization that, unfortunately, leaves out important figures, including Jan Patočka, a former student of Husserl and Heidegger, who was among the signatories and spokespersons of Charter 77, the program presented by a civic movement of Czech intellectuals in 1977 to protest against the State's violation of human rights.
3 Schütz's *Phenomenology of the Social World* represents one of the main works of classical social phenomenology. Despite being influenced by Husserl, Schütz was also quite critical of Husserl's transcendental approach. Indeed, when the second volume of Husserl's *Ideas* came out posthumously in 1952, Schütz wrote a critical review that highlighted the need, among other aspects, to deepen the phenomenology of sociality and social groups (Schütz 1953, p. 413). More recently, Schütz's social phenomenology has been used to investigate critical race theory and intergroup life (Barber 2001; Camara 2021), while his phenomenological insights have widely inspired research on social and collective intentionality (see, for an overview, Szanto 2020 as well as Salice and Schmid 2016 for contemporary debates on collective intentionality).
4 This includes some notable exceptions. For example, in the 1960s, Italian phenomenologist Enzo Paci developed a phenomenological account of Marxist praxis inspired by and modelled upon Husserl's phenomenology (see Paci 1972). The relation between Marxism and French Existentialism (particularly Sartre and Merleau-Ponty) deserves specific and separate attention, as both Sartre and Merleau-Ponty engaged Marxist thought and developed, over the years, unorthodox positions both towards one another's respective political affiliations and towards the French Communist Party. See especially, Sartre, *Search for a Method* (1957), and *Between Existentialism and Marxism* (1974), as well as Merleau-Ponty's *Humanism and Terror: An Essay on the Communist Problem* (1947), and *Adventures of the Dialectic* (1955).
5 Arendt's distinction between the private and the public space is closely related to Arendt's interpretation of the Ancient Greek world as based on a stark separation between housework (characterized by female and slave labour) and political activity (reserved for free men). Arendt's account has been extensively criticized for projecting onto modern politics the paradigm of the Ancient Greek *polis,* overlapping and confusing

the distinction between the social and the political in the modern world. It is, however, important to notice that, despite the privileging of the Ancient Greek tradition, Arendt's analysis seeks first and foremost to bring to light the possibility for political action out of the web of practical activities in which individuals are always involved. For further discussion see Taminiaux 2001 and Loidolt 2018. For a feminist critique and appraisal of Arendt, see Young 2005, pp. 123–54 and Guenther 2013 respectively.

6 For Arendt, this argument can also be extended to the labourer prior to the modern age as well as to the businessman of contemporary, capitalistic society. Both subjects – in different ways – do not inhabit the public world of action, but rather a world defined by activities concerned with the production of material, tangible outputs.

7 As Pitkin (1988, p. 332) notes, Arendt is ambiguous about whether action, and hence freedom, is only possible in the public realm, or whether freedom and action are also possible in the private realm.

8 While Patterson confines his study to historical forms of slavery, which were state-sanctioned and hence considered legitimate, the concept of social death also applies to the victims of contemporary, illegal slavery, such as sex-trafficking and deportation. Indeed, the fact that modern-day slavery operates through clandestine international slave routes adds an extra dimension to the social death experienced by the modern-day slave.

9 Scholars such as Bernasconi 1996 and Gines 2014a have noted Arendt's inattentiveness to the issues of race and racism. This stems from a controversial paper that Arendt wrote, entitled 'Reflections on Little Rock' (Arendt 1959), which discussed the federal government's enforcement of integration in the public schools of Little Rock, Arkansas. Arendt was criticized for seemingly siding with white parents in this dispute and for misunderstanding, even dismissing, the demands to equality and fairness brought about by Black parents and children. For a discussion, see Johnson (2009) and Dodd (2009).

10 For example, Lisa Guenther, José Medina, Gayle Salamon, Iris Young, Susan Bordo, Luna Dolezal, Sara Ahmed, and Sandra Bartky, among others, all utilize insights from Foucault in their work.

11 A similar discussion is offered by Bülent Diken in his analysis of the stranger, belonging, and identity, especially in relation to discourses about nationhood (Diken 1998).

12 A recent example of this is the case of a Black Yale student, Lolade Siyonbola (Griggs 2018). Siyonbola was having a nap in her dormitory common room when a white student discovered her and called the police. According to one of the officers who attended the scene, 'She called us (and) said there's somebody who appeared they weren't ... where they were supposed to be' (Griggs 2018).

13 For a discussion of epistemic injustice in relation to different forms of knowing, see Shotwell 2017.

14 See on this also Lee 2020.

15 Stawarska also speaks of 'gendered feminine' speech, addressing the overlapping lack of credibility produced by gender, nationality, and foreign speech.

16 See in this connection Ferguson 2020.

17 See also, in this context, Medina 2013.

18 https://takebackthenight.org/history/

19 This would explain why attempts to restrict the right to public protest are problematic, as they directly undermine the ability to fight for social justice through public assembly.

20 Indeed, this phenomenon obscures the fact that 'homelessness' is only possible within a system of private property that renders every space and every object someone's property (part of their 'home').

References

Aaltola, E. (2014) Varieties of Empathy. *Topoi* 33: 243–53.

Adler, A. (2013) *Understanding Human Nature*, trans. Wolfe, W. B. London: Routledge.

Adorno, T. (1977) The Actuality of Philosophy. *Telos* 31 (Spring 1977): 120–33.

Ahmed, S. (2000). *Strange Encounters: Embodied Others in Post-Coloniality*. London: Routledge.

— (2006) *Queer Phenomenology: Orientations, Objects, Others*. Durham: Duke University Press.

— (2007) A Phenomenology of Whiteness. *Feminist Theory* 8(2): 149–68.

Al-Saji, A. (2010a) Bodies and Sensings: On the Uses of Husserlian Phenomenology for Feminist Theory. *Continental Philosophy Review* 43: 13–37.

— (2010b) The Racialization of Muslim Veils: A Philosophical Analysis. *Philosophy and Social Criticism* 36(8): 875–902.

— (2014) A Phenomenology of Hesitation: Interrupting Racializing Habits of Seeing, in Lee, E. S. (ed.) *Living Alterities. Phenomenology, Embodiment, Race*. Albany: SUNY Press, pp. 133–72.

— (2009) A Phenomenology of Critical-Ethical Vision: Merleau-Ponty, Bergson, and the Question of Seeing Differently. *Chiasmi International* 11: 375–98.

Alcoff, L. M. (2000) Phenomenology, Post-Structuralism, and Feminist Theory on the Concept of Experience, in Fisher, L. and Embree, L. (eds) *Feminist Phenomenology*. Dordrecht: Kluwer Academic Publishers, pp. 39–56.

— (2006) *Visible Identities: Race, Gender, and the Self*. New York: Oxford University Press.

Allen, A. (1999) Solidarity After Identity Politics: Hannah Arendt and the Power of Feminist Theory. *Philosophy and Social Criticism* 25(1): 97–118.

Allen, A. and Mendieta E. (2019) *The Cambridge Habermas Lexicon*. Cambridge: Cambridge University Press.

Allen, J. (1982–3) Through the Wild Region: An Essay in Phenomenological Feminism. *Review of Existential Psychology and Psychiatry* 18(1–3): 241–56.

Anzaldúa, G. (1983) La Prieta, in Moraga, C. and Anzaldúa. G. (eds) *This Bridge Called my Back* (2nd edn). Watertown, MA: Persephone Press.

— (1987) *Borderlands / La Frontera: The New Mestiza*. San Francisco: Aunt Lute Books.

Appiah, K. A. (1996) Race, Culture, Identity: Misunderstood Connections, in Appiah, K. A. and Gutmann, A. *Color Conscious: The Political Morality of Race*. Princeton, NJ: Princeton University Press, pp. 30–105.

— (2006) How to Decide If Races Exist. *Proceedings of the Aristotelian Society* 106: 365–82.

Arendt, H. (1951) *The Burden of Our Time*. London: Secker & Warburg.

— (1961) *Between Past and Future: Six Exercises in Political Thought*. London: Faber.

— (1970) *Men in Dark Times*. London: Jonathan Cape.

— (1972) *Crises of the Republic*, San Diego–New York–London: A Harvest Book.

— (1973) *The Origins of Totalitarianism*. New York: Harcourt Brace and Company.

— (1974) *Rahel Varnhagen. The Life of a Jewish Woman*. New York: Harcourt Brace Jovanovich.

— (1990) *On Revolution*. London: Penguin Books.

— (2018) *The Human Condition* (2nd edn). Chicago: Chicago University Press.

Atkin, A. (2012) *Philosophy of Race*. Durham: Acumen.

Baldwin, J. (1998) *Collected Essays (Notes of a Native Son, Nobody Knows My Name, The Fire Next Time, No Name in the Street, The Devil Finds Work, Other Essays)*. New York: Library of America.

Barber, M. D. (2001) *Equality and Diversity. Phenomenological Investigations of Prejudice and Discrimination*. Amherst: Humanity Books.

Bartky, S. L. (1990) *Femininity and Domination: Studies in the Phenomenology of Oppression*. New York: Routledge.

Bauer, N. (2001) *Simone de Beauvoir, Philosophy, and Feminism*. New York: Columbia University Press.

Beauvoir, S. de (2011). *The Second Sex*, trans. Borde, C. and Malovany-Chevallier, S. New York: Vintage Books.

— (2018) *The Ethics of Ambiguity*, trans. Frechtman, B. New York: Open Road Media.

Bedorf, T. and Herrmann, S. (eds) (2020) *Political Phenomenology. Experience, Ontology, Episteme*. London and New York: Routledge.

Behnke, E. A. (2010) The Socially Shaped Body and the Critique of Corporeal Experience, in Morris, K. J. (ed.) *Sartre on the Body*. Basingstoke: Palgrave Macmillan.

Bergo, B. (2018) Husserl and the Political. A Phenomenological Confrontation with Carl Schmitt and Alexandre Kojève, in Bedorf, T. and Herrmann, S. (eds). *Political Phenomenology: Experience, Ontology, Episteme*. New York: Routledge, pp. 121–51.

Berlin, I. (1969) *Four Essays on Liberty*. Oxford: Oxford University Press.

Bernasconi, R. (1996) The Double Face of the Political and the Social: Hannah Arendt and America's Racial Divisions. *Research in Phenomenology* 26: 3–24.

— (2000) Toward a Phenomenology of Human Rights, in Jung, H. Y. and Embree, L. (eds) (2016) *Political Phenomenology. Essays in Memory of Petee Jung*. Dordrecht: Springer.

— (2020) Dialectical Praxis and Decolonial Struggle: Sartre and Fanon's contributions to Political Phenomenology, in Bedorf, T. and Herrmann, S. (eds) *Political Phenomenology. Experience, Ontology, Episteme*. London and New York: Routledge, pp. 17–31.

Bernasconi, R. and Cook, S. (eds) (2003) *Race and Racism in Continental Philosophy*. Bloomington: Indiana University Press.

Bernet, R. (2000) The Encounter with the Stranger: Two Interpretations of the Vulnerability of the Skin, in Bloechl, J. (ed.) *The Face of the Other and the Trace of God. Essays on the Philosophy of Emmanuel Levinas*. New York: Fordham University Press, pp. 43–61.

— (2002) Unconscious Consciousness in Husserl and Freud, *Phenomenology and the Cognitive Sciences* 1: 327–51.

Bernstein, R. J. (2011). Hannah Arendt's Reflections on Violence and Power. *Iris* III (5): 3–30.

— (2018) *Why Read Hannah Arendt Now*. Cambridge: Polity.

Bettcher, T. M. (2021) Trans Phenomena, in Weiss, G., Murphy A. V., Salamon, G. (eds) *50 Concepts for a Critical Phenomenology*. Evanston: Northwestern University Press, pp. 329–36.

Bloechl, J. (2011) Words of Welcome. Hospitality in the Philosophy of Emmanuel Levinas, in Kearney, R. and Semonovitch, K. (eds) *Phenomenologies of the stranger. Between Hostility and Hospitality*. New York: Fordham University Press, pp. 232–41.

Bordo, S. (1988) Feminist Skepticism and the 'Maleness' of Philosophy. *Journal of Philosophy* 85(11): 619–29.

— (1993) *Unbearable Weight: Feminism, Western Culture and the Body*, Berkeley, CA: University of California Press.

Bornemark, J. and Smith, N. (eds) (2016) *Phenomenology of Pregnancy*. Stockholm: Södertörn University.

Bornstein, K. (1994) *Gender Outlaw: On Men, Women and the Rest of Us*. London: Routledge.

Butler, J. (1988) Performative Acts and Gender Constitution: An Essay in Phenomenology and Feminist Theory. *Theatre Journal* 40(4): 519–31.

— (1989) Sexual Ideology and Phenomenological Description, in Allen, J. and Young, I. M. (eds) *The Thinking Muse: Feminism and Modern French Philosophy*. Bloomington, IN: Indiana University Press.

— (1990) *Gender Trouble: Feminism and the Subversion of Identity*. New York: Routledge.

— (1993a) *Bodies That Matter: On the Discursive Limits of 'Sex'*. New York: Routledge.

— (1993b). Endangered/Endangering: Schematic Racism and White Paranoia, in Gooding-Williams, R. (ed.) *Reading Rodney Black: Reading Urban Uprising*. New York: Routledge, pp. 15–22.

— (1997) *The Psychic Life of Power: Theories in Subjection*. Stanford: Stanford University Press.

— (2004a) *Undoing Gender*. New York: Routledge.

— (2004b) *Precarious Life: The Powers of Mourning and Violence*. London: Verso.

— (2005) *Giving an Account of Oneself*. New York: Fordham University Press.

— (2009) *Frames of War: When is Life Grievable?* London: Verso.

— (2015) *Notes Toward a Performative Theory of Assembly*. New York: Fordham University Press.

Cacho, L. (2012) *Social Death: Racialized Rightlessness and the Criminalization of the Unprotected*. New York: New York University Press.

Calcagno, A. (2014) *Lived Experience from the Inside Out. Social and Political Philosophy in Edith Stein*. Pittsburgh: Duquesne University Press.

— (2018) On the Vulnerability of a Community: Edith Stein and Gerda Walther, *Journal of the British Society for Phenomenology* 49(3): 255–66.

Camara, E. (2021) *The Critical Phenomenology of Intergroup Life. Race Relations in the Social World*. Lanham: Lexington Books.

Carel, H. (2016) *Phenomenology of Illness*. Oxford: Oxford University Press.

Carr, D. (2014) The Emergence and Transformation of Husserl's Concept of World, in Heinämaa, S., Hartimo, M. and Miettinen, T. (eds) *Phenomenology and the Transcendental*. London: Routledge.

Casey (2014) Walling Racialized Bodies Out: Border Versus Boundary at La Frontera, in Lee, E. S. (ed.) *Living Alterities: Phenomenology, Embodiment, Race*. Albany: SUNY Press, pp. 233–54.

Crenshaw K., Gotanda N., Peller G., and Thomas K. (1995) *Critical Race Theory. The Key Writings that Formed the Movement.* New York: The New York Press.

Collins, P. H. (2000) *Black Feminist Thought: Knowledge, Consciousness, and the Politics of Empowerment* (2nd edn). New York: Routledge.

— (2015) Intersectionality Definitional's Dilemmas. *Annual Review of Sociology* 41: 1–20.

— (2020) Controlling Images, in Weiss, G., Murphy, A. V. and Salamon, G. (eds) *50 Concepts for a Critical Phenomenology*. Evanston, IL: Northwestern University Press.

Combahee River Collective. (2014) A Black Feminist Statement. *Women's Studies Quarterly*, 42(3/4): 271–80.

Conte, J. (2020) Sex versus Gender. *Oxford Bibliographies.* DOI: 10.1093/OBO/9780199756384-0153.

Crenshaw, K. (2012). *On Intersectionality: The Seminal Essays.* New York: New Press.

Crowell, S. (2000). Who is the Political Actor? An Existential-Phenomenological Approach, in Thompson, K. and Embree, L. (eds) *Phenomenology of the Political*. Dordrecht: Kluwer, pp. 11–28.

d'Entrèves, M. P. (1994) *The Political Philosophy of Hannah Arendt.* London: Routledge.

Dahlstrom, D. O. (2013) *The Heidegger Dictionary.* London: Bloomsbury.

— (2021) Experiencing Others: Stein's Critique of Scheler, *American Catholic Philosophical Quarterly*, 95(3): 433–53.

Davis, H. D. (2020) The Phenomenological Method in Weiss, G., Murphy A. V., Salamon, G. (eds) (2020) *50 Concepts for a Critical Phenomenology*. Evanston: Northwestern University Press, pp. 3–9.

Derrida, J. (2003) *The Problem of Genesis in Husserl's Philosophy*, trans. Hobson, M. Chicago: University of Chicago Press, pp. 154–7.

Dewey, J. (1929) *Experience and Nature.* London: George Allen & Unwin.

Diken, B. (1998) *Strangers, Ambivalence and Social Theory.* Aldershot: Ashgate.

Dodd, J. (2009) *Violence and Phenomenology.* London and New York: Routledge.

Dolezal, L. (2015) *The Body and Shame: Phenomenology, Feminism, and the Socially Shaped Body.* Lanham, MD: Lexington Books.

Douglass, F. (1982) *Narrative of the Life of Frederick Douglass, An American Slave.* Harmondsworth: Penguin.

Drummond, J. (2000) Political Community, in Thompson, K. and Embree, L. (eds) (2000) *Phenomenology of the Political*. Dordrecht: Kluwer, pp. 29–54.

Du Bois, W. E. B. (2007) *The Souls of Black Folk.* Oxford: Oxford University Press.

Edelglass, W. et al. (2012) *Facing Nature: Levinas and Environmental Thought.* Pittsburgh: Duquesne University Press.

Enke, A. (ed.) (2012) *Transfeminist Perspectives in and Beyond Transgender and Gender Studies.* Philadelphia, PA: Temple University Press.

Fanon, F. (1963) *The Wretched of the Earth*, trans. Farrington, C. New York: Grove Press.

— (1965) *A Dying Colonialism*, trans. Chevalier, H. New York: Grove Press.

— (1986) *Black Skin, White Masks*, trans. Markmann, C. L. London: Pluto Press.

— (1994) *Toward the African Revolution. Political Essays*, trans. Chevalier, H. New York: Grove Press.

Feinberg, L. (1998) *Trans Liberation: Beyond Pink and Blue.* Boston: Beacon Press.

Ferguson, M. (2020) Hermeneutical Justice in Fricker, Dotson, and Arendt. *Epoché: A Journal for the History of Philosophy* 25(1): 21–34.

Fielding, H. A. (2017) A Feminist Phenomenology Manifesto, in Fielding, H. A. and Olkowski, D. E. (eds) *Feminist Phenomenology Futures.* Bloomington: Indiana University Press, pp. 7–22.

Fink, E. (1981) Operative concepts in Husserl's phenomenology, in McKenna, W., Harlan, R. M., and Winterset, L. E. (eds), *Apriori and World.* The Hague: Martinus Nijhoff Publishers.

Fischer, L. (2000) Introduction: Feminist Phenomenology, in Fischer, L. and Embree, L. (eds) *Feminist Phenomenology.* Dordrecht: Springer, pp. 1–16.

Foucault, M. (1978) *The History of Sexuality, Volume I*, trans. Hurley, R. New York: Pantheon Books.

— (1980). *Power/Knowledge: Selected Interviews and Other Writings*, trans. and ed. Gordon, C. Brighton: Harvester.

— (1986) *The Care of the Self, Volume III of the History of Sexuality*, trans. Hurley, R. New York: Pantheon Books.

— (1995) *Discipline and Punish: The Birth of the Prison*, trans. Sheridan, A. New York: Vintage Books.

— (1997) *The Essential Works of Michel Foucault, Volume 1: Ethics: Subjectivity and Truth.* ed. Rabinow, P. New York: The New Press.

— (2001) *The Hermeneutics of the Subject. Lectures at the Collège de France 1981–1982*, ed. Ewald, F. and Fontana, A., trans. Burchell, G. New York: Palgrave Macmillan.

Freeman, L. (2011) Reconsidering Relational Autonomy: A Feminist Approach to Selfhood and the Other in the Thinking of Martin Heidegger. *Inquiry* 54:4, 361–83.

Fricker, M. (2007) *Epistemic Injustice: Power and the Ethics of Knowing.* Oxford: Oxford University Press.

Friedan, B. (1992) *The Feminine Mystique.* London: Penguin Books.

Frye, M. (1983) *The Politics of Reality: Essays in Feminist Theory*. New York: Crossing Press.

Fuss, D. (1989) *Essentially Speaking*. London: Routledge.

Fussi, A. (2018) *Per una teoria della vergogna*. Pisa: Ets.

Gagne, P., Tewksbury, R. and McGaughey, D. (1997) Coming out and Crossing over: Identity Formation and Proclamation in a Transgender Community. *Gender and Society* 11(4): 478–508.

Gallagher, S. and Zahavi, D. (2012) *The Phenomenological Mind. An Introduction to Philosophy of Mind and Cognitive Sciences*. London and New York: Routledge.

Gilson, E. (2014) *The Ethics of Vulnerability: A Feminist Analysis of Social Life and Practice*. London: Routledge.

Gines, K. T. (2014a) *Hannah Arendt and the Negro Question*. Bloomington, IN: Indiana University Press.

— (2014b) Comparative and Competing Frameworks of Oppression in Simone de Beauvoir's *The Second Sex*. *Graduate Faculty Philosophy Journal* 1–2, pp. 251–73.

Gordon, L. R. (1995) *Fanon and the Crisis of European Man: An Essay on Philosophy and the Human Sciences*. New York: Routledge.

— (1999) *Bad Faith and Antiblack Racism*. New York: Humanity Books.

— (2015) *What Fanon Said. A Philosophical Introduction to his Life and Thought*. New York: Fordham University Press.

— (2020) Bad Faith, in Weiss, G., Murphy A. V., Salamon, G. (eds) *50 Concepts for a Critical Phenomenology*. Evanston: Northwestern University Press.

Griggs, B. (2018) A Black Yale Graduate Student Took a Nap in Her Dorm's Common Room. So a White Student Called Police. *CNN*, 12/05/2018.

Groenhout, R. (2017) Beauvoir and the Biological Body, in Hengehold, L. and Bauer, N. (eds) *A Companion to Simone de Beauvoir*. Oxford: Wiley Blackwell, pp. 73–86.

Grosz, E. (1994) *Volatile Bodies: Towards a Corporeal Feminism*. London: Routledge.

Guenther, L. (2006) *The Gift of the Other. Levinas and the Politics of Reproduction*. Pittsburgh: Duquesne University Press.

— (2013) *Solitary Confinement*. Minneapolis-London: University of Minnesota Press.

— (2017) Epistemic Injustice and Phenomenology, in Kidd, I. J., Medina, J. and Pohlhaus, G. (eds) *The Routledge Handbook of Epistemic Injustice*. London: Routledge, pp. 195–204.

— (2020) Critical Phenomenology, in Weiss, G., Murphy A. V., Salamon, G. (eds) *50 Concepts for a Critical Phenomenology*. Evanston: Northwestern University Press.

— (2021) Six Senses of Critique for Critical Phenomenology. *Puncta. Journal of Critical Phenomenology* 4/2: 5–23.

Gurley, S. W. and Pfeifer, G. (eds) (2016) *Phenomenology and the Political.* London and New York: Rowman and Littlefield.

Gutmann, A. (1996) Responding to Racial Injustice, in Appiah, K. A. and Gutmann, A. (eds) *Colour Conscious: The Political Morality of Race.* Princeton: Princeton University Press, pp. 106–78.

Haney, K. (2000) Edith Stein: Woman and Essence, in Fischer, L. and Embree, L. (eds) *Feminist Phenomenology.* Dordrecht: Springer, pp. 213–36.

Haslanger, S. (2012) *Resisting Reality. Social Construction and Social Critique.* Oxford: Oxford University Press.

Hegel, G. W. F. (1977) *Phenomenology of Spirit,* trans. Miller, A. V. Oxford.

Heidegger, M. (1993) *Basic Writings,* ed. Krell, D. F. New York: Harper Collins.

— (1995) *The Fundamental Concepts of Metaphysics. World, Finitude, Solitude,* trans. McNeill, W. and Walker, N. Bloomington: Indiana University Press.

— (2001) *Being and Time,* trans. Macquarrie, J. and Robinson, E. Oxford and Cambridge, MA: Blackwell.

Heinämaa, S (2003) *Toward a Phenomenology of Sexual Difference.* London and New York: Rowman & Littlefield.

— (1997) What Is a Woman? Butler and Beauvoir on the Foundations of the Sexual Difference, *Hypatia* 12(1): 20–39.

— (2011) A Phenomenology of Sexual Difference: Types, Styles, and Persons, in Witt, C. (ed.) *Feminist Metaphysics. Explorations in the Ontology of Sex, Gender, and the Self.* Dordrecht: Springer.

— (2014) 'An Equivocal Couple Overwhelmed by Life': A Phenomenological Analysis of Pregnancy. *PhiloSOPHIA. A Journal of Continental Feminism* 4(1):12–49.

Heinämaa, S. and Rodemeyer, L. M. (2010) Introduction. *Continental Philosophy Review* 43: 1–11.

Herrmann, S. (2019) The Struggle for a Common World: From Epistemic Power to Political Action with Arendt and Fricker, in Bedorf, T. and Herrmann, S. (eds). *Political Phenomenology: Experience, Ontology, Episteme.* New York: Routledge, pp. 277–99.

Heyes, C. (2000) *Line Drawings: Defining Women through Feminist Practice.* Ithaca, NY: Cornell University Press.

Hinsch, C. (1970) The Personal is Political, in Firestone, S. and Koedt, A. (eds) *Notes From the Second Year: Women's Liberation: Major Writings of the Radical Feminists.* New York: Radical Feminism, pp. 76–7.

Holland, N. J. (2001) 'The Universe Is Made of Stories, Not of Atoms':

Heidegger and the Feminine They-Self, in Holland, N. J. and Huntington, P. (eds) *Feminist Interpretations of Heidegger*. Pennsylvania: Pennsylvania University Press, pp. 128–48.

— (2020) The They, in Weiss, G., Murphy A. V., Salamon, G. (eds) *50 Concepts for a Critical Phenomenology*. Evanston: Northwestern University Press.

hooks, bell. 2015. *Ain't I a Woman: Black Women and Feminism*. London: Routledge.

Husserl, E. (1960) *Cartesian Meditations*, trans. Cairns, D. The Hague: Martinus Nijhoff.

— (1970) *The Crisis of European Sciences and Transcendental Phenomenology. An Introduction to Phenomenological Philosophy*, trans. Carr, D. Evanston: Northwestern University Press.

— (1981) *Shorter Works*, ed. McCormick, P. and Elliston, F. A. Notre Dame: University of Notre Dame Press.

— (1988) *Aufsätze und Vorträge (1922–1937)*, ed. Nenon, T. and Sepp, H. R. The Hague: Kluwer.

— (1989) *Ideas Pertaining to a Pure Phenomenology and to a Phenomenological Philosophy. Second Book*, trans. Rojcewicz, R. and Schuwer, A. Dordrecht-Boston-London: Kluwer.

— (1997) *Thing and Space*, trans. Rojcewicz, R. Dordrecht: Springer.

— (1999) *The Idea of Phenomenology*, trans. Hardy, L. Edmund Husserl Collected Works. Vol. VIII. Dordrecht: Springer.

— (2001a) *Logical Investigations*, trans. Findlay, J. N., revd. Moran, D. Vol. 1. London and New York: Routledge 2001.

— (2001b) *Analyses Concerning Passive and Active Synthesis*, trans. Steinbock, A. J. Dordrecht: Kluwer 2001.

— (2002) Philosophy as Rigorous Science, trans. Brainard, M. *The New Yearbook for Phenomenology and Phenomenological Philosophy* 2, pp. 249–95.

— (2004) *Ideas I*, trans. Dahlstrom, D. O. Indianapolis and Cambridge: Hackett Publishing Company.

— (2008) Edmund Husserl's Letter to Lucien Lévy-Bruhl, trans. Staehler, T. and Moran, D. *The New Yearbook for Phenomenology and Phenomenological Philosophy* VIII.

Jardine, James (2015) Stein and Honneth on Empathy and Emotional Recognition. *Human Studies* 38: 567–89.

— (2017) Elementary Recognition and Empathy. A Husserlian Account. *Metodo. International Studies in Phenomenology and Philosophy. Special Issue on Intersubjectivity and Recognition* 5(1): 143–70.

Jensen, R. T. (2009) Motor Intentionality and the Case of Schneider. *Phenomenology and the Cognitive Sciences* DOI 10.1007/s11097-009-9122-x.

Johnson, C. (1993) A Phenomenology of the Black Body. *Michigan Quarterly Review* 32(4): 599–613.

— (2009) Reading Between the Lines: Kathryn Gines on Hannah Arendt and Antiblack Racism. *The Southern Journal of Philosophy* 47: 77–83.

Judd-Beer, L. (2016) Women's Existence, Woman's Soul: Essence and Existence in Edith Stein's Later Feminism, in Calcagno, A. (ed.) *Edith Stein: Women, Social-Political Philosophy, Theology, Metaphysics and Public History*, pp. 35–48.

Jung, H. Y. and Embree, L. (eds) (2016) *Political Phenomenology. Essays in Memory of Petee Jung*. Dordrecht: Springer.

Karkazis, K. (2008) *Fixing Sex: Intersex, Medical Authority, and Lived Experience*. Durham: Duke University Press.

Käufer, S. and Chemero, A. (2015) *Phenomenology. An Introduction*. Cambridge. Malden: Polity.

Kristeva, J. (1982) *Powers of Horror. An Essay on Abjection*, trans. Roudiez, L. S. New York: Columbia University Press.

Kearney, R. and Semonovitch, K. (eds) (2011) *Phenomenologies of the Stranger. Between Hostility and Hospitality*. New York: Fordham University Press.

Keating, A. and González-López, G. (2011) *Bridging: How Gloria Anzaldúa's Life and Work Transformed Our Own*. Austin: University of Texas Press.

Kendi, I. X. (2016) *Stamped from the Beginning. The Definitive History of Racist Ideas in America*. New York: Nations Books.

Kruks, S. (2001) *Retrieving Experience: Subjectivity and Recognition in Feminist Politics*. Ithaca, NY: Cornell University Press.

— (2006) Merleau-Ponty and the Problem of Difference in Feminism, in Olkowski, D. and Weiss, G. (eds) *Feminist Interpretations of Merleau-Ponty*. Pennsylvania: Pennsylvania State University Press, pp. 25–48.

Leder, D. (1990) *The Absent Body*. Chicago: Chicago University Press.

Lee, E. (2014) Bodily Movement and Responsibility for a Situation, in Lee, E. S. (ed.) *Living Alterities: Phenomenology, Embodiment, Race*. Albany: SUNY Press, pp. 233–54.

— (2020) Model Minority, Weiss, G., Murphy A. V., Salamon, G. (eds) *50 Concepts for a Critical Phenomenology*. Evanston: Northwestern University Press, pp. 231–6.

Lee, N.-I. (1993) *Edmund Husserls Phänomenologie der Instinkte*. Dordrecht: Springer.

Legrand, D. (2010) Myself with No Body? Body, Bodily-Consciousness and Self-Consciousness, in Schmicking, D. and Gallagher, S. (eds), *Handbook of Phenomenology and Cognitive Science*. Dordrecht: Springer, pp. 181–200.

— (2015) Anorexia and Bodily Intersubjectivity. *European Psychologist* 20(1): 52–61.

Levinas, E. (1969) *Totality and Infinity: An Essay on Exteriority*, trans. Lingis, A. Pittsburgh: Duquesne University Press.

— (1991) *Otherwise than Being or Beyond Essence*, trans. Lingis, A. Pittsburgh: Duquesne University Press.

Lewontin, R. (1972) The apportionment of Human Diversity. *Evolutionary Biology* 6: 381–98.

Lipps, T. (1909). *Leitfaden der Psychologie*. Leipzig: Verlag von Wilhelm Engelmann.

Loidolt, S. (2016) Hannah Arendt's Conception of Actualized Plurality, in Szanto, T. and Moran, D. (eds) *Phenomenology of Sociality. Discovering the We*. London and New York: Routledge, pp. 42–55.

Loidolt, S. (2018) *Phenomenology of Plurality: Hannah Arendt on Political Intersubjectivity*. London and New York: Routledge.

Lorde, A. (1984) *Sister Outsider: Essays and Speeches*. New York: Crossing Press.

Luft, S. and Wehrle M. (eds) (2017) *Husserl-Handbuch. Leben-Werk-Wirkung*. Stuttgart: J. B. Metzler.

Lugones, M. (1987) Playfulness, 'World'-Traveling, and Loving Perception. *Hypatia* 2(4): 3–19.

— (2003) *Pilgrimages/Peregrinajes: Theorizing Coalition against Multiple Oppressions*. New York: Rowman & Littlefield.

McGowan, J. (1993) *Hannah Arendt: An Introduction*. Minneapolis: University of Minnesota Press.

McIntyre and Smith (1989) Theory of Intentionality, in Mohanty, J. N. and McKenna, William R. (eds) *Husserl's Phenomenology: A Textbook*. Washington, DC: Center for Advanced Research in Phenomenology and University Press of America, pp. 147–79.

McMullin, I. (2013) *Time and the Shared World. Heidegger on Social Relations*. Evanston: Northwestern University Press.

McRuer, R. (2006) *Crip Theory. Cultural Signs of Queerness and Disability*. New York and London: New York University Press.

Marder, M. (2014) *Phenomena – Critique – Logos. The Project of Critical Phenomenology*. London and New York: Rowman & Littlefield.

Martinez, J. (2000) *Phenomenology of Chicana Experience and Identity: Communication and Transformation in Praxis*. Lanham: Rowman & Littlefield.

Marx, K. (1987) Economic and Philosophic Manuscripts of 1844, in *The Marx Reader*, ed. Tucker, R. C. New York and London: Norton & Company.

Mascat, J. M. H. (2014) Hegel and the Black Atlantic: Universalism, Humanism and Relation, in Dhawan, N. (ed.) *Decolonizing Enlightenment: Transnational Justice, Human Rights and Democracy in a Postcolonial World*. Opladen: Verlag Barbara Budrich, pp. 93–114.

Mason-Schrock, D. (1996) Transsexuals' Narrative Construction of the 'True Self". *Social Psychology Quarterly* 59(3): 176–92.

McCoul, A. and Grace, W. (1993) *A Foucault Primer. Discourse, Power, and the Subject.* London and New York: Routledge.

Merleau-Ponty, M. (1964) Eye and Mind, trans. Dallery, C., in *The Primacy of Perception and Other Essays on Phenomenological Psychology, the Philosophy of Art, History and Politics.* Evanston: Northwestern University Press, pp. 159–90.

— (1968) *The Visible and Invisible*, trans. Lingis, A. Evanston: Northwestern University Press.

— (2012) *Phenomenology of Perception*, trans. Landes, D. A. London and New York: Routledge.

Mills, C. (2007) White Ignorance, in Sullivan, S. and Tuana, N. (eds) *Race and Epistemologies of Ignorance.* Albany: SUNY Press, pp. 13–38.

— (2014) Materializing Race, in Lee, E. S. (ed.) *Living Alterities: Phenomenology, Embodiment, Race.* Albany: SUNY Press, pp. 19–41.

Mooney, T. (2017) Repression and Operative Unconsciousness in *Phenomenology of Perception*, in Legrand, D. and Trygg, D. (eds) *Unconsciousness Between Phenomenology and Psychoanalysis.* Dordrecht: Springer.

Moran, D. (2005) *Edmund Husserl Founder of Phenomenology.* Cambridge-Malden: Polity.

— (2011) 'Even the Papuan is a Man and not a Beast': Husserl on Universalism and the Relativity of Cultures. *Journal of the History of Philosophy* 49(4): 463–94.

— (2012) *Husserl's Crisis of European Sciences and Transcendental Phenomenology. An Introduction.* Cambridge: Cambridge University Press.

— (2015) Between Vision and Touch: from Husserl to Merleau-Ponty, in Kearney R. and Trenor, B. (eds) *Carnal Hermeneutics.* New York: Fordham University Press, pp. 214–34.

Morris, D. (2020) Horizons, in Weiss, G., Murphy A. V., Salamon, G. (eds) *50 Concepts for a Critical Phenomenology.* Evanston: Northwestern University Press.

Murphy, A. V. (2012) *Violence and the Philosophical Imaginary.* Albany: State University of New York Press.

Ngo, H. (2017) *The Habits of Racism. A Phenomenology of Racism and Racialized Embodiment.* Lanham: Lexington Books.

Oksala, J. (2016) *Feminist Experiences: Foucauldian and Phenomenological Investigations.* Evanston, IL: Northwestern University Press.

Oliver, K. (2001) *Witnessing: Beyond Recognition.* Minneapolis: University of Minnesota Press.

— (2008) Beyond Recognition: Merleau-Ponty and the Ethics of Vision, in

Weiss, G. (ed.) *Intertwinings. Interdisciplinary Encounters with Merleau-Ponty*, pp. 131–52.

Ortega, M. (2016) *In-Between. Latina Feminist Phenomenology, Multiplicity, and the Self*. Albany: State University of New York Press.

Outlaw, L. (1996) *On Race and Philosophy*. New York: Routledge.

Paci, E. (1972) *The Function of the Sciences and the Meaning of Man*, trans. Piccone, P. and Hansen, J. E. Evanston: Northwestern University Press.

Parekh, S. (2008) *Hannah Arendt and the Challenge of Modernity. A Phenomenology of Human Rights*. London and New York: Routledge.

Petherbridge, D. (2013) *The Critical Theory of Axel Honneth*. Lanham: Lexington Books.

— (2016) What's Critical about Vulnerability? Rethinking Interdependence, Recognition, and Power. *Hypatia* 21(1).

— (2017) Racializing Perception and the Phenomenology of Invisibility, in Dolezal, L. and Petherbridge, D. (eds) *Body/Self/Other: The Phenomenology of Social Encounters*. Albany: SUNY Press.

— (2022) Habit, Attention and Affection: Husserlian Inflections, in Bortolan, A. and Magrì, E., *Empathy, Intersubjectivity, and the Social World. The Continued Relevance of Phenomenology. Essays in Honour of Dermot Moran*. Berlin: De Gruyter.

Pitkin, H. F. (1998) *The Attack of the Blob. Hannah Arendt's concept of the social*. Chicago and London: University of Chicago Press.

Preester, H. de (2013) Merleau-Ponty's Sexual Schema and the Sexual Component of Body Integrity Identity Disorder. *Medicine, Healthcare and Philosophy* 16: 171–84.

Price, J. (2015) *Prison and Social Death*. New York: Rutgers.

Pugliese, A. (2009) Triebsphäre und Urkindheit des Ich, *Husserl Studies* 25: 141–57.

— (2015) *Il movente dell'esperienza. Costituzione, pulsione ed etica in Edmund Husserl*. Milan: Mimesis.

Ratcliffe, M. (2008) *Feelings of Being: Phenomenology, Psychiatry and the Sense of Reality*. Oxford: Oxford University Press.

— (2010) The Phenomenology of Mood and the Meaning of Life, in Goldie, P. (ed.) *The Oxford Handbook of Philosophy of Emotions*. Oxford: Oxford University Press, pp. 349–72.

— (2012) Phenomenology as a Form of Empathy. *Inquiry* 55 (5): 473–95.

— (2015) *Experiences of Depression. A Study in Phenomenology*. Oxford: Oxford University Press.

Rich, A. (1977). *Of Woman Born: Motherhood as Experience and Institution*. London: Virago.

— (1980) Compulsory Heterosexuality and Lesbian Existence. *Signs: Journal of Women in Culture and Society* 5(4): 631–60.

Robillard, A. B. (1999) *Meaning of a Disability. The Lived Experience of Paralysis*. Philadelphia: Temple University Press.

Rodemeyer, L. M. (2020) The Natural Attitude. In Weiss, G., Murphy A. V., Salamon, G. (eds) (2020) *50 Concepts for a Critical Phenomenology*. Evanston: Northwestern University Press.

Rubin, H. (2003) *Self-Made Men: Identity and Embodiment Amongst Transsexual Men*. Nashville: Vanderbilt University Press.

Salamon, G. (2010) *Assuming a Body: Transgender and Rhetorics of Materiality*. New York: Colombia University Press.

— (2018) What is Critical about Critical Phenomenology? *Puncta: Journal of Critical Phenomenology* 1, pp. 8–17.

Salice, A. and Schmid, H. B. (eds) (2016) *The Phenomenological Approach to Social Reality. History, Concepts, Problems*. Dordrecht: Springer.

Sartre, J.-P. (1989) *No Exit and Three Other Plays*, trans. Gilbert, S. New York: Vintage Books.

— (1992) *Notebooks for an Ethics*, trans. Pellauer, D. Chicago and London: University of Chicago Press.

— (1995) *Anti-Semite and Jew*, trans. Becker, G. J. New York: Shocken Books.

— (2003) *Being and Nothingness*, trans. Barnes, H. E. London and New York: Routledge.

— (2008) *Black Orpheus*, in Sartre, J.-P: *The Aftermath of War (Situations III)*, trans. Turner, C. Oxford: Seagull Books, pp. 259–329.

Sawicki, M. (1997) *Body, Text, and Science. The Literacy of Investigative Practices and the Phenomenology of Edith Stein*. Dordrecht: Springer.

Scheler, M. (1973a) *Formalism in Ethics and Non-Formal Ethics of Values*, trans. Frings, M., Funk, R. L. Evanston: Northwestern University Press.

— (1973b) *Selected Philosophical Essays*, trans. Lachterman, D. R. Evaston: Northwestern University Press.

— (2017) *The Nature of Sympathy*, trans. Heath, P. London and New York: Routledge.

Schilder, P. (1999) *The Image and Appearance of the Human Body*. London: Routledge.

Schütz, A. (1944) The Stranger. An Essay in Social Psychology. *American Journal of Sociology* 49(6): 499–507.

— (1953) Edmund Husserl's Ideas, Volume II. *Philosophy and Phenomenological Research* 13(3): 394–413.

— (1967) *The Phenomenology of the Social World*, trans. Walsh, G. and Lehnert, F. Evanston: Northwestern University Press.

Sheets-Johnstone, M. (2011) *The Primacy of Movement*. Amsterdam: John Benjamins B.V.

— (2015) Embodiment on Trial. A Phenomenological Investigation. *Continental Philosophy Review* 48: 23–39.

Shelby, T. (2005) *We Who are Dark: The Philosophical Foundations of Black Solidarity*. Cambridge, MA: Harvard University Press.

Shotwell, A. (2009) A Knowing that Resided in my Bones: Sensuous Embodiment and Trans Social Movement, in Campbell, S., Meynell, L. and Sherwin, S. (eds) *Embodiment and Agency*. Pennsylvania: Pennsylvania University Press.

— (2017) Forms of Knowing and Epistemic Resources, in Kidd, I. J., Medina, J. and Pohlhaus, G. (eds) *The Routledge Handbook of Epistemic Injustice*. London: Routledge, pp. 79–88.

Shrage, L. (ed.) (2009) *You've Changed: Sex Reassignment and Personal Identity*. Oxford: Oxford University Press.

Silverman, H. J. (1987) Merleau-Ponty's Human Ambiguity, in Silverman, H. J., *Inscriptions. After Phenomenology and Structuralism*. Evanston: Northwestern University Press, pp. 63–92.

Simonsen, K. and Koefoed, L. (2020) *Geographies of Embodiment. Critical Phenomenology and the World of Strangers*. Los Angeles: SAGE.

Slatman, J. and Yaron, G. (2014) Toward a Phenomenology of Disfigurement, in Zeiler, K. and Käll, L. K. (eds) *Feminist Phenomenology of Medicine*. New York: SUNY, pp. 223–40.

Smith, C. (2009) *The Prison and the American Imagination*. New Haven: Yale University Press.

Spelman, E. (1990) *Inessential Woman: Problems of Exclusion in Feminist Thought*. London: Women's Press.

Spiegelberg, H. (1965) *The Phenomenological Movement. A Historical Introduction*. Vols. 1–2. The Hague: Martinus Nijhoff.

Staehler, T. (2016) Passivity, Being-With and Being-There: Care During Birth. *Medicine, Health Care and Philosophy* 19(3): 371–9.

Stanghellini, G. et al. (eds) (2019) *The Oxford Handbook of Phenomenological Psychopathology*. Oxford: Oxford University Press.

Stawarska, B. (2009) *Between You and I: Dialogical Phenomenology*. Athens: Ohio University Press.

— (2017) Unhappy Speech and Hearing Well, in Fielding, H. A. and Olkowski, D. E. (eds) *Feminist Phenomenology Futures*. Indiana University Press.

— (2018) Subject and Structure in Feminist Phenomenology: Re-Reading Beauvoir with Butler, in Shabot, S. C. and Landry, C. (eds) *Rethinking Feminist Phenomenology. Theoretical and Applied Perspectives*. London: Rowman and Littlefield International.

Stein, E. (1964) *On the Problem of Empathy*. The Collected Works of Edith Stein. Vol. 3, trans. Stein, W. Washington, DC: ICS Publication.

— (1996) *Essays on Woman*. The Collected Works of Edith Stein. Vol. 2, trans. Oben, F. M. Washington, DC: ICS Publications.

— (2000) *Philosophy of Psychology and the Humanities*. The Collected

Works of Edith Stein. Vol. 7, trans. Baseheart, M. C., and Sawicki, M. Washington, DC: ICS Publication.

Steinbock, A. J. (1995) *Home and Beyond: Generative Phenomenology after Husserl*. Evanston: Northwestern University Press.

Stoller, S. (2017) What is Feminist Phenomenology? Looking Backward into the Future, in Fielding, H. A. and Olkowski, D. E. (eds) *Feminist Phenomenology Futures*. Bloomington: Indiana University Press, pp. 328–54.

Stone, A. (2007) *An Introduction to Feminist Philosophy*. Cambridge: Polity.

— (2017a) Hegel and Twentieth-Century French Philosophy, in *The Oxford Handbook of Hegel*. Oxford: Oxford University Press, pp. 697–717.

— (2017b) Beauvoir and the Ambiguities of Motherhood, in Villa, D. (ed.) *The Cambridge Companion to Hannah Arendt*. Cambridge: Cambridge University Press.

Stone, S. (1991) The Empire Strikes Back: A Posttranssexual Manifesto, in Epstein, J. and Straub. K. (eds) *Body Guards*. London: Routledge.

Stryker, S. and Whittle, S. (eds) (2006) *The Transgender Studies Reader*. New York: Routledge.

Sullivan, N. (2003) *A Critical Introduction to Queer Theory*. Edinburgh: Edinburgh University Press.

Sullivan, S. (1997) Domination and Dialogue in Merleau-Ponty's *Phenomenology of Perception*. Hypatia 12(1): 1–19.

— (2001) *Living Across and Through Skins. Transactional bodies, Pragmatism, and Feminism*. Bloomington: Indiana University Press.

— (2006) *Revealing Whiteness. The Unconscious Habits of Racial Privilege*. Bloomington: Indiana University Press.

Summa, M. (2014) *Spatio-Temporal Intertwining. Husserl's Transcendental Aesthetics*. Dordrecht: Springer.

Szanto, T. (2020) Phenomenology and Social Theory, in Kivisto, P. (ed.) *The Cambridge Handbook of Social Theory*. Cambridge: Cambridge University Press.

Szanto, T. and Jardine, J. (2017) Empathy in the Phenomenological Tradition, in Maibom, H. L. (ed.) *The Routledge Handbook of Philosophy of Empathy*. London and New York: Routledge, pp. 86–97.

Taminiaux (2001) Athens and Rome, in Villa, D. (ed.) *The Cambridge Companion to Hannah Arendt*. Cambridge: Cambridge University Press.

Thompson, K. and Embree, L. (eds) (2000) *Phenomenology of the Political*. Dordrecht: Kluwer.

Titchkosky, T. and Michalko, R. (2012) The Body as the Problem of Individuality: A Phenomenological Disability Studies Approach, in Goodley, D. et al. (eds) *Disability and Social Theory: New Developments and Directions*. Basingstoke: Palgrave Macmillan, pp. 127–42.

Toombs, S. K. (1992) *The Meaning of Illness. A Phenomenological Account of the Different Perspectives of Physician and Patient*. Dordrecht: Springer.

Waldenfels, B. (2002) Levinas and the Face of the Other, in Critchley, S. and Bernasconi, R. (eds) *The Cambridge Companion to Levinas*. Cambridge: Cambridge University Press, pp. 63–81.

Webber, J. (2009) *The Existentialism of Jean-Paul Sartre*. London and New York: Routledge.

— (2018) *Rethinking Existentialism*. Oxford: Oxford University Press.

Wehrle, M. (2019) 'There is a Crack in Everything'. Fragile Normality: Husserl's Account of Normality Re-Visited. *Phainomenon: Journal of Phenomenological Philosophy* 28: 49–76.

Weiss, G. (1999) *Body Images: Embodiment as Intercorporeality*. London and New York: Routledge.

— (2003) The Body as a Narrative Horizon, in Cohen, J. J. and Weiss, G. (eds), *Thinking the Limits of the Body*. New York: SUNY.

— (2008a) *Refiguring the Ordinary*. Bloomington and Indianapolis: Indianapolis University Press.

— (2008b) Can an Old Dog Learn New Tricks? Habitual Horizons in James, Bourdieu, and Merleau-Ponty, in Weiss, G. (ed.) *Intertwinings. Interdisciplinary Encounters with Merleau-Ponty*. Albany: State University of New York Press.

— (2014) Ambiguity, in Diprose, R. and Reynolds, J. (eds) *Merleau-Ponty. Key Concepts*. London and New York: Routledge, pp. 133–41.

— (2016) De-Naturalizing the Natural Attitude: A Husserlian Legacy to Social Phenomenology. *Journal of Phenomenological Psychology* 47: 1–16.

— (2018) Race and Phenomenology (or Phenomenologizing Race), in Taylor, P. C., Alcoff L. M., Anderson L. (eds) *The Routledge Companion to the Philosophy of Race*. London and New York: Routledge, pp. 233–44.

— (2021) Feminist Phenomenology, in Hall, K. Q. and Ásta (eds) *The Oxford Handbook of Feminist Philosophy*. Oxford: Oxford University Press. DOI: 10.1093/oxfordhb/9780190628925.013.5.

Weiss, G., Murphy A. V. and Salamon, G. (2020) *50 Concepts for a Critical Phenomenology*. Evanston: Northwestern University Press.

Welton, D. (1987) Introduction, in Welton, D. and Silverman, H. J. (eds), *Critical and Dialectical Phenomenology*. Albany: State University of New York Press, pp. xii–xxi.

Wollstonecraft, M. (1992) *A Vindication of the Rights of Woman*. London: Penguin.

Yancy, G. (ed.) (2004) *What White Looks Like: African-American Philosophers on the Whiteness of Philosophy*. New York: Routledge.

— (ed.) (2010) *The Center Must Not Hold: White Women Philosophers on the Whiteness of Philosophy*. Lanham: Lexington Books.

— (ed.) (2015) *White Self-Critically Beyond Anti-Racism: How Does it Feel to be a White Problem?* Lanham: Lexington Books.

— (2017) *Black Bodies, White Gazes: The Continuing Significance of Race in America* (2nd edn). Lanham: Rowman & Littlefield.

— (2020) Confiscated Bodies, in Weiss, G., Murphy A. V., Salamon, G. (eds) *50 Concepts for a Critical Phenomenology*. Evanston: Northwestern University Press.

Young, I. M. (2005) *On Female Body Experience: 'Throwing Like a Girl' and Other Essays*. Oxford: Oxford University Press.

Zack, N. (1993) *Race and Mixed Race*. Philadelphia: Temple University Press.

— (2002) *Philosophy of Science and Race*. New York: Routledge.

Zahavi, D. (2001) Beyond empathy. Phenomenological Approaches to Intersubjectivity, *Journal of Consciousness Studies* 8(5–7): 151–67.

— (2011) Shame and the Exposed Self, in Webber, J. (ed.) *Reading Sartre. On Phenomenology and Existentialism*. London and New York: Routledge, pp. 211–26.

— (2014) *Self and Other. Exploring Subjectivity, Empathy, and Shame*. Oxford: Oxford University Press.

— (2019) *Phenomenology. The Basics*. London and New York: Routledge.

— (2020) *Self-Awareness and Alterity. A Phenomenological Investigation. A New Edition*. Evanston: Northwestern University Press.

Zahavi, D. and Loidolt, S. (2022) Critical Phenomenology and Psychiatry. *Continental Philosophy Review* 55: 55–75.

Zahavi, D. and Kriegel, U. (2015) For-me-ness: What it is and what it is not, in Dahlstrom, D. O., Elpidorou, A., and Hopp, W. (eds) *Philosophy of Mind and Phenomenology: Conceptual and Empirical Approaches*. London: Routledge.

Zaner, R. M. (1981) *The Context of Self. A Phenomenological Inquiry. Using Medicine as a Clue*. Athens: Ohio University Press.

Zurn, P. (2020) Social Death, in Weiss, G., Murphy A. V., Salamon, G. (eds) *50 Concepts for a Critical Phenomenology*. Evanston: Northwestern University Press, pp. 309–14.

Index